Ma

CH00982924

JOHN P J KENNEY, BA, CIPM, MSc, Head of Business and Management School, Ealing College of Higher Education, London

EUGENE L DONNELLY, DIP ECON (OXON), CERT ED, MIPM, Assistant Dean, Faculty of Business Studies and Management, Middlesex Polytechnic

MARGARET A REID, MA, CIPM, Principal Lecturer, School of Management and Business Studies, Leeds Polytechnic

In writing Manpower Training and Development the authors have drawn freely from their industrial backgrounds as personnel managers and training consultants responsible for training in large and small organizations at levels ranging from operative to senior management. This, together with their Business School teaching and examining experience, has enabled the authors to be sensitive to the needs of students and practitioners in the training field.

Manpower Training and Development
An introduction

Second edition

John Kenney
Eugene Donnelly
Margaret Reid

Institute of Personnel Management
Central House, Upper Woburn Place, London WC1H 0HX

To our families

First published 1972
by George G Harrap and Co Ltd
© *J P J Kenney and E L Donnelly 1972*

Second edition published 1979
©*Institute of Personnel Management 1979*

Printed in Great Britain by Martin's of Berwick

ISBN 0 85292 257 4

Contents

Preface to the second edition

In this edition we have rewritten much of the text, particularly those sections relating to training legislation, and the young worker. We have also taken the opportunity to extend the coverage of systematic training and the training function in organizations.

We should like to thank colleagues in industry and education for their suggestions which have been helpful to us in this edition.

November 1979

Preface to the first edition

This book has been written at the request of the Institute of Personnel Management to introduce students with limited industrial or commercial experience to the field of manpower training and development. The comments we received while drafting the book suggest that it may also prove useful to specialist training officers moving into a new area of training.

Our philosophy is straightforward. We believe that training contributes to society by the development of individual potential and by improving the effectiveness of organizations. For the latter it is essentially an investment in manpower and as such it must meet the same stringent criteria which are applied to any form of investment.

The book is in three main parts. The first five chapters deal with the training function, the factors which determine training policies and the use of training resources, the identification of organizational and individual training requirements and the design and evaluation of training programmes. Chapters 6 to 13 examine the ways in which training can be applied to categories of employee from operative to management levels. The last chapter reviews the evolution of training in this country following the 1964 Industrial Training Act.

We appreciate that the text can serve only as an introduction to the fundamentals of a rapidly developing field, but we would hope that it may stimulate readers to pursue the main themes in greater detail, in specialist books and periodicals.

No book is the completely original work of its authors, and we acknowledge with gratitude the valuable help we have received from our colleagues, both in industry and in our Colleges at Ealing and Hendon. In particular we would like to thank S J Dalziel, Manager, Central Information and Training Services Division of the Hotel and Catering Industry Training Board, and former Vice President, Education and Training, of the Institute of Personnel Management; J K Prior, Deputy Staff Controller of the Prudential Assurance Company Limited; B J G Alner, Master in charge of Counselling, Collyer's School, Horsham; and M D C Campbell, Assistant Director, Training, Organization and Manpower Planning, the Institute of Personnel Management, all of whom have advised us on the text but cannot be held responsible for our views and opinions.

E Ashman has earned our thanks for her rapid and very accurate typing of the manuscript, and finally, we wish to express our gratitude to our wives for their many helpful comments during the preparation of the book.

February 1972

Foreword

In his foreword to the first edition of Manpower Training and Development seven years ago the Secretary of State for Employment said that training by its very nature must be associated with development and change. Since then much development and change has continued to take place with far-reaching implications for training and for the national training system. We have seen the implementation of the 1973 Employment and Training Act and the establishment of the Manpower Services Commission. We have experienced the increasingly serious economic and unemployment situation and the measures which have and are being taken to tackle its causes and effects. We see the beginnings of the impact of major technological advances in the application of micro-electronics.

Within training itself the recent report of the Training of Trainers Committee has reinforced the need for training to be seen to contribute effectively to the business or the organization. It has provided a much needed framework for trainers of all kinds to be better selected, trained and integrated with their organization's policies, objectives, priorities and structures.

This second edition of Manpower Training and Development is timely in that it reflects these and other changes, not least among them being the increased awareness of the need to learn to adapt to change itself and the development of ways in which people can be helped to do this. That the main content of the book remains the same, however, is a useful reminder that underlying all these changes is a core of systematic training analysis and practice which still needs to be applied more than it sometimes is. The worth of books like Manpower Training and Development is that they show how a systematic approach to training can benefit organizations and give readers a practical understanding of what steps are needed. I am sure that the book in its revised form will continue to serve this purpose.

The current review of the Employment and Training Act, being carried out by the Manpower Services Commission, and the implementation of the government's policies for improving industry's growth and competitiveness will provide yet more challenges for relevant and effective training efforts by organizations. Manpower Training and Development should make a valuable contribution to meeting these challenges.

The Rt Hon James Prior MP
Secretary of State for Employment

17 October 1979

Chapter 1

Approaches to Training

Manpower as a resource — education and training —
changes in attitudes to training — fundamental
aspects of training

MANPOWER AS A RESOURCE

Commercial and industrial organizations operate in a dynamic
business environment. Market, technological, personnel and
other changes have far-reaching effects on companies and
unless they are prepared and able to move with the times their
competitiveness is eroded and their opportunities for growth
curtailed. However, as Burns and Stalker★ (1966) point out,
organizations often find it difficult to adjust to change, so one of
management's prime responsibilities is to develop organizations to meet the challenge of the future. This responsibility is
exercised by assessing the resources and opportunities available,
defining business objectives and efficiently managing the
resources allocated to meet these goals.

One of the most important resources available to an organization, and many would say the most important, is its employees.
Their competence and commitment largely determine the
objectives that an enterprise can set for itself and its success in
achieving them. This fact of industrial and commercial life is
not new, but since the last war economic, technological and
social changes have forced employers to pay particular attention
to their manpower policies and practices. The rapid evolution
of personnel management as a major business function is itself a
direct result of the growing managerial concern for the more
effective use and development of human resources.

For many years managements have recognized that it makes
good business sense to have progressive manpower policies for

★References are to be found on p.269 *et seq* under name and year.

welfare, remuneration, recruitment and industrial relations. More recently, notably since the mid-1960s, companies have become aware of the need to adopt a positive and systematic approach to employee training and development, a part of the manpower function which had been neglected in many companies.

The terms 'training' and 'development' are open to differing interpretations. We define training as helping an individual to learn how to carry out satisfactorily the work required of him in his present job. Development we define as preparing the individual for a *future* job. Both are achieved by creating learning conditions in which the necessary skill and knowledge can be effectively acquired by the learner.

EDUCATION AND TRAINING

A number of writers, including Tannehill (1970) and Stringfellow (1968), have discussed the nature of education and training in industry and have pointed to the problems which arise from the different meanings attributed to these two words. The word education, for example, is at times narrowly used to mean the formal process of studying a syllabus of work, which usually involves attendance at an educational institution. It is also used in the very much broader sense of 'life itself is the best educator', where the meaning conveyed is that of developing an individual's personality, attitudes and knowledge of self — largely or wholly independent of institutionalized education.

Similarly, the word training is used both as a synonym for education and, in our view more appropriately, in the restricted sense of learning behaviour which is usually capable of precise definition.

Distinguishing between the purpose and methods of education and those of training is not always easy, as the two overlap. However, as we shall see later, there are differences which are of more than academic and semantic interest. Indeed, the assumptions of employers and employees about the nature of education and training, what each aims to achieve, and by what means, have led to costly mistakes. A classic example of this was the assumption made by many companies about the value of young graduates as potential senior managers. The practice of employing graduates fresh from university and giving them a general manager's view or a 'tour' of the company proved to be a singularly unsuccessful method of developing potential top executives. It had been thought that graduates would be able to

2

learn the company's business in a short time and rise rapidly in the management hierarchy, but in a great many cases this simply did not happen. There were two main reasons for the failure of this kind of graduate training scheme: first, that companies had set too high a premium on graduates' educational achievements and had assumed that this would correlate with success in business and secondly, the 'tour' approach to training graduates was not strictly training, but rather an in-company educational programme. The trainees learnt a great deal about the company yet acquired little or no practical expertise in managing others.

The expectations which some companies have of staff who have attended short training courses provides another common example of the failure to understand the nature of education and of training. Some employers believe that attendance on a fortnight's course should be sufficient to convert a clerk into an office supervisor, or to turn a research chemist into a leader of a research team. Such confidence in the effectiveness of two weeks of training is sadly misplaced! Appropriate training courses may be necessary to provide the techniques and other information which new managers require. What they also need is on the job training, possibly over a long period of time, to fit them for their new responsibilities.

Bearing these examples in mind, and remembering also that education and training are both concerned with promoting and guiding learning, we can consider how training and education differ and yet can complement each other. They differ in four main areas: in the degree to which their objectives can be specified in behavioural terms; in the time normally needed to achieve these objectives; in their methods of learning; and in the learning material involved. A characteristic of training objectives is that they are capable of being expressed in behavioural terms. They can and should specify the work behaviour required of a trainee at the end of his training, ie the criterion behaviour (see page 66). Another characteristic of a training objective in a business setting is that it is job rather than person orientated and this often implies a uniformity of performance behaviour.

Educational objectives are less amenable to definition in behavioural terms because, as Glaser (1965) puts it, 'they are too complex or because the behaviours that result in successful accomplishment in many instances are not known'. In the absence of behavioural performance standards, educational objectives have to be couched in more general or abstract terms. They aim to provide the learner with a basic understanding which he is expected to interpret and apply in his own way to specific situations. Educational objectives seek to stimulate personal development and so can be thought of as 'person' rather than 'job' orientated. This holds true for both vocational and general education.

The following examples illustrate the differences between educational and training objectives. The training requirements for a sewing-machine operator should specify the hand movements etc which a trainee operator must learn and the output level which she must reach before she is regarded as trained. The objectives of a Master of Business Administration degree course (MBA) can do little more than state that by studying behavioural science, accountancy, economics and related subjects, the student will learn the relevance of these disciplines both to general and to particular business situations. The satisfactory completion of an MBA means that the student can demonstrate the application of certain principles and techniques in solving examination problems. His improved grasp of the business world should help him to be a successful manager in practice as well as in theory, but the former cannot be guaranteed.

The second point of difference between education and training lies in the time needed to achieve their respective objectives. A training objective can normally be reached in a relatively short period of time, while often many years are needed to accomplish educational objectives. For example, a young girl starting work in an office can be trained to touch-type in a matter of months, but 10 or more years of schooling would be needed for her to develop an acceptable general standard of education and for her to achieve a level of maturity as an individual.

Some approaches to learning are more appropriate to education than to training, and it is useful to refer to Tannehill's (1970) distinction between mechanistic and organic learning. Mechanistic learning is achieved as a result of stimuli and responses and is reinforced by practice. Training, as opposed to educational programmes are usually designed on the assumption that mechanistic learning is involved.

Organic learning involves a change in the individual rather than in what he can do. Organic learning is much less amenable

4

to external direction and its outcome is very difficult to predict.

Finally, there is the difference in the learning content of training and educational programmes. As we have seen, training provides the trainee with knowledge and skills necessary to carry out specific work tasks. It is geared directly to this end and is essentially practical and relevant to the job. Most, if not all, of the material to be learnt, such as details of work methods, techniques and procedures are derived from within the company. In contrast, educational programmes contain theoretical and conceptual material aimed at stimulating an individual's analytical and critical faculties. Detail, although important, is included to illustrate principles and relationships. Moreover, the content of an educational programme is widely based and frequently derived from different sources and disciplines.

These various differences, although significant, should not obscure the fact that education and training are both concerned with the development of human potential or talent. They are complementary parts of the same process, and it is difficult to imagine any training which does not have some educational effect and vice versa — in short, some of each exists in both.

This interdependence of education and training has been stressed by the former Central Training Council (1966a) (see page 239):

> The increasingly complex industrial environment, the rapid pace of technological change, and intense international competition demand a work force which is both highly trained and educated. In recent years, it has therefore become generally recognized that a programme combining education and training is essential if people in industry are to be equipped to carry out their work effectively as well as to have the opportunity to advance to more demanding and responsible work.

In practice the extent to which a formal educational element is included in training programmes varies widely. It figures prominently in what are sometimes called career programmes, where employees, such as trainee accountants or technologists, are prepared over an extended period of time for responsible positions in the company. In contrast, many job training programmes, with their shorter-term objectives and emphasis on specific behaviour change, include little or no formal educational requirements. This is certainly the case for unskilled and most semi-skilled jobs, although there is a growing tendency,

5

strongly supported by training boards (see chapter 15) to encourage young employees to attend relevant further-education courses.

CHANGES IN ATTITUDES TO TRAINING

Wellens (1968) has argued that changes in managements' attitudes to training are both predictable and permanent and that they depend primarily upon the state of technology in a society. The increasing complexity of business and industry in the United Kingdom has reached a stage where the ratio of professional and skilled jobs is such that only by pursuing a policy of training can employers ensure that their staff's skills keep pace with technological progress. Add to this the impact of recent legislation and a better understanding by many managers of what systematic training can offer a business, and the training function qualifies, as Wellens puts it, 'for a place in the main-stream of management'.

The Training Services Agency (TSA)★ (1977a) has stressed that:

> the whole environment in which training and the trainer has to operate has changed rapidly and in all probability will continue to change, eg the increasing stimulus and direction from the TSA and MSC (Manpower Services Commission); increasing external demands through legislation; develop-ment of levy-grant or exemption polices from ITBs (Indus-trial Training Boards); availability of investment monies; inflation; competition in the market; and increasingly impor-tant, unemployment and the changing values and expecta-tions of the work force, especially among young people.

These changes are not, of course, confined to the UK and the effect of technology on the training function is highlighted in the EEC. Preliminary guidelines on Community Social Policy (1971):

> Progress is itself gradually raising the general level of skills; the faster rate of progress is tending to blur the nature of these skills by the swift and radical change in machinery, materials and methods of work and organization. Knowledge, know-how, techniques and acquired attitudes are quickly left behind and re-adaptation, which was recently the exception, is becoming the rule. As a result, occupational skills can no longer be defined solely by reference to the job and the nature

★Abbreviations are to be found on p.258

6

of the operation involved. They are now seen as the permanent ability to adapt to the technical pattern of work.

Management's attitude to training in a growing number of companies is clear cut. Training is seen as an activity capable of making a major contribution to the achievement of company objectives. In this situation training will be taking place, where needed, at all levels in the organization, from the boardroom to the shop-floor. But in too many companies the traditional *laissez-faire* attitude to training still survives.

Unsystematic Training
The Training Boards have done much to extend the use of successful training practices, but many companies still pay 'lip service' and barely satisfy minimum training board requirements, with the result that their training has the following features:

it is not an integral part of the company's operations
it has a low priority and is, at best, a peripheral management responsibility; employees are largely responsible for their own training; managers, for example, are appointed for their technical abilities, and are expected to pick up their managerial skills with little or no formal help
management development is practically non-existent and the training officer is inappropriately placed in the hierarchy to advise or take any active part in the training of management staff
more attention may be paid to the presentation of documentation and written programmes than to the actual training
management is under the impression that, whilst properly organized training costs money, unstructured training, which relies on informal or unplanned assistance from fellow employees, is inexpensive; however, this is likely to be a fallacy, as the costs of the latter are difficult to estimate and control because they are hidden in lost production hours, longer learning times, faulty work, poor utilization of machinery and sometimes damage to equipment, labour turnover, and possibly lack of applicants capable of being trained.

Systematic Training
In contrast to the unstructured approach, systematic training is
7

an important ingredient in a company's manpower strategy and is a sound business investment. Systematic training can be defined as the process of:

IDENTIFYING what training is needed

PLANNING appropriate training programmes to meet this need

IMPLEMENTING the training and ensuring that employees are assisted to acquire the skills and knowledge they need in the most efficient manner

EVALUATING as far as possible the effectiveness of the particular training programme and satisfying any residual training requirements, *see* figure 1.1 below:

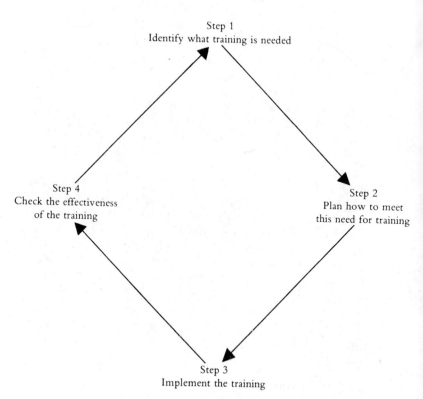

Figure 1.1
The systematic training process

Step 1
Identify what training is needed

Step 4
Check the effectiveness
of the training

Step 2
Plan how to meet
this need for training

Step 3
Implement the training

This four-step sequence, which is sometimes referred to as the training cycle, can be applied to:

training at the level of the organization or department
training for specific occupations
training of individuals at all levels in the organization, from school-leaver to managing director, and whether newly appointed or with long service in the organization.

Variations on this approach, developed to meet different training requirements, are described in subsequent chapters. The following simplified example illustrates the main steps in the systematic training sequence applied to a typical situation, the training of new employees, and also illustrates the parts played by a line manager and the training specialist.

The works manager of a successful electronics manufacturing business has decided to meet an increasing demand for his company's products by introducing shiftwork. New staff are to be engaged and will need training, as it is most unlikely that they will have had suitable previous experience. It is assumed that relevant job specifications and training programmes are not available in the company. The sequence would be as follows:

Step 1: identify what training is needed
With the cooperation of the departmental manager, the training officer carries out a training analysis of the work to find out precisely what the new staff will be expected to do and, in particular, to identify those parts of the job which they are likely to find difficult to learn and where work errors are costly. This analysis clarifies the performance standards to which the new staff must be trained and so provides the objectives for the training programme. For example, 'to construct twenty 'A' type radio units per hour with a maximum reject rate of three per cent'.

The training officer then works out a training programme, taking into account the trainees' present and required levels of competence. Any difference between what the recruits have to be able to do and what they can already do, can be thought of as a 'learning gap' — shown diagrammatically in figure 1.2 on page 10. The tops of the columns represent the levels of competence which trainees have to achieve in the various tasks, and the shaded areas indicate a particular trainee's ability in these tasks at the beginning of training. The training programme should bridge the gap between trainees' initial performance and that of experienced staff.

9

Step 2: plan the training programme

Having identified what training the recruits require, the training officer decides with line management how to meet this need, bearing in mind relevant company policies and other constraints.

The programme specifies: the skills and knowledge required; the time-table of the training sessions and who will be responsible for them; where the training will take place; and the resources needed. In helping to prepare the programme the training officer uses his specialist knowledge and experience to keep costs to the minimum compatible with efficient training.

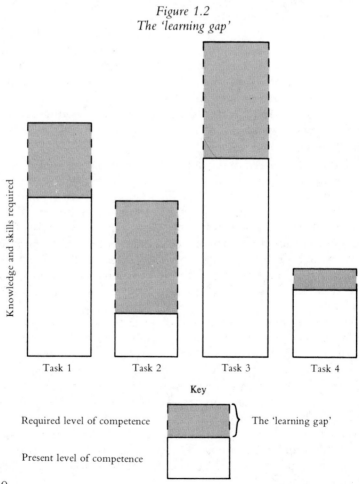

Figure 1.2
The 'learning gap'

Step 3: implement the training
The training is then carried out according to the programme, with adjustments being made where necessary to suit the learning rates of individuals: training times may therefore vary depending on the trainees' abilities to reach the required standard. Instruction is given by trained staff in the training area or school (off-the-job training) and at the workplace (on-the-job training).

Records are kept of the trainees' progress for immediate control purposes, such as rearranging the programme to cater for recruits finding certain parts more difficult to learn and others easier than had been anticipated, and to provide feedback on the effectiveness of the training.

Step 4: evaluate the effectiveness of the training
The programme is reviewed at intervals and on completion by the training officer, the line management and, if appropriate, by the trainees themselves. Any lessons that can be learnt from these reviews, such as changes in the method of instruction or training times, are built into future programmes. In this way experience is used to improve the efficiency of training in the company. A discussion of the ways in which the effectiveness of training programmes can be tested is given in chapter 6.

To summarize, the key features of systematic training are that it is:

based on an analysis of a need for training and geared to specific performance standards of work

planned and controlled at all times whether off- or on-the-job

implemented by managers and specialist staff who have themselves been trained to train

evaluated to check its effectiveness.

FUNDAMENTAL ASPECTS OF TRAINING
Our approach so far has been based on a model which may appear somewhat mechanistic in the face of reality. To redress the balance and to place the following chapters in context, it is necessary to consider some fundamental aspects of the nature of training.

Bass and Vaughan (1966) define learning as a 'relatively permanent change in behaviour that occurs as a result of practice or experience'. People cannot be brought together into an organization to achieve any kind of common purpose without learning taking place. As a result they will change their

11

behaviour in various ways. For instance, at the simplest level, they learn and use each other's names, technical terms, etc and, at a more sophisticated level, they learn about the behaviour of their colleagues, supervisors and management and thus develop attitudes which can have complex effects on behaviour. They learn by imitating other people, by seeing and interpreting what happens in the organization and by the cumulative experience of trial and error. In this sense, therefore, as King (1964) has stressed, learning is an inevitable organizational feature, the question is, how far is it possible and desirable for this learning to take place as a result of formal training?

This may seem a simple point to make, but it has several important implications. First, if we accept the scope of Bass and Vaughan's definition of learning, formal training can and must encompass much more than the provision of courses and off-the-job training, ie it includes any activity which provides organizational experience relevant to training objectives. Such activities range from short periods of work in different organizations, jobs or roles to problem-solving discussion groups or projects.

The second implication is that the training officer is really intervening in a continuing learning process and, therefore, requires diagnostic and analytical skills of a far higher order than is commonly realized.

The third is that people learn by example and the influence of a superior upon his subordinate is very powerful. It is particularly strong when the superior holds the key to what may be termed the rewards and punishments of the organization. Successful training normally requires active management support — ideally it should start at the top and filter down through the organization, the superior being involved in the training of his subordinate. McGregor (1960) maintains that:

> Every encounter between a superior and subordinate involves learning of some kind for the subordinate (and should for the superior too). The attitudes, habits, and expectations of the subordinate will be reinforced or modified to some degree as a result of every encounter with the boss . . . Day by day experience is so much more powerful that it tends to overshadow what the individual may learn in other settings.

Fourthly, off-the-job training requires reinforcement on return
12

to the workplace and not only the attitude of the superior but the whole organization's climate is a powerful influence in determining whether training is really transferred to the working situation. For instance, it is difficult for a manager to put into practice what he has just learned about the adoption of a participative and democratic style if the company structure and atmosphere is autocratic. During courses for supervisors, a common cry is 'It's our managers you ought to have here'. However, in realistic situations it is not always possible to start at the top, as we shall discuss later. It is, nevertheless, always necessary to take the organization's climate into consideration — an induction course will have little value if the new entrant finds that the picture which was painted during the first few days has little resemblance to the organization as he later experiences it.

The fifth implication is that training may be likened to a game of skittles, where aiming at one target may have repercussions in a variety of other areas. It may be impossible to train one group of people efficiently without changing the behaviour of another group. For example, for a variety of reasons most of the early ITBs put their first efforts into operative or craft training, but soon found that, in order to gain the proper benefit from the trained operators, it was necessary to start training the supervisors. What appear to be inefficiencies on the part of one section of employees may, in fact, indicate training needs for someone else — for instance, lack of speed by operators may be caused by their having to cope with poor materials or poorly maintained equipment. Training can sometimes act as a catalyst in triggering off change in other parts of the organization, and can have unexpected consequences — in one instance, a complete redefinition and reappraisal of the organization structure resulted from an in-company training course for managers.

The sixth is that everyone in the organization, not least management, is learning something about training and developing an attitude towards it. As learning, however inefficient and haphazard, is taking place anyway (and the cost of this type of learning is usually hidden) the advantages of systematic training have to be 'sold' and clearly demonstrated. This is no easy task and because organizations are all different there is no one recipe for success. The credibility of the training officer is an important factor; this may come originally from his personality, but it can ultimately only be maintained by successful training results.

The starting point is crucial, and it needs little imagination to see why the recommendation that training should start at the top is not always practicable. It is a question of weighing up the situation and deciding whether to start where the most serious problems and priorities appear to be, or where success seems to be the most likely, or to begin in an idealistic fashion at the top.

The seventh, McGregor (1960) suggests that 'knowledge cannot be pumped into human beings the way grease is forced into a fitting on a machine. The individual may learn; he is not taught. Programmes do not produce managers; we cannot produce managers as we do products — we can only grow them'. Although skill and knowledge are required to devise training programmes to meet specific needs, the most difficult task is often to gain enthusiasm and whole-hearted cooperation, because people will only learn if they want to do so. It is all too easy to pay lip service to training. We could extend McGregor's horticultural analogy a little further and suggest that a gardener will succeed in cultivating a delicate plant if he starts by allowing it to grow in appropriate conditions and encourages and feeds it to help it bloom. Earlier in this chapter we described a systematic training cycle, but we must never lose sight of the fact that commitment comes from involvement and if we involve people we must attempt to use their suggestions, even if they do not accord with a neat and tidy model. In a sense, this increases the necessity for a training officer to be fully conversant with systematic methods so that he can adapt them to specific situations.

The final implication is that people learn from the organization and that, as Greiner (1972) maintains, 'their behaviour tends to be determined primarily by previous events and experience, not by what lies ahead'. He extends this analogy to the organization itself and suggests that a company can become 'frozen in its present state of evolution, or ultimately in failure, regardless of market opportunities . . . (because of) . . . the inability of management to understand its organization development problems'. He quotes an example: 'Key executives of a retail chain store hold on to an organization structure long after it has served its purpose, because their power is derived from this structure. The company eventually goes into bankruptcy'. A lengthy analysis of the relationship between organization development (OD) and training is inappropriate here but is discussed by Thakur, Bristow and Carby (1978). However,

14

learning (as defined by Bass and Vaughan) is involved in OD, and if we recognize that training can include group activities which might trigger off change, then there is a very close link between training and organization development. A somewhat sophisticated assessment of training needs therefore would include, not only details of the future development of individuals, but also a framework for discussion of the future potential of the organization and the changes in climate and structure which would be necessary to achieve it. The simplest example of this is to be found in the small, established company which is owner-managed. Training boards have found that such an organization may appear to have no training needs — all employees know their jobs as the company has been running the same way for years. If, as a result of training, the owner-manager sees the potential of his company in a different light and, for example, installs new methods, then the company may require, not only new skills, but a new organization structure. Training and organization development needs can therefore arise at the second level when a fresh assessment may be required. The whole operation must be seen as a dynamic process, not as a once and for all event.

Our aim in this chapter has been to set the scene: in the four-step training cycle we have outlined a useful approach to any type of training problem; at the same time, we have indicated the need for its adaptation and the need for the training officer to use diagnostic and innovative skills in dealing with complex situations. These points will serve as a background for the chapters which follow.

Chapter 2

The Training Function in the Organization

The benefits and costs of training — company training
staff, their roles and their training

THE BENEFITS AND COSTS OF TRAINING

Systematic training is a sound business investment. This is an
important statement but to a businessman it poses three questions:

1 What benefits can a company obtain from investing in
   training?
2 What costs are involved in training?
3 How can a company ensure that its training is successful?

What benefits can a company obtain from investing in training?

In general terms the following benefits can be expected,
although, as we point out on page 18 training is only one of
many variables which influence business activities:

training helps employees to learn their jobs quickly and effectively. It also helps to minimize the costs incurred by
employees while learning their jobs

existing employees can be helped by training to improve
their work performance and to keep up to date in their
specialist fields. The standard or quality of work required
by the company is more likely to be achieved and maintained if employees are well trained

a greater volume of work can be expected from trained staff,
partly because they work more rapidly and partly because
they make fewer mistakes

16

a reduction in work errors benefits a company in two other ways. First, management can spend more time on planning and development activities instead of correcting mistakes. Secondly, costs of correcting errors, often involving overtime, are eliminated

labour turnover among new staff, if caused by ineffective learning and inadequate training, can be reduced. Staff who are helped by efficient training to learn their jobs rapidly are more likely to achieve a high level of job satisfaction soon after joining the company and so tend to remain longer, Jones and Moxham (1969)

retention of staff is an advantage to a company only so long as the skills and knowledge of its employees contribute to the company's operations. By retraining staff, new abilities replace obsolescent ones

training in safe working practices reduces accidents, resulting in social and financial benefits to both the employees and the company

a company needs a flexible workforce to operate efficiently when staff are absent through sickness or on holiday. Training increases staff versatility by widening their range of expertise to include related jobs

a company with a reputation for providing good training tends to attract better applicants

employees are less likely to become frustrated and leave if opportunities for further training and development are available within the company.

To this list must be added the social and private benefits which result from training. The advantages to society of having a well trained national workforce are very real. Without such expertise in its working population, the high standard of living of technology-based societies such as that of the UK would not be possible. It is the dearth of a well educated and trained work force as well as a shortage of financial and other resources which mark underdeveloped countries.

Finally, there are the private benefits enjoyed by those who have been trained. Training increases the value of an employee in the labour market and this usually provides both the individual and his family with a higher standard of living. There are also important non-financial benefits which trained people enjoy, including higher status, a greater degree of job security (trained staff are a valuable asset which employers are loath to lose), better promotion prospects, and, because their work talents are fully used, greater job satisfaction.

The various benefits which flow from systematic training are desirable and impressive. However, training may solve some problems but create others if it is not integrated into the policies and operations of the company. Many companies have found, to their cost, that it is insufficient to provide first-class training opportunities without also recognizing that training adds to their employees' market value. So careful attention must be paid to the broader context of a firm's personnel and total operating policies if the benefits of training are to accrue to the company bearing the cost of the training and not to another employer. For example, remuneration, staff development and physical working conditions must be at least as attractive as those offered by competitors if investment in training is to pay dividends.

It is often difficult to quantify the precise benefits which unequivocally result from a particular investment in training because there are many variables affecting a business and it is frequently impossible to isolate and measure the contribution made by any one of these, such as training. In a number of situations, however, improved performance can with certainty be attributed to training. Such examples are usually drawn from operative training where there are often fewer and identifiable variables (see Seymour 1966). The following example illustrates the more usual situation.

As part of its expansion programme a Birmingham manufacturing company decided to recruit additional sales staff and give them a thorough training. This was the first time that the company had run training programmes for new representatives. On completion of training, and after several months in the field, these new salesmen proved to be extremely successful, with their sales results being very much better than had been anticipated. To what extent could this success be attributed to training? Many other factors could have combined to produce the satisfactory outcome. The quality of the salesmen recruited may have improved; production or delivery difficulties may have put competitors at a disadvantage during the period when the new salesmen were doing well; the advertising support for the company's products may have become more effective; special price or discount arrangements may have assisted the salesman; the quality of sales management may have been

18

improved, and so on. This example is typical in that training was one of a number of possible variables influencing the final result. The problem lies in isolating the contribution made by training as opposed to the other variables in business.

This problem is not restricted to training: it occurs in a similar form in other important business activities such as industrial relations and advertising. A company which enjoys good industrial relations may reasonably attribute this in part to its joint management and union consultative machinery, but this cannot be proved. Similarly, it is considered sound business practice to assist sales effort with advertising support, but again, apart from the general argument that a company failing to advertise its products is likely to face falling sales, it is often very difficult to specify the precise benefits of advertising.

Training is in a similar position. It is common sense to help people to learn their jobs, and companies that do not train their staff risk foregoing the benefits which systematic training would otherwise bring. However, the common sense argument justifying an investment in training is crude and is no substitute for an analysis of the costs and benefits that are likely to result. The more evidence of this kind that is available, difficult though it may be to produce, the less dependence need be placed on value judgement. The problems of assessing the benefits of training are discussed further in chapter 6.

What costs are involved in training?

The list of advantages noted in the previous section may well convince businessmen that investment in training is worth serious consideration — even after taking into account the practical difficulties involved in assessing the benefits of training in a particular. case. Yet these advantages only become commercially meaningful if related to the resources needed to achieve them.

What then does training cost a company? An obvious starting point is to examine a company's training budget, as this might be expected to provide information on the amount and type of training expenditure. Although apparently obvious, such a move is not always very illuminating for two main reasons. First, companies do not necessarily have a separate budget for training. Their planned expenditure in this area may be limited and is included under other headings. Secondly, even if a company has a training budget, many of its training costs are incurred in the day to day running of the business. These costs are difficult to identify and are therefore not itemized in financial statements.

One possible way of looking at training costs is that adopted by an economist, who would argue that the true cost of training to a company is not the financial expenditure incurred — ie the money costs — but the opportunity costs involved. Garbutt (1969) has put it this way: 'the opportunity which a firm foregoes may be a better measure of its cost than its accountancy procedure. In other words, we may spend a hundred pounds on training but if in doing so we lose the opportunity to make two hundred pounds then the opportunity cost of training is two hundred pounds'. However, as Garbutt continues: 'measures of opportunity cost are hard to establish and even harder to agree between conflicting interests'. The opportunity cost approach is therefore not usually a practical one for a businessman trying to identify training costs, except where the level of investment in training is very high.

An alternative way of tackling the problem is to consider the costs that a company is forced to incur as a direct result of employees having to learn their jobs (learning costs), and then seeing how these costs can be minimized by expenditure on training (training costs). Talbot and Ellis (1969) have pointed out that learning costs are unavoidable and will be incurred by a company whenever learning is taking place whether the employee is being formally trained or not. Examples of learning costs include: payments made to employees when they are first learning their jobs or attending a refresher course; the cost of materials wasted, sales lost or incorrect decisions made as learners practise; and the cost of reduced output caused by the slowing-down effect which learners have on the people with whom they are working.

Training costs, on the other hand, are those deliberately incurred by the company to facilitate learning and thereby reduce learning costs. Examples of training costs include: part of a manager's salary for the time he spends in coaching his staff; the emoluments of training officers, instructors and their supporting staff; the capital and running costs (heating, lighting, rates) of a training centre; training aids such as projectors, films, books, programmed learning texts; and payments of fees to consultants, colleges and other outside bodies.

Ideally the relationship between learning costs and training
20

costs should be such that both are minimized, since expenditure on training is only justified if it reduces the costs of learning. However, since learning costs are to some extent unavoidable, there must be an upper limit to the amount of training expenditure which is appropriate in any situation. Incurring additional training costs beyond this point would have no effect in reducing the costs of learning.

In reality, companies can rarely exercise the fine degree of control needed to optimize their training expenditure in this way because decisions normally have to be made on incomplete information. In the past, senior managers and accountants have not always realized the wider significance of learning and training costs and have not given these items due prominence in their costing systems. As a result, many companies lack the financial information necessary to identify and control these two sets of costs more accurately.

For example, certain obvious items of training expenditure such as the salaries of training staff can be readily identified, but others, such as the cost of mistakes made by an inadequately trained invoice clerk (delays in receiving settlements, loss of goodwill, overtime working needed to amend and send out correct invoices, etc), or the loss of overhead recovery from plant under-utilized through shortage of skilled staff, often remain hidden in the general operating costs of a business.

In theory any cost incurred by a company can be identified, but the process of collecting and analyzing data itself costs money and is only justifiable if the value of the information produced makes the process worthwhile. Broadly speaking, a sophisticated system of costing training and learning activities is unnecessary in small companies, but becomes increasingly important in larger organizations where expenditure under these headings is considerable. What is important is that management recognizes the relationship between learning and training costs in the company and knows their relative order of magnitude. It is then a matter of company policy to decide the degree of detailed information necessary for the effective control of these costs.

Hall (1976) examines the ways in which cost benefit analysis (CBA) can be used as an evaluative tool in industrial training: CBA is shown as a concept with both costing and general value overtones not only for industry but also for the worker and the economy. He also investigates the applicability of CBA as a decision-taking tool in organizational analysis and examines the problems generated by its application (*see also* page 104).

To summarize, training should be considered an investment in manpower aimed at reducing learning costs. The question asked at the beginning of this section, 'What does training cost a company?' would therefore be more meaningfully phrased as 'Is the level of training investment appropriate?'

How can a company ensure that its training is successful?
Apart from the requirements that training must be systematically based, three further conditions must be met if a business is to obtain maximum benefit from its training: management must accept responsibility for training; the training function must be appropriately organized within the company; and the roles of the training officer must be defined.

Management's responsibility for training
Although, as we shall see, there are different types of managerial responsibility for training, every manager is responsible for the training and development of his own staff. A company should ensure that its managers accept the importance of this personal role in training and that their success in it will have a bearing on their own career prospects. Unlike other training responsibilities, this cannot be delegated and so every manager requires appropriate expertise in this area.

We can now briefly consider how training decisions and activities vary with the level of management.

Top management in large companies is not concerned with the day-to-day aspects of training. These are matters of immediate importance to departmental managers and are delegated to them for action, with the exception of two critical training responsibilities: formulating company training policies and management training and development.

A company's training policies include such items as the extent of training in a business, priority areas and the resources to be made available to translate policies into practice, (*see* chapter 4). While executives and other staff contribute to the development of policies, final decisions are made by top management.

Management training and development is the other major area of responsibility of top management and this is discussed in chapter 14. Experience has shown that success at this level
22

depends heavily on top management's personal commitment.

Middle and junior managers are responsible for implementing company training policy within their own spheres of influence. There are certain aspects of training which require their personal attention, such as on-the-job coaching of their staff, and others which they normally delegate. For example, much of the detailed work involved in analysing departmental training requirements and in preparing programmes is dealt with by a training officer, with the help and cooperation of line management.

The structuring of training within companies
The responsibilities for training in small companies rest with the owner or manager, but in medium sized and large organizations it is often necessary to establish a training department to provide line management with the necessary specialist service.

There is no one correct way of structuring training within a firm and companies have evolved different forms of organization which have been equally successful in meeting their particular requirements. Whatever form of organization is adopted, the main criterion to be satisfied is that the training department contributes effectively to the running of the business. How this is achieved will depend on the particular circumstances in the company.

Apart from a limited number of companies with a full-time training specialist on the board of directors, the training department is organized so that its manager reports to a senior executive with wider responsibilities than training alone. In practice, as the following structures illustrate, the head of the training department is normally accountable to one of three senior managers: the personnel manager, the chief executive or the relevant line manager (where training is restricted to a group of employees in the company).

The training officer within the personnel department
We have already demonstrated that training is an essential part of an organization's manpower function and that it cannot be effective if isolated from related activities such as the selection and recruitment of staff. In general, therefore, the more closely training is integrated within the personnel function, the more beneficial it will be. This is not to say that the training officer should invariably report to the company personnel manager,

whether this is advisable will depend on the personnel department.

Where the personnel department has a dynamic and progressive outlook and is successfully led by professionally-trained staff, the central training function will usually be part of it. On the other hand, where a company's personnel department has only a limited development and influence, a dependent training function is unlikely to prosper and the training officer may be more effective if made directly responsible to the chief executive of the company or to a senior line manager.

Traditionally, company personnel departments have been responsible for staff training, but in practice the pressures of full employment following the Second World War forced many personnel managers to give priority to the recruitment, remuneration and industrial relations aspects of their work. The result was that training rarely received the attention it deserved. This pattern has been changed significantly in recent years as personnel managers and line management have come to recognize the need to integrate the training and the personnel functions. The advantages of this structure can be considered under the following headings.

Manpower planning: a company's estimated requirements for various categories of employee have direct implications for the training specialist. He needs to know the numbers and types of future training programmes required for new and existing staff, and for re-training where jobs change or become obsolete (*see* chapter 3).

Recruitment: the contribution of a training department in this important area will largely depend on the extent to which the company's recruitment policy is to engage ready-trained employees or to develop its own. However, if the role of the training department is wider than that of simply responding to the demands for the training of new staff, it will also influence recruitment policy. For example, an analysis of the long-term training requirements of a large department store indicated that the age structure of its management was unbalanced. There were insufficient employees with appropriate experience and in the right age range to succeed the present key staff. The training officer therefore recommended that future recruitment must compensate for this imbalance.

Selection procedures: the feedback from the training officer on the progress of new recruits during training helps validate recruitment and selection procedures.

Remuneration: a company's remuneration policy and practice should recognize the enhanced value of the employee who has successfully completed training. This can be overlooked if personnel and training staff are not working closely together.

Staff development: a company's system of staff appraisal indicates the strengths and weaknesses of individual employees, and at the same time identifies how training can help improve work performance. Appraisal and training must be recognized as part of the same process of staff development.

Promotion: promotion plans for staff at all levels in the organization invariably have training connotations. In some cases the training required is limited, in others an anticipated promotion may necessitate the grooming of an employee over a period of months or years. Planning an employee's promotion, deliberately increasing his responsibilities, assisting him where necessary with training and matching his improved performance with increased pay, are all part of the same process and are best dealt with as such.

Personnel records: company personnel records contain employee's work histories and, more important in many cases, details of staff training and development plans. A central and up-to-date source of this information is a basic requirement for effective personnel practice. Decentralization of records to various sub-functions, apart from being expensive, presents problems in keeping several sets of records up-to-date and increases the potential misuse of confidential information.

The above indicates some of the advantages that a company gains from having a high-level personnel department, co-ordinating training and other manpower activities in a single personnel system. However, for the reasons given at the beginning of this section, placing training under the wing of the personnel department is not necessarily desirable, and other ways of structuring it may be more appropriate.

The training officer reporting to the chief executive of the company
An example of this is the organization in which the managing director wishes to be personally responsible for the training function and so makes the training officer directly responsible

to him. This type of structure is common in medium-sized firms and in some very large organizations, where the importance of the training function makes it necessary for the training officer to have direct access to the chief executive. A training officer in this situation, by reporting to the top and having the ear of the managing director, will almost certainly have a great deal of informal authority within the company. If the chief executive gives personal support to the training officer, then the latter is less likely to meet opposition in the day to day implementation of training. This structure also has its limitations. Managing directors are busy people and cannot always devote adequate time to training matters. Decisions may be delayed or made without their implications being fully appreciated.

The training officer reporting to a line manager
In a company where training is restricted to one category of employee, the training officer is often responsible to the departmental manager concerned. A common example is the sales training officer who reports to the sales manager.

In this structure, training can be closely related to the needs of the department and it may be the most suitable temporary arrangement where training is restricted. However, it should only be considered an interim arrangement until training is introduced into other parts of the firm when the need for a co-ordinated company training effort will become apparent. At this stage one of the previously mentioned structures could be more appropriate.

COMPANY TRAINING STAFF: THEIR ROLES AND THEIR TRAINING
Training director: in very large organizations the importance of the training function may be such that it is controlled by a full-time training director. Few companies have so far appointed full-time training directors, and in many businesses accountability for training at board level is carried as an additional part-time responsibility by the director of another function such as personnel or production.
Group training manager: this title has two different meanings. It may refer to the senior training specialist in a multi-company organization who is responsible for the training function at group level. The 'group training manager' in this sense

advises the group board of directors on training matters and guides the work of training officers in the constituent companies of the group.

Group training manager can also refer to the training specialist in charge of a 'group training scheme'. Small companies, because of their size and limited training facilities, often lack the expertise and breadth of training opportunities necessary for effective training of their employees. One solution to this problem is for such companies with similar training needs to form a training group. Member companies benefit by pooling training resources and sharing the services of the group training manager appointed to co-ordinate and develop the group. He is normally assisted by part-time and sometimes full-time training instructors; the larger group schemes also employ specialist training officers.

The company or general training officer: the training needs of a company employing between approximately five hundred and a thousand staff are often sufficient to require a full-time training officer, who is normally responsible for all types of training and is assisted by full-time and part-time instructors.

The specialist training officer: in companies with large numbers of employees requiring specialized training, it is necessary to appoint specialist training officers. They may be specialists in any aspect of training.

The part-time training officer: there is no need to employ a full-time training officer where there are few people requiring training — as in most small companies. In this situation a line manager acts as a part-time training officer in addition to being responsible for another function. In some companies the personnel officer includes training among his responsibilities, but often it is the company secretary, work study, sales or production manager who is in charge of training.

The roles of training staff

As Rodger, Morgan and Guest (1971) have shown, training officers have many roles to perform and these are mainly determined by the following factors:

the status and importance of the training function in the organization expressed by top management's interest and support. This is a major variable and depends on the degree to which training is regarded as an important contributor to efficient management the extent to which there is a requirement and demand for training in the company. This varies with the size of the firm and the complexity of its operations. It also depends upon the natural development of training in the firm which can change the role of the training specialist over quite short periods of time. When training is first introduced, much of the training officer's time is spent analysing needs. Later, the emphasis switches to designing and running training programmes, structuring learning situations, or helping to initiate change and organization development

the managerial calibre of the training officer, his seniority in the management hierarchy and his acceptability as a person to his fellow managers

the professional expertise of the training officer and his effectiveness in providing the service which management require.

The various combinations of these factors result in a wide spectrum of training practice. At one end is the senior training specialist who is deeply involved in the policy making processes of his company, and whose role is that of consultant to the board of directors and senior management. His major responsibility is to help identify and achieve the organizational changes necessary for the company to reach its objectives and he assists in the diagnosis of problems which appear to have training solutions. He is actively concerned with management training and development.

Reddin (1968) has described a training specialist with this top-level responsibility as a 'Manager of Organizational Development', whose: 'client is not the individual alone but, in addition, the department and the organization. He is interested in training's contribution to overall effectiveness, not simply to individual effectiveness' As yet few training specialists in this country have this corporate training role.

At the other end of the spectrum is the training officer working in a company where the training function is little developed. He has junior management status and limited authority. He is in no position to influence organizational development in the way described by Reddin, and his responsibilities typically include the training of junior staff and the maintenance of training records. His contact with management training is probably limited to making administrative arrangements for managers to attend external courses.

28

Between these two extreme types of training officer, there are of course many others, intermediate in their authority, status and in the tasks for which they are responsible. For a useful list of training activities *see* appendix 1 on page 259.

The different roles of training officers can be classified as follows (Local Government Training Board (1976)):

Management of Training: training officers with this responsibility are concerned with long-term planning and policy formulation. They 'must be aware of the environmental factors affecting the development of the organization and be able to suggest training to meet changed circumstances'. They will be involved in the 'establishment, development and acceptance of the training function . . .'. They will participate in all stages from the formulation of training policy to its achievement'.

Application of systematic training: for example, assessing training needs, formulating training plans, implementing training, advising departments and individuals, planning courses and participating in them, choosing external courses.

Training administration: records, administration of courses etc.

It is not suggested that any of these roles are exclusive. This classification is in line with the core competencies of training staff outlined by the TSA (1977a) in which the specific knowledge and skills are grouped under the role elements of direct training, organizing/administrating, determining/managing, consulting/advisory.

A number of common know-hows (built-in abilities to put understanding into practice) are suggested as necessary for all four roles; know-how about learning, about people, about the organization, about trainer roles, and about diagnosis and problem solving. It is suggested that it is know-how about learning which uniquely characterizes the trainer.

The training of training officers
There was a remarkable increase in the number of companies employing training officers following the establishment of ITBs in 1964. Many of the newly-appointed training officers were previously in other service functions or in line management and so required conversion training for their new jobs.

In 1964, when the Industrial Training Act (*see* chapter 15) became law, there were very few courses available for training

29

officers. The leader in the field was the British Association for Commercial and Industrial Education (BACIE), which for some years had run short courses in specific training topics. BACIE and IPM sponsored the pilot programmes for training officers which were later used as the basis for the Introductory Training Officers courses recommended to all ITBs by the former Central Training Council (1966b).

Introductory courses provided a minimum national basic training for newly-appointed training officers. The courses were usually of a 'sandwich' type, with two 'at college' periods separated by an 'in company' stage during which the course members carried out a project. The demand for these courses grew rapidly in the 1960s as Training Boards strongly encouraged new training officers to attend them. However the Training of Trainers Committee (Manpower Services Commission (1978b) recommended the replacement of the introductory course by a range of core competency modules.

Introductory courses for training officers largely satisfied the immediate post-1964 demand for training specialists, but there remained the longer term need to attract more graduates to a career in training. This need was investigated by the former Central Training Council (1967a) and it recommended the development of six months and longer post-graduate courses in industrial training. In 1968 the Foundry Industry Training Committee and the Ceramics, Glass and Mineral Products Industry Training Board sponsored the country's first post-graduate diploma course in industrial training. (Kenney and Donnelly, 1969)

A later development, reflecting the growth of professionalism, was the increased provision of specialist training and development papers in the Institute of Personnel Management's professional examination structure and the introduction of the Institution of Training Officers' examination scheme.

These advances in the field of training officer training would not have been possible a decade earlier, when there was neither the demand for this kind of training nor, indeed, sufficient expertise available to provide it. However, by the early 1970s the combined experience of industry, ITBs, colleges and consultants, had created a new technology of training which provided the basis for more effective and advanced training on a national scale.

The pattern of training for training officers is evolving and

substantial changes in the present arrangements will be necessary as the function itself develops. Moreover, while the peak
demand for initial training officer training has passed, there is
some evidence to show that many training officers see training
as an interim profession and not as a lifetime career. Rodger,
Morgan and Guest (1971), in their study of training officers
found, for example, that six years was the average length of
time which their respondents had spent in training. If this
proves to be the general pattern, then a regular, if lower,
demand for training officer training can be expected.

It is important to consider the individual nature of the needs
of each training officer, and the necessity for 'job-centred practical training . . . to enable skills and knowledge learned to be
applied and developed at work'. Local Government Training
Board, (1976).

Three stages are identified by this training board:

Induction training: this is required by newly appointed training
officers. It is recommended that they should take part in a
diagnostic course with two in-college periods, and that this
should be followed by an initial programme of short courses
and job-centred practical training. The initial programme for
a completely inexperienced training officer is unlikely to span
less than twelve months.

Further development: planned development of the training officer
should continue while he is in post and he should therefore
always have an individual training and development programme which is regularly reviewed and updated. This can
include: short courses, guided reading, secondments and
attachments, visits, participation on committees etc, and
project work.

Career development and professional qualifications: those who see
their long-term career in the training function and aspire to
posts concerned with the management of training should be
encouraged to become professionally qualified by taking the
examinations of the appropriate professional body, or possibly a post-graduate course in industrial training. The choice
would depend upon the specific needs of the individual. In
some cases the need may be for a more general management
qualification in which case a Diploma in Management
Studies would be appropriate.

The Training of Trainers Committee (Manpower Services
Commission 1978b) state that:

training staff need to be professionals capable of understanding and fitting into the business environment in which they work. As well as relating to training matters this professionalism can extend to technical, managerial or personnel expertise, and there is therefore no one ideal preparation suitable for everyone in a training role. For those who intend to make a full time career in training or allied personnel fields, the membership requirements of the Institute of Personnel Management or the Institution of Training Officers are a relevant and desirable objective . . . It was not, however, felt desirable to establish a common national scheme of individual accreditation, but instead the MSC should set up a voluntary scheme whereby any organization willing to comply with the Code of Practice in relation to core competency programmes should be able to register voluntarily and to derive certain benefits from doing so.

In this chapter we have looked at training mainly from a company viewpoint. We have stressed the value of the systematic approach and outlined how a company can gain maximum benefit from its investment in training. What must not be forgotten is that employees' attitudes to training are very varied and do not necessarily coincide with those of the company — no matter how well intentioned the latter may be.

The self-made manager who learnt his job in the school of hard experience sometimes has no time for training, while the bright school-leaver sees training as a means of achieving his ambition and tries to find a job in a firm which is prepared to train him. Training to a trades unionist may be viewed as a possible threat to the over-supply of skilled labour, and at other times considered the right of all employees as a means of bettering themselves. To some people attendance on a training course is a status symbol, or a holiday from work, or a reward for past services, while others interpret being asked to attend a training course as a criticism of their work and take umbrage at the suggestion that they need training.

Finally, we would mention that training is not always pleasant and acceptable to those on the receiving end. It can show up weaknesses, it can lead to a sense of failure and it often requires great effort to achieve results. These points should never be forgotten by those responsible for training.

Chapter 3

Assessing Training Needs: the Organization

Training assessment at organization level — the impact of legislation — the role of the assessor — carrying out a company-wide assessment

The purpose of a training assessment is to provide an objective analysis of the organization's training requirements. This enables senior management to draw up a training policy so that training resources are used effectively to develop manpower for present and future requirements. Training assessment, as Nadler (1971) has pointed out, is an essential requirement for the effective development of an organization's human resources.

When describing systematic training in chapter 1, we explained that the first step in the cycle is to identify the training requirement. This is critical as it provides the information on which the training is based and the latter can be no better than the quality of the analysis permits. It is important, therefore, to understand the analytical techniques which have been developed to identify and assess training requirements in companies.

TRAINING ASSESSMENT AT ORGANIZATION LEVEL

There are two main types of analysis. First, organization or macro-analysis directed towards broad-based objectives, such as the investigation of the training requirements of all categories of staff in a company, or of a single employee category such as technicians. Secondly, individual job or micro-analysis, where the objective is to identify the skill and knowledge required for a

33

particular job.

These two distinct but complementary types of analysis require different techniques and methods and those used in analysing jobs for training purposes are discussed in chapter 5. In this chapter we describe the various stages in carrying out a company-wide training needs assessment, the role of the assessor, the sources of information and help that he uses, and the interpretation of the information he collects, *see* Boydell (1976). First, it may be helpful to describe some of the reasons for the assessment of organizational training needs.

Establishment of a training department

A company which has appointed a training officer for the first time may be aware of some of its training requirements, yet rarely possesses all the information necessary to formulate an appropriate training policy and plan of action. In these circumstances the new training officer may carry out a training audit to assess the strengths and weaknesses of the company's present training activity and to find out how training can contribute more effectively to the organization's objectives. While it is desirable that the assessment is company-wide, in practice this depends on the training officer's terms of reference. If he has responsibility for training throughout the organization, an overall assessment is necessary. For the training officer with a more restricted responsibility, the initial assessment would be correspondingly less comprehensive. The scope and effectiveness of a needs analysis is determined largely by the level of support it receives from management.

In general, the newly-formed training department is concerned with meeting immediate and short-term training needs. When these are under control, the company can turn its attention from the present training needs to those of the future.

Assessing an organization's long-term training needs

It is still the exception for companies to attempt long-range business forecasting but where this is the practice, manpower planning plays a key role. Manpower planning can be defined as 'a strategy for the acquisition, utilization, improvement and preservation of an enterprise's human resources' (Department of Employment and Productivity (1968)) — a strategy in which training plays an integral part. Manpower specialists, (including the training officer) working with other functional specialists

34

and line management, analyse the organization's business objectives and predict the categories and numbers of staff required to run the company in the future, taking into consideration factors such as market and technological changes, productivity bargaining, investment programmes, competitors' activities and government policies.

The anticipated pattern of employment is then compared with the existing workforce, and after making adjustments for retirements and other staff losses, it is possible to estimate where surpluses or shortages of qualified staff are likely to occur. This is the first step in developing a comprehensive manpower policy for the company which, by co-ordinating recruitment, training, re-training, and other personnel activities, will help to ensure that appropriately trained staff are available when required, (see Bramham (1978)).

Assessments are up-dated at intervals to ensure that a company's training policy and practice are in line with technological, market, economic and other developments likely to affect the business. For small companies the approach to assessing training needs is less sophisticated than the above.

The need to budget for training expenditure

A company training officer reviews his organization's training requirements annually when preparing his budget and training plans for the following year. On these occasions he does not carry out a detailed assessment of the kind described on page 41, since much of the information gathered during such a major investigation is unlikely to change in the short-term. The annual review of training requirements therefore builds on the findings of the earlier assessments.

Previously identified training requirements

A training officer is often asked to investigate a training requirement which has been identified in outline but not yet analysed in any depth. For example, when an airline decides to buy a new type of aircraft, the jobs of some of its pilots, navigators and maintenance engineers will change considerably. The training implications of the decision to buy new aircraft must be assessed if the airline is to minimize changeover problems. Priorities, costs and training methods must be determined at an organizational level and subsequently, detailed training programmes prepared.

35

Hidden training needs

Problems in organizations which stem from inadequate training are often attributed to other causes and not recognized by management as training needs. For example, an investigation into the backlog of work in the accounts department of a rapidly expanding company showed that the root of the trouble was not, as the chief accountant had claimed, a shortage of staff, but a deterioration in the quality of accounts clerks which the company was able to employ. Previously, the recruitment position in the area had been favourable and new employees had not needed formal training. When the labour market was tighter, less able staff were recruited and still no attempt was made to train them. The newcomers were eventually able to do the work without training but they took much longer to learn it and in the process made many more mistakes than their predecessors.

As a further illustration, newsagents were frequently complaining that they did not receive delivery of a certain evening paper in time to sell all the copies. This was found to be due to the fact that the editorial department were so keen to have their news hot from the press that they only released copy to the composing room at the very last minute and the paper was therefore late. The problem was resolved by the editorial staff having some work experience in the composing room and thus able to understand the compositors' difficulties.

Incorrectly identified training needs

A training officer should approach an assessment objectively, not being unduly influenced by the initial information which he receives in a particular brief. On occasions he will find that a difficulty which was presented to him as being caused by lack of training is in fact not a training problem. For example, the training officer in a civil engineering company was asked to prepare a training programme for supervisors in the sub-contracting department. On investigation he found that the supervisors' apparently inadequate performance was caused by the irregular flow of work into the department. The problem was an organizational one and could not be solved by supervisory training.

We have already demonstrated (page 13) how apparent poor performance by one group of people may indicate training needs in an entirely different part of the organization. It is therefore necessary to obtain and analyse all relevant facts; hasty conclusions leading to incorrect training priorities could make the situation worse by frustrating those who are already working under difficulties beyond their control.

Partial training needs

A training officer's help is often sought in tackling such problems as reducing customers' complaints about the quality of goods or removing bottle-necks in a production department: the assumptions being that the employees concerned have not been trained to do their jobs correctly. While this could be the case, an investigation may show that inadequate training is only partly responsible for the poor quality of work or slow working: the major causes may be poor supervision, discontent over pay, or recruitment of unsuitable employees. The training officer has to distinguish between those problems which are wholly or partly due to ineffective training and are therefore likely to have training solutions, and those which result from non-training factors for which other answers must be found.

THE IMPACT OF LEGISLATION

It is obvious that training is not going to be effective if it is carried out purely because the law says so, ie to comply with minimum requirements. However, as well as laying down certain statutory obligations which not only the training officer but every manager and employee representative should know, recent legislation highlights a number of important aspects of training which merit careful attention for their own sake and for their possible effect on organizations. In general these aspects concern all levels of the organization hierarchy and are therefore better included as part of the overall training assessment than treated as entirely separate items.

Health and Safety

The Health and Safety at Work etc Act 1974 specifies that it is the duty of every employer to provide 'such information, instruction, training and supervision as necessary to ensure, so far as is reasonably practicable, the health and safety at work of his employees' (Part I Sec 2). Subsequent sections of the Act are concerned with a written statement of policy on health and safety and the 'arrangements' (which presumably include training) for its implementation, together with the appointment in

37

'prescribed cases' of employee representatives and safety committees. The philosophy of the Act is clearly supportive of employee participation and consultation and this has training implications. This trend is in line with developments in ITB policies described on page 56. For a more detailed discussion of the training implications of this Act (*see* Howells and Barrett (1975)).

It must be emphasized that Part I Sec 2 of this Act (quoted above) mentions the provision of 'supervision'. It is now generally recognized that safety training must be an integral part of the company's training schemes and must be included in programmes for supervisors and managers as well as in induction courses and in operator training. School leavers are particularly at risk and require special attention. For an excellent publication on safety training *see* Iron and Steel ITB (1976)

Industrial relations

Legislation such as the Trade Union and Labour Relations Act 1974 and the Employment Protection Act 1975 have far reaching implications for training. How little training there has been for either side in this important aspect of business is described in the CIR Report No 33 (1972a) where the point is also made that most current industrial relations training consists of imparting broad general knowledge and insufficient attention is paid to the specific knowledge and skill requirements of individual jobs. It is also claimed that those who are actively involved in industrial relations play little part in the training. A further suggestion in the CIR Report is that all those concerned should be consulted about their industrial relations training needs.

It is now increasingly accepted that the inept handling of relatively minor problems can lead to major industrial issues. Furthermore, if a case is brought against an organization at an Industrial Tribunal, it is extremely damaging if top management cannot support the actions of their subordinates. In addition to a knowledge of the law, skill in devising the procedures necessary to comply with it and training in company policies and practices as well as in union agreements is a necessity. A number of ITBs have made recommendations for industrial relations training, eg Food, Drink and Tobacco (1977). For a practical guide, *see* the Commission on Industrial Relations (1972b).

38

Worker participation

The trend towards increased worker participation also has training implications of which the most obvious is the training of employee representatives. The Employment Protection Act places the employer under a responsibility to allow a trade union 'official' time off with pay during working hours to take part in industrial relations training relevant to his duties. There have also been considerable developments in shop steward training, particularly that sponsored by the TUC. The large number of shop stewards and the comparatively high rate of turnover indicate the extent of this problem. Important as this training is, however, it is only one aspect of an enormous training need. Participation can only be truly successful where the organizational climate is suitable and in some cases this would be the consequence of a far reaching programme of organization development in which training would play a most important role. Effective participation involves numerous managerial and supervisory skills and in some cases genuine attitude change, as well as a certain amount of education of the whole workforce so that they can make a fair appraisal of the work of their representatives. None of this can be achieved overnight. The training officer should be aware of these trends when considering organizational training needs.

Race relations

The harmful results of failure to deal effectively with major issues in this field are becoming more apparent by the day. Training will not solve such problems in an organization but it has an important contribution to make. Awareness of the special needs of particular groups of workers is likely to be most effectively achieved when included as an integral part of the company's training plans for managers, supervisors and other employees. Then there are the obvious needs relating to job centred training. The Race Relations Act 1976 encourages positive action to promote entry of racial groups into new areas of work by stipulating that an employer or trade union can provide training facilities exclusively for a particular racial group to fit them for work in which they are unrepresented. Another important aspect is induction to the organization and to the trade union, including knowledge of all relevant procedures. This training can help to prevent the painful consequences that may otherwise arise from later misunderstandings. Language

39

teaching may be necessary and there is evidence that such programmes must be supported by the English speaking population and related to shop floor practice, Leppard and Kaufman (1972). For a discussion of the advantages and costs of language training *see* Carby and Thakur (1977).

Advice on problems ranging from provision of language training to courses for managers and shop stewards can be obtained from the Race Relations Employment Advisers at the Department of Employment Regional Offices. There is also a National Centre for Industrial Language Training which has an information service, a centre with audio visual materials and a staff training programme.

THE ROLE OF THE ASSESSOR
While the above description of organization training needs assessments is not exhaustive, it should be sufficient for the reader to appreciate that differing types of assessment call for assessors with different abilities and experience. For example, the analytical and personal skills, and the authority necessary to assess the training requirements for semi-skilled work would normally be within the competence of a junior training officer. An assessment of a company's total training needs, including those of its management, presents a more difficult problem. The seniority of the assessor carrying out this latter investigation requires that he is informed of the company's plans, and has access to personal and other confidential data, such as performance appraisal details and promotion plans.

The diagnosis of training needs on an organizational scale requires a high order of ability in analysis, evaluation and communication. Talbot and Ellis (1969) make the point that:

> the provision of mere routine training answers to traditional problems will not be sufficient. The requirement is for a much more extensive diagnostic skill which looks beyond the learning processes of individuals and of groups and assesses the impact of this on the business's needs for growth and adjustment.

Over and above the routine techniques described later, the assessor must know how and when to enlist the help of other company specialists, such as manpower planners or operational researchers, in predicting training and re-training needs. He must also be able to take a fresh view of the organization and see what effect its structure, policies and practices have on the optimum use of its employees' abilities. To what extent, for example, does the organization provide promotion plans, career paths or job opportunities within and across depart-'ments, and what training is, or should be, available to help staff move along these paths? The assessor working at this level must be able to propose company training priorities and assist in the development of training policies to make the best use of the organization's manpower.

In addition to knowing the techniques of assessment, it is very important that the training officer is acceptable as a person to his top management and to the management hierarchy in general. Without this, he would lack the personal authority to complete the assessment satisfactorily and the chances of his recommendations being implemented would be reduced.

The assessor must be prepared for non-training problems which he will from time to time uncover when carrying out an assessment. Internal company politics, personality clashes between managers, bad discipline in a department, are examples of problems which may not have training solutions but do have implications for the trainer. There is no one way of handling these kinds of situations, but the assessor is advised to keep to his brief impartially and diplomatically. At the same time he must not ignore the fact that these problems exist in the company and that they may create a hostile attitude to training.

CARRYING OUT A COMPANY-WIDE ASSESSMENT

A number of ITBs (*see* Ceramics, Glass and Mineral Products ITB (1968a), Paper and Paper Products ITB (1969) and Chemical and Allied Products ITB (1970a)) have published guides on training needs assessment and figure 3.1 shows the sequence which a training officer would normally follow. The main steps are:

Step 1: preparation for the assessment
The importance of preparation as a key to the success of a training needs assessment cannot be overstressed. The training officer must prepare himself by ensuring that he has a clear brief, specifying the precise objectives of the assessment. This brief should cover such points as the scope, objectives and time-span of the assessment, the degree to which it is confidential, the authority which the training officer is given for access to

41

Figure 3.1
Stages in an organization training needs assessment

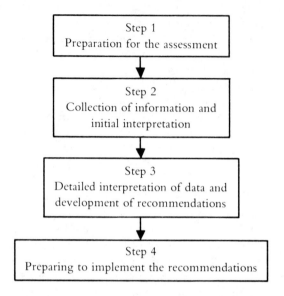

relevant company information, when the results are required and to whom the assessment report is to be sent.

When he is quite clear as to what he has to do, his next step is to prepare the employees who are likely to be affected by the investigation. This is necessary for three reasons. First, the training officer is in effect acting as a consultant and must rely on the cooperation of managers and others to help him carry out the assessment. It is, therefore, important that the purpose of the assessment, and how and when he proposes to carry it out, are fully discussed in advance with the appropriate staff. He should, for example, make it clear that the assessment is *not* part of an Organization and Method (O and M) or work measurement investigation. As the first stage in the training cycle, the assessment has an important part to play in the formation of attitudes and in selling any resultant training activities.

Secondly, during the assessment a training officer asks searching questions. This may cause adverse reaction from some employees who may adopt a less than cooperative attitude if, as can easily happen, they misconstrue the training officer's motives. This is particularly likely if the organizational climate is unsettled. An assessment taking place soon after a company has been taken over, or during an industrial dispute, may well run into difficulties which are not of the training officer's own making. Even if the organizational climate is generally favourable, he should nonetheless explain the purpose of the assessment to the staff concerned and obtain their cooperation. Training needs are often weak spots in an organization and those concerned tend to be sensitive when questioned about them, especially if they regard the investigation as implied criticism.

A third reason for a training officer advising those involved of the impending assessment is that, given advance notice, they can collect the information which the assessor will require from them, for example, by preparing labour turnover figures or up-dating job specification sheets or organization charts, if available. This can save everyone a great deal of time and brings forward the completion date of the assessment.

Finally in this first step, the training officer has to decide where to start the assessment. This has already been discussed and the most appropriate starting point in any given case depends on variables, such as staff availability, the purpose of the assessment, the personal choice of the assessor and the degree to which line management are prepared to cooperate with him.

It is useful at the beginning of a company-wide training needs assessment to have an organization chart showing the relationships of different departments and the formal lines of responsibility. Many organizations do not have such charts and the training officer may have to draw up his own as he progresses with the assessment. It is important to remember that organization charts often show much less information than may at first be apparent. To be of value to the assessor, they must be up-to-date and indicate, where possible, the real areas of responsibility and lines of communication, not just those of the formal organization.

Step 2: collection of information and its initial interpretation
Although in theory, information has first to be collected before it is interpreted, in practice it is artificial to separate these two processes, as they tend to take place simultaneously. The training officer interprets the facts and opinions that he gathers about the organization as he records them, at times seeking more detail and at others deciding further information is irrelevant. Later (step 3) he assesses the data more critically in relation to

the broader picture which has emerged.

In carrying out the assessment, the training officer collects information about the training needs of the organization and its training resources. There is a very close connection between these two since the extent to which resources are or can be made available provides a major constraint on the training which the company can carry out. (Training resources are described in chapter 4). Companies are often faced with the problem of competing claims for limited training resources. The assessor needs to indicate: training priorities, the basis for these priorities and how, if resources are not available, the need for qualified staff can be satisfied, for example, by recruiting ready-trained employees or possibly by redesigning jobs.

Methods of collecting information: depending on the type of assessment, the assessor obtains his information:

> from analysing company records (such as personnel statistics, accident records, training reports, and staff appraisal forms), and policy statements on manpower, marketing, production, etc
> by formal and informal interviewing
> from direct observation of work and by keeping his eyes open as he proceeds with the assessment
> from a training committee, which can provide information on training requirements in a company and the priority areas.

The assessor often has to ferret out his own information, since it is not necessarily available in the form in which he needs it. For example, job specifications prepared for recruitment purposes are useful but are, at best, only a starting point for any training analysis (*see* page 66).

Sources of information: there is no one correct sequence in which to collect relevant data when carrying out a training needs assessment. The following are likely to be the main sources:

> external influences
> top management
> personnel department
> other service departments
> departmental managers and their staff.

External influences: an organization's training needs can be considerably influenced by the external environment in which

44

the company operates. These include competitors' labour requirements, market changes, the difficulty of recruiting staff, the general economic climate and government policies. The assessor does not normally carry out detailed investigations into all these factors, but he must be aware of them and discuss their possible training implications with the appropriate executives.

Top management: the training officer, if possible, begins the assessment by finding out from top management the company's short and long-term objectives, bearing in mind that his aim is to identify how, when and where investment in training can help an organization to achieve its objectives. However, objectives are not always defined nor will they necessarily be disclosed to the training officer.

For example, a company may not have precise written aims, but the training officer must be given information about its present and future operations by senior management if the assessment is to be meaningful in terms of the organization's requirements. Otherwise, he would have no objective means of assessing the significance of the data he collects, no certain basis for determining priorities and other training recommendations, and therefore no satisfactory way of measuring the standards and effectiveness of existing and future training.

Furthermore, if the organization's goals have not been clarified it is probable that the company's structure is inappropriate and that operating problems occur because managers are unknowingly working to different ends. This can give rise to situations where training is apparently being applied successfully to remedy a problem. In reality it is only a palliative which treats the symptoms of a problem while its cause — for example, an out-dated policy, remains unaltered.

The training officer therefore obtains from top management indications of any anticipated variations in the business such as technical, product or market changes, future capital expenditure, or predicted adjustments in the labour force. These have training implications if they result in a demand for new expertise, or an increased requirement for existing categories. The assessor records these changes in detail and notes when they will be implemented, their scope and estimated effect. Armed with this information, he will know what to look for when discussing training needs with managers of departments affected by these changes.

Personnel department: the training officer must be familiar with the company's personnel policies, practices and plans. Recruitment, selection procedures, industrial relations, remuneration, promotion policies and training are inter-dependent and therefore relevant to the assessor. A personnel department can supply valuable information, including job specifications, recruitment plans, the industrial relations climate, bonus payment systems and promotion policy. In addition, it can provide employee statistics of three main kinds: labour turnover, length of service of leavers, age distribution all by department and section. These statistics are of fundamental importance in an assessment and are illustrated on pages 47 and 48.

Labour turnover: labour turnover statistics are of interest to an assessor because where there is a high turnover of new staff there is also a substantial need for induction and job training for recruits. An investigation of the reasons for high labour turnover may reveal that it is caused by inadequate training (*see* below) or by non-training problems. Some of the latter — such as low wages or inadequate supervision — the company may choose to solve; if it fails to do so, a disproportionately heavy expenditure on training is the penalty.

At times, companies find that the cause of a high labour turnover lies outside their control. An example of this is the employment of young office workers in central London, where, in spite of attractive salaries and work conditions, it is quite common for junior staff to change jobs after a few months. Faced with this situation the assessor might recommend the introduction of training, not because it would reduce labour turnover significantly but because, by training new employees systematically, they would reach a level of competence more rapidly. If the average length of service of office juniors were six months and by sitting-next-to-Nellie training they took two months to master their jobs, they would give on average only four months' efficient work to their employers. If, with the systematic approach, training times were reduced to about a month, even though the new staff still left after approximately six months in the firm, for five of these months they would be pulling their weight if the training is cost effective.

It should be remembered that labour turnover as an index of labour instability is only meaningful if related to small groups of employees. When dealing with large numbers of staff, marked variations in labour turnover tend to be evened out and their significance lost. Further caution is necessary in deciding what constitutes a 'high' or 'low' figure. Comparisons should be made only with situations within the same industry and area and with similar recruitment problems.

Length of service of leavers: as noted above, the absence or inadequacy of training in a company can cause labour turnover. If staff are not correctly trained and find the work too difficult to learn unaided, an unstable labour force results. This is found by examining the 'length of service of leavers' to check whether, as in figure 3.2, many staff have left within a short period of joining the firm. Even if the assessor finds this pattern in the figures, he should not automatically assume that inadequate training is to blame, as non-training reasons, such as poor selection or tight bonus times may be the cause.

Figure 3.2
Statistics showing the length of service of
leavers (taken over a one-year period)

Job	Sex	Length of service					
		Up to 3 months	4 to 8 months	9 to 23 months	years	Over 5 years	Total
Sales Assistant	F	48	25	9	6	4	92

As with labour turnover figures, the assessor should initially regard leavers' length of service data as general pointers for further investigation. Finding out why employees leave a company is not easy. They are often reluctant to give the real reason and a 'reason for leaving' book can be misleading unless interpreted by experienced staff.

Age distribution: the purpose of an age distribution analysis, in this context, is to discover how many employees in a department or staff category fall within certain age groupings and to interpret the training implications of any imbalance in the age structure.

A department may have a very young labour force, in which case both inexperience and staff mobility are likely to create considerable demands for training. Conversely, it may be staffed largely by older employees, perhaps with a number of its key personnel approaching retirement. Figure 3.3 (male supervisors) illustrates the latter situation. The training officer should check that plans have been made to provide successors. An ageing workforce is not revealed by labour turnover statistics; on the contrary, a low staff turnover suggests little training is required. The training officer must therefore use both turnover and age distribution statistics in assessing an organization's training needs.

Figure 3.3
Statistics showing age distribution

Job	Sex	Age range						
		Under 25	26-30	31-40	41-50	51-60	61-65	Total
Office supervisor	M	1	2	2	5	7	8	25
„ „	F	—	3	3	2	1	—	9

An assessor normally has little difficulty in obtaining these various manpower statistics if the company has a personnel department. His task is more difficult where no such department exists as the information has then to be extracted from pay and other records. This is much less satisfactory and usually results in incomplete and, therefore, less useful information.

Help from other service departments in the organization: in medium and large companies there are usually other specialists from whom the training officer can obtain information. For example, the Accounts, O and M, Work Study, Quality Control and Research and Development departments all have data about the company's activities which can be of direct value to the assessor.

The Accounts department may be able to provide such details as: training expenditure in the company, with a breakdown by department; the system of recording training costs and the company's training budget. A review of company training, expressed in financial terms, provides the assessor with a valuable measure of the scale on which training is taking place. However, the level of expenditure must be carefully interpreted. For example, a department's high training costs can be due to inefficient training or it can be fully justified; while low expenditure can indicate inadequate training or little requirement for it.

The records in the O and M and the Work Study departments can be an important source of information for the training officer. Work procedures, job specifications and grades, training times and work standards provide a clear picture of the structure and work of a department. Moreover, since these specialists are concerned with analysing existing work as well as implementing new systems, they can often suggest where training requirements already exist in the company, and where in the future training is likely to be needed.

Similarly, the assessor can be helped by the Quality Control and the Research and Development departments. The former can provide quality standards for particular work and indicate where employees have difficulty in achieving these standards. Research and Development staff will know of anticipated technological changes and when they are likely to be introduced in the company. They may also be able to predict some of the manpower implications of the proposed changes, such as the grades of employee that will be required

49

in the future and the feasibility of re-training existing staff for new jobs.

The costs of unsystematic training are often hidden but are usually well worth investigating, both to help sell an improved scheme and to use as a yardstick in later evaluation. They are expressed in items such as inadequate machine utilization, damage to machinery, scrap, time taken by supervisors or Nellie in instruction, sometimes in lack of recruits and, as already mentioned, in labour turnover and length of training time. For a more detailed discussion of this aspect see King (1964).

Departmental managers and their staff: the assessor is by this stage well prepared to start the major part of his investigation, his discussions with line management. Using the information already collected about the company's current operations and its objectives, he visits, in turn, all departmental managers and obtains answers to the following questions:

Present training arrangements in the department

> Who is responsible for training?
> What training has the nominee had to do this job?
> What is the scope of the present training?
> What plans are there for training new and existing staff?
> Do these cover job and career training?
> Are these arrangements regarded as satisfactory?
> How much is training costing the department?

The quality of the present training

> Have training programmes been based on identified needs?
> Have training standards been established and, if so, on what basis?
> How are trainees assessed?
> What records of training are kept, and why?
> Are training resources adequate, and what is the basis for their allocation?

Departmental management's attitude to training

> Is the manager well-informed about the training in his department?
> Is he aware of the company's training policy?
> Does he regard it as satisfactory?
> Has he developed his own departmental policy? For example, is it his practice to train staff to be able to do more

50

than one job?

Can senior management, or the training department, give him any further assistance?

Are there any training problems which are particular to the department?

Future training requirements

What training needs have been recognized in the department and

What plans have been evolved to meet them?

Which requirements should have priority?

What departmental and other resources will be required to meet these needs?

The assessor then interviews the junior managers who are usually directly involved in day to day training and are well-qualified to talk about the quality of existing arrangements, and to recommend improvements. Junior management's close involvement in training is vital, since they are one of the company's most important training resources. These discussions also give the training officer an opportunity to assess these managers' actual and potential performance as trainers.

Other employees who can help the training officer in his assessment are staff currently under training or who have recently completed their training. The consumer's point of view is often very illuminating!

Having collected data under these different headings, the training officer has a comprehensive record of the department's present arrangements, its anticipated training needs and priorities and the resources required to meet them. He then repeats this process in all departments of the company.

Step 3: Detailed interpretation of data and development of recommendations

At this stage in the assessment the training officer reviews the information he has collected and begins to piece together the results of the training audit. He works through his assessment notes and assembles the material which is particularly relevant and disregards that which is now seen to be of marginal significance. At times, he will find gaps and discrepancies in his data necessitating a return to particular information sources. He attempts to weigh the relative importance of the training needs

51

which have been identified, initially on a departmental basis and subsequently for the company as a whole.

The ranking of training priorities is a difficult but important part of the assessment process. It is difficult because the assessor has to exercise his judgement in deciding between different priorities, although he is helped in his decisions by reference to criteria such as: the terms of his brief; the company's existing training policy; the availability of resources which particular training programmes will require and the benefits which they are expected to yield.

The ranking of training requirements is important because a company's training budget is rarely large enough to meet every need. The training officer has, therefore, to synthesize his findings and express them as recommendations for action. His recommendations should be:

   justified, with supporting evidence of actual training needs listed in priority terms

   feasible, in that the necessary resources are likely to be available

   costed and, if appropriate, should indicate whether or not the proposed training is eligible for grant or is likely to gain exemption from levy (*see* chapter 15)

   acceptable to senior management

   within the company's training policy, or where policy changes are needed, reasons given

   practical and acceptable to those implementing the recommendations

   specific, in naming who is responsible for implementing the training and when it is required.

These recommendations and the evidence on which they are based are normally contained in a report prepared by the assessor for management. In writing the assessment report, the training officer bears in mind such points as: the initial and the likely subsequent readers of his report; the use of confidential information collected during the assessment; how to express criticism of managers who have apparently failed to train their staff and the general principles of good report writing, *see* British Association for Commercial and Industrial Education (1977).

The contents of an assessment report refer to a training situation which prevailed at the time it was written and as circumstances change the assessment becomes progressively outdated. A training officer must, therefore, carry out a detailed overall assessment of his company's training needs at intervals and, in between times, undertake minor assessments as necessary.

Step 4: preparing to implement the recommendations
When the assessment report is completed, the training officer still has two key tasks to perform. First, to follow up his recommendations and help to get them accepted by the company and second, to see that they are implemented.

No experienced training officer assumes that all his assessment recommendations will be adopted by the company. Some managers will accept the assessor's specialist advice enthusiastically and use the training department's services fully. Others will disagree with particular findings or recommendations, but will be open to persuasion if the training officer can substantiate his points with facts and figures. The apathetic manager, who superficially accepts the results of the assessment but takes no positive steps to implement them, is more difficult to win over.

The assessor should be prepared to spend a great deal of time discussing, persuading and selling his wares using the support of senior management, keen departmental managers, the training committee and, if appropriate, his Training Board adviser. If the training officer does not carry his fellow managers with him, much of the value of an assessment is lost since an assessment is essentially a seed-sowing exercise for subsequent training.

Chapter 4

Training Policies and Resources

Training policies — policy development — company
training plans — training resources

In this chapter we consider the relationship between the broad
training requirements of an organization and its training
policies. We also examine how these two factors determine the
content of a company's training plan and some of the typical
resources required to implement it.

TRAINING POLICIES

Companies have very different policies for training. A growing
number have policies designed to gain the maximum benefit
from training, while in contrast there are still many organizations where the systematic approach is unknown and management do not accept responsibility for training. The majority of
organizations lie somewhere between these extremes, with
training which is variable in quality, limited in scope, and to a
greater or lesser extent, lacking in direction. Training priorities
are determined on an *ad hoc* rather than a planned basis.

A company's training policies represent the commitment of
its directors to training and are expressed in the rules and
procedures which govern or influence the standard and scope of
training in the organization. Training policies are necessary:

to provide guide lines for those responsible for planning and
implementing training
to ensure that a company's training resources are allocated to
priority requirements
to provide for equality of opportunity for training throughout the company and

to inform employees of training and development opportunities.

These points are illustrated in an example of a company's statement of its general training policy on page 57 and in the following examples of specific training policies:

> during the year all managers and supervisors will attend a
> seminar on the company's industrial relations procedures
> junior office staff should be encouraged to attend appropriate
> day release further education courses.

POLICY DEVELOPMENT

An organization's policy for training, in common with other
business functions, often results from an organic growth of
rules and procedures established to deal with particular problems. These decisions tend to be made on a piecemeal basis and,
with the passage of time, some of them are accepted as prece-
dents and become company policy. The development of
policies in this way is beneficial only if they are comprehen-
sively reviewed at regular intervals. Such reviews are necessary
as the circumstances which give rise to policies can change
markedly, often over short periods of time. A comprehensive
review of a company's training policies therefore assesses the
appropriateness of existing rules and procedures to the training
needs of the organization and indicates where alterations may
be necessary.

A company may be prompted to carry out such a review for
reasons other than to update its existing training policies. The
decision may be linked to the introduction of systematic training, or to a sudden demand for training caused, for example, by
successful productivity bargaining (Chemical and Allied Products ITB (1970b), or by new legislation (*see* page 37).

A change in the economic climate can be another reason for a
review. Although it is clearly preferable for a policy to antici-
pate contingencies such as retraining stemming from fluctua-
tions in trading, it is difficult for equitable guidelines to be
drawn up objectively by all parties, if important decisions have
to be taken in a potentially emotive environment.

Whatever the reasons for the review, it is essential that training policies contribute directly to an organization's objectives.
As Tavernier (1971) stresses: 'Any policy regarding training
(must) be in harmony with the company's personnel policies on

recruitment, salaries, promotion and security of employment . . .'. A company's directors are responsible for deciding training policies, although the effectiveness of their decisions will be increased if they have consulted their subordinates. The requirements of line management should be fully considered and, as we have stated in chapter 2, the training officer plays an important part in this process. A recent development has been the general move towards effective employee consultation and participation in top level decision making and this means that there is increasing involvement of trade union and other worker representatives in the formulation of company training policies.

ITBs regard a written training policy as an important criterion for exemption from the payment of levy, but it is interesting to note that some boards have gone further and require participation in the planning of training eg:

> . . . the policy should contain provisions, appropriate to the company, for employees or their representatives to participate in formulating and evaluating training plans, Clothing and Allied Products ITB (1977).

There are obvious benefits in involving employees in this way: the board of directors' decisions can be more effective if they are consonant with the values and expectations of the organization they direct.

Deciding training policies can prove to be a difficult task for directors, especially if they are doing so for the first time, and if they do not have the advice of a training officer with previous experience at this level. In such cases, assistance may be necessary from consultants, including advisers from ITBs. Most Boards have published recommendations suggesting the questions which companies should be asking (and answering!), when structuring training policies.

In framing their policies for training, directors have first to decide what contribution they want the training function to make to the achievement of the company's objectives. For example, where a system of Management by Objectives is in operation, the training policy is completely integrated with corporate strategy: Humble (1973). The type of policy will vary from one organization to another and depend on such factors as:

the objectives of the business
the directors' personal views on training and the extent to
    which they are informed about systematic methods

information which is available about the organization's training needs
the size of the company
the labour market situation and the alternative means of procuring skilled and qualified staff other than by training
the company's former and current policies and practices
the calibre of its training staff
the resources the company can allocate to training.

Before 1964, it was fairly unusual for training policies to be written let alone published, because management had not in general been sufficiently interested in training, and the expertise required to produce relevant policies on a company-wide basis was often lacking. Moreover, many boards of directors were cautious of publicly committing themselves to policies which were untried and which they considered were better handled, at least initially, on a less formal basis. Now, ITBs require a written policy and, as we have noted, recent legislation obliges employers to provide a written policy on safety, which by implication should include reference to training provisions.

For the reasons mentioned above, the contents of training policy statements vary with the approach and requirements of different organizations. In all cases, however, the statement should provide clear guidelines for those concerned with training. The following is an example of a company's general policy statement on training:

The directors recognize the important contribution which training makes to a company's continuing efficiency and profitability. They further recognize that the prime responsibility for training rests with management. The company training officer is responsible for advising and assisting all managers on training matters and is accountable to the managing director.

The company's training policy refers to all employees and aims to:

provide induction training for new staff and for those transferred to new departments
ensure that appropriate training is available to enable individuals to reach a satisfactory performance in their jobs
provide the training required by those selected for promotion so that they are appropriately prepared for their new responsibilities

provide information, instruction and training to ensure the
health and safety of all employees.

There are a number of advantages to be gained from making the
content of the training policy widely known in the company. It
communicates the directors' intentions, it helps those responsible for implementing training, it clarifies the role and function
of the training specialist, it indicates in general terms the training opportunities available to employees and, if the contents are
progressive, publication enhances employer-employee relations.

COMPANY TRAINING PLANS

A company's training plan lists the training which it intends to
implement in a given period of time. A plan is produced as a
result of a three-fold process incorporating training needs,
policies and resources.

The organization's requirements for training are identified
when preparing the annual training budget, or from a detailed
investigation of the kind indicated in the previous chapter.
These training needs are then appraised against the criteria
contained in the company's training policies; a process which
may eliminate some requirements from the proposed plans. For
example, a proposal for certain managers to attend a day release
Diploma in Management Studies course would be excluded if
there are to be no exceptions from a company's policy that staff
over the age of 21 are not granted day release. Finally, training
priorities have to be established because there are usually insufficient resources available for all the training which has been
requested.

In such circumstances decisions have to be made as to what
training is to be included in the plan. For example, a company
which has limited training resources but which is introducing
an important new range of products in the coming year would
give a high priority to product training for its sales force, if
necessary, at the expense of training in other fields which is less
urgent and can be postponed without serious repercussions.

A company's training plan is, therefore, the outcome of
co-ordinating its training needs, policies and resources. A typical plan contains the following factors:

details of the projected training for categories of staff on a
company basis (eg management trainees)

details of departmental training requirements eg clerical and
  supervisory training in the accounts department, technician training in the laboratories, shop steward, operative
  and management training in the factory
against each item of training the plan specifies who is responsible for seeing that it is implemented, how much it will
  cost and when it will take place
departmental and company budget figures for training: these
  can be divided into training which is continuing and to
  which the company is already committed, for example,
  craft trainees who are part-way through their courses, and
  other training.

TRAINING RESOURCES

Training resources can be thought of as the input required to
enable a training plan to be implemented. They include people
(eg training officer and external course organizers), facilities (eg
a training room), aids and materials.

All training resources ultimately cost a company money.
Many of these costs appear in a training budget, but others are
rarely identified as training costs. Whether the costs are identified or not, the training officer is responsible for advising on
the best use of resources to facilitate learning. To do this he
requires an up to date knowledge of the resources available to
his company and how they can best be employed. Some of these
are discussed below.

Internal resources
Training specialists
An experienced training officer is potentially one of the major
contributors to his organization's training operations. The
extent to which his skills and knowledge are put to profitable
use depends in practice on many variables, in particular on his
technical competence and on the degree of cooperation which
he receives from fellow managers.

Trainers
The role of trainers (or instructors) is discussed in chapter 6.
They act as the essential link between the learner and the training programme and all companies require them to implement
training. Trainers include managers (when coaching their own
staff), company tutors overseeing trainee technologists, craft

59

apprentice supervisors and operator instructors.

Training budget
Many of a training officer's activities depend on the availability
of finance, so the preparation of a budget is a very important
aspect of his job. The content and size of a training budget
depends on many factors, including the way in which the
organization views the training function, the level of its training
activity and the tenacity of its training officer. It can also vary
from year to year, depending upon the profitability of the
company, or in a public concern upon government policy and
funds. This is an added problem, because it is sometimes during
a difficult period that training or retraining needs can be
greatest. It is always necessary to plan well ahead and to assess
the situation carefully so that whatever finance is available goes
to the real priorities.

The growth of training in many companies makes it necessary for training costs to be isolated for budget purposes and to
assist in training evaluation (*see* chapter 6). The reader is referred
to Garbutt (1969) and to Talbot and Ellis (1969) for detailed
examples of components of training budgets. While these vary
from one organization to another, all require appropriate systems of forecasting and controlling the financial resources
needed for training.

Singer (1977) has specified certain main requirements for
budget and budgetary control in this function:

   adequate training plans
   the expenses incurred in achieving the training plan must
      have been identified and estimated
   the responsibility for items of expenditure must have been
      allocated between training specialists and other managers
   account classifications must have been made so that expendi-
      ture can be allocated to specific cost areas
   cost information must be recorded accurately and a
      mechanism for feeding back the collated information must
      be present so that individuals can take corrective action
      when required.

Training facilities
These include training centres or areas, which range from country mansions for management development programmes,
through apprentice schools, to a part of a shop, office or work-

60

shop set aside for training. The size and type of facilities depend on company requirements and policy.

Training aids
Professional training staff use the products of educational technology, such as closed-circuit television, overhead projectors, programmed learning texts and audio-visual materials. These can be powerful learning aids but, as Powell (1978) has stressed, they must be chosen and used skilfully to avoid being regarded as gimmicks.

Company training information
An organization with a systematic approach to manpower development has a wide range of data covering its training operations ie job descriptions and specifications, training programmes, employees' training histories, reports on company training needs and training plans. This information bank is a useful asset in, for example, improving future programmes or reducing the time needed for job training analysis.

External resources
These can be grouped under the following main headings: private sector courses and consultants, group training schemes, professional associations, public sector education and training services.

Private sector courses and consultants
Since the Industrial Training Act there has been a boom in the training course industry with numerous organizations offering a bewildering variety of courses on almost every aspect of training. Selecting the right course is a difficult but important task for a training officer, if his company is to benefit from what can be a considerable financial outlay.

Nelson (1966) has examined criteria for selecting training courses (*see also* Ceramics Glass and Mineral Products ITB (1969)) and the questions which a company should ask when considering their use. These include:

Is the cost of the course related to its anticipated benefits?
Has the course clearly defined objectives?
Are they realistic in the time available?
Do the instructional methods employed seem suitable to meet the objectives eg do they teach knowledge or skill?

To what extent does the course content coincide with the company's specific requirements and what experience and other qualifications do the course tutors possess?

Advice in choosing an appropriate course is also available from the information departments of organizations such as the Institute of Personnel Management, British Association for Commercial and Industrial Education, British Institute of Management and ITBs. Consultants are a valuable source of expertise, especially to companies new to systematic training. Organizations considering the use of training consultants should apply similar criteria to those used in selecting courses.

Group training schemes
These are formed by a group of employers, normally in a similar industry, who join together to establish joint training facilities, which they would be unable to justify economically on an individual basis. A number of group schemes (approximately 60) existed before the Industrial Training Act, and many more (over 700) have been formed under the auspices of the ITBs. These schemes offer employers, particularly small employers, the facilities of a training officer, instructors, and (usually) an off the job training centre. Traditionally, the group scheme concentrates mainly on craft training, particuarly first year off the job training, but some schemes cover the whole spectrum of training and many also assist with employee selection.

Professional associations
The rapid growth of professionalism in many fields of employment in recent years has led to the creation of numerous professional bodies. The training officer needs to be familiar with those professional associations relevant to his company. They can supply detailed information on the education and training programmes which lead to membership qualifications. In addition, many professional bodies run or sponsor post-qualification courses to assist their members to keep up to date in specialist fields, courses a company could not normally run internally.

Public sector education and training services
Colleges offer vocational courses in a very wide range of subjects and skills. Many of these courses are geared to national

examination syllabuses, but there is a trend for colleges to provide courses to meet regional and individual company requirements. The availability of courses 'tailor-made' to meet companies' specific training needs is well advanced in management training, where it is closely associated with consultancy, Kenny and Marsh (1969). Increasingly, colleges are regarded by industry as 'resource centres' rather than providers of standard courses.

The Manpower Services Commission (MSC)

The Training Services Division of the MSC is responsible for the administration of Skillcentres. These developed from the Government Training Centres and, whilst preserving the original functions of rehabilitation for the disabled and accelerated vocational training for craft and semi-skilled occupations, they have undergone a major expansion under the TSD.

A Training Opportunities (TOPS) scheme has been designed to help those over 19 years of age who, having been away from the education system for at least three years, wish to undergo training which will assist them to change their careers; or to help those who have been made redundant to embark on a new career. A very wide range of college and university-based courses is available under the TOPS scheme, ranging in content from engineering and construction to clerical and management subjects. It is intended to pay special attention to people with specific needs, such as the disabled, the long term unemployed, immigrants, redundant workers, young people, and to have particular regard to the employment needs of women.

Training within industry

TWI was started as a public service just after the Second World War and quickly gained a nation-wide reputation. The original TWI courses were concerned with four main areas of a supervisor's job: job instruction, job relations, job methods and job safety. The range has now been broadened and includes in addition: training and communication skills, office supervision and special courses for the retail trade, for export staff, and for operator and clerical instructors. Many of the courses are arranged in-company and are conducted by a TWI training officer, or by a specially trained member of the firm. The job analysis technique from the job instruction course is very widely used and an example is given on page 78.

Training Boards are responsible to the Training Services Division of the MSC, and the assistance they offer companies is described in chapter 15.

Trade unions
The expansion in training courses for shop stewards and union officials has already been mentioned. Some of these courses are sponsored jointly by employers' associations and trade unions and are usually orientated towards a particular industry. Most courses, however, are arranged by the TUC or by trade unions sometimes in conjunction with colleges. A training officer might do well to make his directors consider the consequences of their union representatives being better trained in the knowledge and skills of industrial relations than are their managers!

Chapter 5

Assessing Training Needs: the Individual

Job training analysis — job characteristics and approaches to analysis — carrying out a job training analysis — analytical techniques — assessing an employee's performance

JOB TRAINING ANALYSIS
In this chapter we consider the analysis of jobs for training purposes — the essential link between defining an organization's training requirements and policies — and the implementation of training programmes for individual employees. We are concerned with two main questions. First, how to identify the skill and knowledge required in a given job or task, and secondly, how to assess the present competence of the employee to be trained.

In the early part of the chapter we look at the different approaches to analysing jobs for training purposes and at some of the techniques which are commonly used. Later we consider briefly how an individual's performance may be assessed.

Job training analysis is the process of identifying the purpose of the job and its component parts and specifying the skill and knowledge required for effective work performance: special consideration is given to those aspects of the job which make it difficult to learn. Such an analysis identifies the performance standards required to set objectives for a training programme and subsequently to evaluate it. Training objectives should, where possible, be expressed in behavioural terms, *see* below.

We call the activity of analysing a job for training purposes job training analysis, to distinguish it from job analyses carried out for recruitment, work study, ergonomic, job evaluation or other purposes. However, since there is some overlap between the results of these different types of job analysis, they may provide useful training information. Similarly, the results of job training analysis can be an aid in recruitment and selection. While much of the early work in expressing training objectives in behavioural terms was associated with programmed learning, the resulting terminology has been adopted more widely, and two terms, 'criterion behaviour' and 'terminal behaviour', are of particular importance for our purposes. Criterion behaviour can be defined as what the trainee is expected to be able to do at the end of his training. It specifies the tasks, procedures, techniques and skills that he should be able to perform and the standards of performance required; for example, on completion of training, the trainee typist should be capable of typing x invoices per hour under typing pool conditions.

Terminal behaviour can be defined as the trainee's actual behaviour or abilities at the end of his training. Ideally, this should be the same as the criterion behaviour and any difference between the two is an indication of the success of the training (see Mager (1962)).

It should be noted that it is not always easy or possible to structure an unambiguous behavioural objective in a training context, but the clearer the objective which results from the analysis, the more likelihood there is of successful training. A trainee cannot be expected to know what he should be learning if the trainer's own objectives are uncertain!

In some areas, such as management training, it is much more difficult to describe training objectives in strict behavioural terms, because they are often more like educational objectives (see page 3). The specific behaviour required may not be known at the time of training, or the possible behavioural outcomes may be too numerous to list. One solution proposed by Gronlund (1970) in such circumstances, is to state the general objective first, and then to clarify it by listing a sample of the specific behaviour which would be acceptable as evidence of the attainment of the objective.

JOB CHARACTERISTICS AND APPROACHES TO ANALYSIS

As Boydell (1977) points out 'Job analysis is a process of examining a job. Thus it is not a particular document, but rather gives rise to certain documents, the product of an analytical examination of the job.'

When a training officer or other analyst begins an analysis he has a certain amount of background information about the job, but he should avoid being unduly influenced by, for example, what the classification or title of the particular job suggests he should find. Work classifications such as managerial, skilled, semi-skilled, and unskilled, beyond conveying a general idea of different types of work, are in themselves of little help to the analyst. As we shall see in later chapters, work categories are difficult to define, since there are no sharp boundaries between them and usage can vary from one industry to another and even between companies in the same industry. Moreover, the terms can be misleading. Work classified as semi-skilled can require a high degree of skill in particular tasks, while the category unskilled is a contradiction in terms because all work, no matter how menial, requires the application of some, albeit low order, skill.

Further confusion can be caused if a job continues, because of tradition rather than fact, to be regarded as belonging to a particular category of work. For example, certain printing industry craft jobs, which have been de-skilled as the result of technological changes, still retain craft status.

In practice, jobs are varied and have many facets. Some jobs consist of few tasks, others of many, some are relatively static and others subject to frequent changes, some require a high degree of discretion while others are mainly prescribed, some necessitate formal education, others none. Additional complications are caused by the wide variety of social and physical environments in which jobs are carried out. A more helpful way forward is to view a job as consisting of the two components mentioned previously, skill and knowledge. This sub-division provides a useful framework in which to collect and organize information about the job. It is also necessary when we start devising training programmes since the objectives, and therefore the techniques of teaching 'skills', are usually different from those of imparting knowledge, as will be seen in chapter 6. It is, however, to some extent, artificial to separate the two components since they are closely interlinked.

A wide variety of skills and knowledge may need to be analyzed. For example: job skills may be manual (psycho-motor), diagnostic, interpersonal (face to face), or decision making. The knowledge component may be technical, procedural (what to do and when), or concerned with company organization. Moreover, jobs vary widely in the range, variety and degree of skills and knowledge needed to perform them, *see* Singleton (1978). With many different combinations of these components occurring in jobs, different analytical approaches and techniques are necessary.

Wellens (1970) has pointed out that job analysis as a means of determining training needs is at its most effective at the lower end of the organization. The discretionary and ever-changing nature of supervisory and managerial jobs means that they cannot be predetermined or prescribed. Indeed, often the most important task facing a manager is to determine what, in fact, he *ought* to be doing and this can involve a complicated balance of priorities. Although a breakdown into tasks and their requisite knowledge and skills can be of some use at supervisory and middle management levels, a total analysis would be never-ending, cumbersome and likely to obscure the critical areas of the job. At management level, therefore, job descriptions and specifications are generally expressed in more general terms, concentrating on objectives, targets and key areas.

Types of analysis
There are three main approaches to analysing jobs for training purposes: the comprehensive, the key task and the problem-centred analysis.

The comprehensive analysis
In this approach, all facets of the job are examined with the aim of producing a detailed record of *every* task in the job, including the skill and knowledge requirements. In carrying out this type of analysis the training officer normally goes through certain stages. First, he checks that the approach is appropriate and that the time and costs incurred are justified, since a less comprehensive and less expensive approach is often adequate. The following criteria need to be satisfied before a comprehensive analysis is carried out:

> the majority of the work tasks which the trainee will have to do are unfamiliar to him, difficult to learn and the cost of error unacceptable
> time and other resources are available for the full analysis of the job to be made

the job is unlikely to be altered and the resultant training programme used frequently by a number of trainees

the job is closely prescribed and the 'correct' method of doing it must be learnt

A situation in which a full analysis is necessary is where new plant is to be installed in a factory and because unfamiliar operating skills are required the staff concerned need re-training. Secondly, having decided that a comprehensive analysis is justified, the training officer initially examines the job to gain an overall picture and to write a job description. This is 'a broad statement of the purpose, scope, responsibilities and tasks which constitute a particular job', Department of Employment (1971). The description contains the job title, the department in which the job holder works, to whom he is responsible, the purpose of his job, a list of his major tasks and, if appropriate, a brief description of any resources for which he is accountable.

As well as marking a stage in the development of the job specification, a job description is a useful document in its own right. It helps to assess the importance of the job and clarifies its purpose and content for the job holder, his superior and others with whom he works. A job description is also useful for recruitment and selection. The third step is to examine the job in depth to produce a job specification. This is a 'detailed statement of the knowledge and the physical and mental activities required to carry out the tasks which constitute the job', Department of Employment (1971).

Examples of techniques used in a comprehensive analysis are described later in this chapter and while there is no single correct approach, a useful sequence is to identify the main responsibilities of the job holder and then to record for each one its constituent tasks, and the skills and knowledge involved in carrying them out. For example, the responsibilities of a garage forecourt attendant include accepting new stock and receiving payment for goods sold. Taking the first of these, a number of separate tasks can be identified, one is the handling of petrol deliveries and another, receiving a consignment of new tyres. Each task is then analysed to find out what knowledge and skill are necessary. In the case of the petrol delivery, the attendant must know the relevant fire precautions and understand their significance, the sequences to be followed in dipping petrol tanks, the paperwork procedures, etc.

On completion of the comprehensive analysis, the training officer will have specified for every task its objective, its frequency, its required standard of performance, and the skill and knowledge needed to achieve it. With this information he prepares a training syllabus and designs a training programme to meet the requirements of the employee (*see* Boydell (1977) and chapter 6).

Key task analysis

As its name suggests, this approach to job training analysis is concerned, not with every task, but solely with the identification and detailed investigation of the key tasks within a job. A key task can be defined as a task in which adequate performance is essential. This approach is used increasingly in the analysis of managerial and other professional jobs, and is appropriate whenever the following apply:

a job consists of a large number of different tasks, not all of which are critical for effective performance, it is assumed that the job holder does not normally require training in minor or non-key tasks

a job is changing in emphasis or in content, resulting in a continuing need to establish priority tasks, standards of performance and the skills and knowledge required.

As in the case of the comprehensive analysis, the key task approach yields a job description (and a limited job specification), in addition to details of the critical tasks in the job.

Problem-centred analysis

This approach differs from those described previously in that no attempt is made to produce a description or specification of either the whole job or of its key tasks. In a problem-centred approach, analysis is limited to a difficulty considered to have a training solution, such as the chief chemist asking the training department to organize a report writing course for technical staff because their reports were unclear and poorly structured. The training officer concentrates his analysis on this particular aspect of the technical staff's work and excludes others unless they are directly relevant to the specific problem. A problem-centred approach to job training analysis is appropriate when:

the need for training is urgent but resources are not available for a comprehensive or key task analysis

a fuller analysis is unnecessary, for example, where an employee's work is satisfactory except in a specific area.

Warr and Bird (1968) have developed an approach to identifying the training needs of junior managers which is basically a
problem-centred type of analysis. They call it 'training by
exception', because the analysis concentrates on those issues
which are exceptions to a supervisor's normally adequate performance.

In implementing any one of these three main approaches, a
training officer will use specific analytical techniques, his choice
depending on the job he is analysing. Commonly used techniques include role analysis, Training Within Industry (TWI)
analysis, manual skills analysis, knowledge analysis, faults
analysis, decisions analysis and inter-personal skills analysis.
Some of these techniques are discussed later.

CARRYING OUT A JOB TRAINING ANALYSIS
The Analyst
A line manager is ideally placed to identify the training needs of
his staff, but he will not necessarily have the experience to carry
out a full analysis. In most companies it is the training officer
who carries out job training analyses. Large organizations may
also employ specialist analysts, for example, a management
analyst for managerial jobs and a manual skills analyst for jobs
having a high manual skills content. We saw in chapter 3 that
the assessment of an organization's training requirements can
be a difficult process and that the assessor needs to be technically
competent and acceptable to those with whom he works. Similar qualities are needed by a job analyst. Analysing jobs requires
an appreciation of learning difficulties, a logical mind, the ability to separate the important from the less important parts of the
job and an imaginative approach in providing training solutions. It also requires the analyst to handle, at least initially, any
difficulties exposed during an analysis. Motivation and discipline problems, misunderstandings caused by ill-defined responsibilities, and inappropriate organization structures can be
uncovered, particularly when an organization first introduces
job analysis. These kinds of problem adversely affect the business and therefore the analyst who, while concentrating on
training matters, has a responsibility to contribute to resolving
such difficulties when appropriate.

Stages in the Analysis

Figure 5.1 shows the main steps in analysing a job for training purposes. The sequence shown in the diagram illustrates a comprehensive job training analysis but the principles involved also apply to the key task and problem-centred approaches.

Figure 5.1
Stages in a comprehensive job training analysis

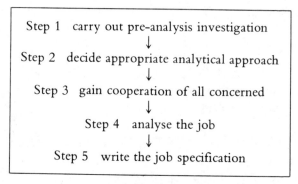

Step 1: carry out a pre-analysis investigation

A number of points are considered before an analysis is started to ensure that it is necessary and justified, since the activity of analysing a job can take many hours to complete, *see* Donnelly and Kenney (1970).

It is first necessary to establish that it is a *training* analysis that is wanted, because a problem which may appear to be due to a lack of training may have other causes, such as excessive work-loads or poor organization.

When it is agreed that the problem is a training one, the next step is to decide whether a training analysis is required. Questions, such as the following, clarify this point:

What is the organization losing in terms of production or services because the employee has not been formally trained?

Is sufficient information already available to make a job training analysis unnecessary (eg from suppliers' manuals)?

How long does it take for an average employee to learn the job without training? If a matter of hours or days, then analysis may be unnecessary.

Having established that a training analysis is needed, a check is

72

made to ensure that the job is unlikely to be changed significantly as a result of the introduction of new work methods or performance standards, alterations to operational policies, or the restructuring of the organization. This check avoids the analysis of obsolescent jobs.

Step 2: decide the appropriate analytical approach
The criteria for selecting an appropriate approach to job training analysis have been discussed previously. At this stage, the techniques of analysis most likely to provide the necessary training information are chosen. For example, a TWI analysis may be appropriate for most of the tasks within a job, with one task requiring a faults analysis in addition (*see* page 79). Choice of analytical techniques tends to be straightforward but care is needed to assess the real, as opposed to assumed, learning difficulties in a job. For example, the Engineering ITB (1971b) has described how, in analysing certain craft jobs, manual skills analysis was thought to be an appropriate technique. Subsequently, it was realized that more importance needed to be given to analysing the planning and decision-making activities rather than to the detailed job knowledge and procedures.

Step 3: gain the cooperation of all concerned
A prerequisite for successful job training analysis is that those who are in any way concerned cooperate with the analyst, and that the general industrial relations climate in the department is favourable. The cooperation of the job holder, his immediate superior (and other managers as necessary), and of staff or trade union representatives is essential, but cannot always be relied upon. Two typical problems which an analyst faces are that managers are too busy to spare the time to assist him, or that if the employee mistrusts the analyst's motives, inaccurate or incomplete data may result. An analyst has to exercise considerable inter-personal skill in explaining the purpose of the analysis, convincing those affected of its value and enlisting their support.

Step 4: analyse the job
The analyst needs to know the sources of information available, the appropriate methods of collecting it, and the depth of analysis required.

Sources of information:
  the job holder, who can often provide the bulk of the data required
  the job holder's superior, who will specify the purpose of the job and the necessary standards of performance (these points may be obvious for work which has a largely pre-scribed content, as in the case of most semi-skilled jobs, but it is often much less clear in other types of work, notably in managerial jobs)
  service departments such as O and M, work study, personnel and cost accounting, can assist the analyst working in a large organization
  company records such as job descriptions/specifications, organization charts, policies, plans, procedures and sales and production records
  suppliers' manuals are an essential source of information for training purposes, particularly when new equipment is purchased which is unfamiliar to the existing staff.

Methods of analysis
As already noted, when analysing a job, the analyst first iden-tifies the job holder's responsibilities and tasks, and then finds out for each task what is done, why it is done and how it is done. This process involves analysing what plans the job holder fol-lows, what cues he uses in initiating, controlling and complet-ing a task or part of a task, and what skills and knowledge are required to respond effectively to the relevant cues at various stages in each task.

The choice of methods will depend upon the characteristics of the job to be analysed, but the following are commonly used, *see also* Talbot and Ellis (1969):

Observation by the analyst: in many cases watching an employee at work provides a great deal of information, particularly about what a job holder does and how he does it, and to a lesser extent why he does it. Very detailed and continuous observation is required when analysing the manual skill used by an operative in complex short cycle repetitive work (*see* page 79). Continuous observation is not normally warranted for jobs in which tasks are repeated at irregular intervals as sufficient information can usually be obtained by random sampling. For example, activity sampling of a manager's work can be an economic and effective means of determining the different activities in which he is involved during the course of a day, week or a longer period of time. However, observation by itself is inadequate and at times not very informative: observing a process operator reading a number of instruments on a control panel is of little help to the analyst.

Self observation: this can be a useful method of collecting data on the purpose and content of a job but relies entirely upon the job holder's willingness to keep a diary or record of his activities. The technique is used in the analysis of managerial and other work characterized by a high degree of discretion. Disadvantages of self-observation are that the observer may be too close to the job to see it objectively and that he may, for his own purposes, under- or over-emphasize certain aspects of his work at the expense of others. As the job holder may be very busy and by the end of the day his recollections may not be strictly accurate, it is essential that the required record is as simple as possible, so that it can be kept up-to-date rather than becoming a chore to be completed later.

Fact-finding interview/discussion: formal and informal interviews or discussions with the job holder and other relevant employees are an essential part of the job training analysis. The analyst should be competent in the use of interview techniques, such as the framing of questions and careful listening, to gain the maximum benefits from this method.

'Do-it-yourself': one way of learning about a job is to try to do it! The analyst, by putting himself in the position of a trainee, experiences at first hand the learning difficulties involved in the job. While this may be impracticable or unnecessary, there are certain situations in which it is a useful method of collecting information. Tasks which are difficult to describe in words, such as those involving a high degree of manual dexterity, are amenable to this form of analysis.

Depth of analysis

Identifying the main responsibilities in a job is usually straightforward, identifying the tasks within a job is also relatively easy, but deciding how much detail is needed about a task and the skills and knowledge required to do it presents a problem for the analyst. This problem is discussed by Annett and Duncan (1968) *see also* Annett *et al* (1971), who argue that:

A major difficulty, and one of the first to be encountered, is

75

that a complete description of the execution of a task will include the information required for training, but will usually include much else as well. What is needed is some explicit rule or guide as to what to record for training purposes and at what level of description to operate. There is a danger that, without some rule as to what to include and what to exclude, essential training information will be buried in a plethora of detail.

The rule which Annett and Duncan propose is to, 'Begin with the most gross description of performance and ask two questions — what is the estimated probability, without training, of inadequate performance, and what would be the estimated cost (in a general sense) to the system of inadequate performance?' They suggest that the analyst should make a progressively more detailed investigation and description of the elements in a task until the limits of the training need is reached. This limit to the analysis will vary from task to task and is reached when it is considered that a particular part of the task can be readily learnt without training, and that should inadequate performance result, it would not be a serious matter. In other words, the task should continue to be broken down and described until both the cost of failure and the probability of failure are negligible. The use of this rule helps in a practical way to avoid unnecessary analysis. It also ensures that due consideration is given to such factors as safety problems, the trainee's ability to learn the job or task and learning difficulties posed by the work.

Finally, the analyst must investigate any learning problems which characterize the environment in which the trainee will eventually apply his skills and knowledge. For example, a trainee barman may find it relatively easy to learn individual tasks off-the-job, but find it very hard to cope with the real work situation in a busy pub, when he has to be competent at serving a round of drinks, pricing them correctly, chatting with the customers he is serving, and avoiding upsetting those he is not — all at the same time!

Step 5: write the job specification
When the analysis has been completed and the data checked, the job specification is drawn up in as much detail as is required. The completed specification provides the yardstick against which a trainee's performance will be measured and any short-fall identified. It also provides the information required to

design and run an appropriate training programme. *see* chapter 6.

ANALYTICAL TECHNIQUES

As mentioned previously, different techniques have been developed to enable the variety of job skills and knowledge to be analysed and recorded for training purposes. To illustrate some of the many techniques which are used in industry and commerce we have chosen the following; TWI analysis, manual skills analysis, faults analysis and inter-personal skills analysis. For further details and examples see the Food, Drink and Tobacco ITB (1972), the Knitting, Lace and Net ITB (1970a) and the Ceramics, Glass and Mineral Products ITB (1968b).

TWI Job analysis

This technique can be applied to any job for which the learning time is a matter of hours or days. It can also be applied to relatively simple tasks which are part of a more difficult job, but it is not suitable for complex work. A TWI analysis is normally undertaken by a TWI-trained supervisor or senior operator.

The analyst watches and questions an operator at work and, using a TWI breakdown sheet (*see* figure 5.2) records in the 'stage' column the different steps in the job. Most semi-skilled jobs are easily broken down into their constituent parts and a brief summary is made of what the operator does in carrying out each part.

The analyst then examines the stages separately and for each one describes in the 'instruction' column and against the appropriate stage, how the operator does it. The description of the operator's skill and knowledge is expressed in a few words. At the same time, the analyst notes in the 'key points' column of the breakdown sheet any special points such as quality standards or safety matters, which should be emphasized to a trainee learning the job. A TWI breakdown sheet serves two purposes. It provides the *pro forma* which aids the analysis, and, when completed, it is used as the instruction schedule.

A TWI analysis is an efficient method of analysing relatively simple jobs. It is a well-proven technique and has been used widely since its introduction into this country from the USA during the 1939-45 war.

Figure 5.2
Training Within Industry (TWI) job breakdown

JOB TITLE: How to make a Job Breakdown

Stage (what to do in stages to advance the job)	Instructions (how to perform each stage)	Key Points (items to be emphasized)
1 Draw-up table	Rule three columns. Allow space for column headings and job title	Use this sheet as example
2 Head the columns	On top line insert the title of job Insert: Column 1 (Stage) Column 2 (Instructions) Column 3 (Key Points)	Headings — summarize what worker needs to know to perform each job
3 Follow through the job to be analysed	After each step, ask yourself — 'What did I just do?' Note places where the worker could go astray. Note items to be emphasized. Note hazards. Stress safety points	Watch for steps which are performed from habit
4 Fill in Columns 1, 2 and 3 as stage 3 above is performed	Make brief and to the point notes	Write notes clearly and concisely
5 Number the stages	Follow the sequence a worker must follow when learning the job	Keep stages in order
6 Follow the job through using directions in Columns 1 and 2	Follow the instructions exactly	Ensure directions are complete — never assume they are
7 Check that all 'Key Points' are included	Record in Column 3 all points where the worker may be confused	Review, and emphasize these 'Key Points' decisively

Reproduced with permission of the
Ceramics, Glass and Mineral Products Industry Training Board

Manual skills analysis
This is a technique, derived from Work Study, and developed by Seymour (1966) to isolate the skills and knowledge employed by experienced workers performing tasks requiring a high degree of manual dexterity.

The technique is used to analyse short-cycle repetitive operations, such as assembly tasks and other similar factory work. Its application, however, is not restricted to the factory nor to semi-skilled jobs. It can be used to analyse any task in which manual dexterity and perception are important features.

In manual skills analysis (MSA), the hand, finger and other body movements of an experienced operative are observed and recorded in great detail as he carries out his work. MSA is a highly specialized technique and should be used selectively: those parts of the job which are relatively easy to learn are analysed in much less depth (a TWI approach may often be adequate), and an MSA is limited to those tasks (or parts of tasks) which involve unusual skills. These are the 'tricky' parts of a job, which, while presenting no difficulty to the experienced operative, have to be analysed in depth before they can be taught to trainees. Figure 5.3 is an example of a typical *pro forma* used in a MSA and illustrates the breakdown of the complex task of filleting raw fish in a food processing factory. It will be seen from this example that an experienced operative's hand movements are recorded in minute detail, together with the cues (vision and other senses) which the operative uses in performing the task. Explanatory comments are added, where necessary, in the 'comments' column.

Special training is needed to apply this level of analysis and to identify the cues on which an operator depends, the senses he employs to pick up these cues, and the use he makes of pertinent cues under normal and other work conditions. For further details of the analysis of manual skills *see* Seymour (1968).

Faults analysis
When analysing a job, information is collected about the faults which commonly occur and especially those which are costly. 'The process of analysing the faults occurring in a procedure, product or service, and specifying the symptom, cause and remedies of each . . .' Department of Employment (1971), is termed a faults analysis. The result of this analysis, a faults specification, provides a trainee with details of faults which he is

79

Figure 5.3
Manual skills analysis

DEPARTMENT: Fish-filleting   TASK: Fillet/trim small plaice   DATE:

Section or Element	Left hand	Right hand	Vision	Other Senses	Comments
Select fish	Reach to trough-grasp fish with T and 1 2 3 4 around belly, p/u and bring forward to board	P/u knife with T and 1 2 3 4 around handle. With sharp edge of blade to right of filleter	Glance ahead for knife position on board	Touch LH on fish	
			Glance ahead for fish position on trough		
		Knife hold:			
Position fish	Place fish on board so that the dorsal fins fall to the edge of the board and the head lies to the right hand side of the filleter	Hold knife handle against first and third joints of the fingers. Place upper part of T (1st joint) against lower blunt edge of knife and the lower part of T against upper edge of handle. Do not grasp knife tightly Do not curl tip of fingers into palm of hand.	Check position of fish	Touch LH on fish	Knife is held in the RH during the complete filleting cycle. If knife is held correctly it should be possible to move the knife to the left and right by 'opening' and 'closing' the knuckles (when T is removed from handle).

LH = left hand
RH = right hand
p/u = pick up
T = thumb
1 = first finger
2 = second finger
3 = third finger
4 = fourth finger
Synchronous movements are recorded on the same line
Successive movements are recorded on succeeding lines

likely to come across in his work, how he can recognize them, what causes them, what effects they have, who is responsible for them, what action the trainee should take when a particular fault occurs, and how a fault can be prevented from recurring.

A faults specification is usually drawn up either in a tabular or 'logic-tree' form *see* Jones (1968), and is useful both for instruction purposes and as an *aide memoire* to an employee after completion of training.

Inter-personal skills analysis
Inter-personal skills are sometimes referred to as interactive, face-to-face, or social skills. Some jobs, such as those of a sales assistant or a receptionist, contain tasks which involve dealing with the public and have a very obvious inter-personal skills content which can determine successful performance. These skills should be analysed if they are to be taught and learned systematically, but in practice, despite their importance, they are rarely analysed in any depth. They are often extremely complex and have proved very difficult to analyse in the absence of adequate tools and methods of analysis however, *see* Argyle (1970). Nonetheless, attempts have been made to identify the cues and responses which characterize the successful use of inter-personal skills and an interesting approach, developed by the Food, Drink and Tobacco ITB (1972) is illustrated in figure 5.4. While at first reading the example may be so obvious that it should be taken for granted, skills such as those described are very often conspicuous by their absence in day to day work situations.

In other types of jobs, eg managerial and supervisory positions, the need for inter-personal skills occurs at the 'interface', ie the relationship with other job holders or because of the demands of team work. Traditional analysis, looking inward at the actual tasks of the job, has a tendency to miss this aspect; it is most likely to be revealed as the result of a problem-centred approach, where lack of coordination and understanding between superior and subordinates, or between colleagues or departments, soon becomes apparent.

It is only necessary to consider how much of a manager's or supervisor's time is spent in dealing with people to realize how important this is. Because of its interactive nature, however, a sequence of behaviour cannot be prescribed and special techniques of analysis are required.

81

Figure 5.4
Analysis of interpersonal skills

JOB: Manageress — Retail confectioner

TASK BREAKDOWN: Interpersonal (Social) Skills

TASK: Handling complaint (returned merchandise)

Stage	Cues (eye, ear, etc.)	Responses (voice, eye, gesture, action)	Attention points
1 Manageress (M) becomes aware of Customer (C)	M sees/hears C enter shop Notes C is carrying something in the shop's bag, notes C's stiffness and lack of response to M's smile	M (busy writing) puts pen down, makes eye contact with C and smiles M also tries to assess C. M decides course of action	M is prepared because she is facing shop entrance while working — stops working to impress C and to prepare for her. M smiles to make initial welcoming contact, M makes subjective judgment about type/mood of C and looks for signals
2 Manageress contacts and greets customer	Notes C's continuing stiffness and hostility	M comes round counter to C — gestures her further into shop. M smiles warmly with direct eye contact, greets C questioningly — by name	M removes barrier of counter to reduce anxiety — encourages C away from other customers. M's greeting designed to get C to talk, to relax and feel important
3 Manageress listens to complaint	Watches C's reactions. Hears complaint (that C's daughter had earlier been sold stale merchandise). M notes C's embarrassment by lack of eye contact. M detects that 'wind is slowly going from C's sails'	Keeps eye contact with C, nods when C makes valid point. M gives C her full attention — allows C to talk until she has had her say	M knows danger of alienating C by interrupting her story M's attention makes C feel important — convinces her M is sympathetic not hostile
4 Manageress deals with complaint	Watches C's visible relief notes sincere thanks	Thanks C for her action. Smiles — offers money back immediately. Moves to till	M's action dispels any remaining hostility/embarrassment
5 Manageress promotes possible future sale	Sees interest in C's eyes: notes enthusiastic response, hears C's daughter is soon to marry	While opening till, chats to C about daughter. Avoids too much eye contact to allow C to relax — hands over money with no reference to original problem	M responds to distract C from original problem and establish firm rapport — could shop cater for wedding?

One such method is that of Rackham et al (1971), who have devised a system of analysing face-to-face behaviour into categories, such as suggesting, building (on the suggestions of others), proposing, criticizing, seeking clarification etc. Trained observers provide participants of group exercises with a detailed breakdown of their behaviour during group task exercises, discuss this with them and provide opportunities for changing their behaviour categories if they so wish. Prior to this the trainers have conducted surveys throughout their organizations to take account of organizational climate and to ascertain which categories of behaviour appear to be associated with managerial success. This information is fed back to their trainees. Some training boards, notably the Air Transport and Travel ITB, are associated with this work. Another method of analysing interactive skills is Transactional Analysis (TA). This really involves a complete theory of personality, and so it is inappropriate to describe it here. For further information *see* Carby and Thakur (1976). TA is seen as a communications tool, whose main purpose is to enable trainees to analyse their own interactions and develop insight and awareness and so increase their effectiveness.

ASSESSING AN EMPLOYEE'S PERFORMANCE

So far in this chapter we have examined the different approaches and techniques used in job training analysis. We have seen that the end product of analysis is a statement of the expectations which a company has of a particular job and of the skill and knowledge necessary for acceptable performance. Information about a job provides the yardstick against which to measure an employee's performance. However, before an individual's training need can be determined, it is necessary to know his present level of competence. In this final section we consider briefly the different ways in which this information can be obtained.

A new employee selected against a personnel specification should have, in broad terms, the necessary ability, achievement and experience, and should require only limited training, *see* Fraser (1966). It is, however, advisable to check this, either by discussion with the trainee, or, if appropriate, by administering a test. Taking account of present knowledge and skill reduces training time, and prevents boredom. It also serves a further purpose in that the new job may be very familiar in most respects but differ in one or two important aspects, and in these, previous experience can hinder performance. This is known as negative transfer of learning, *see* page 94. Possibly the only training which might be required would be to discuss the areas of difference and provide practice in them. With unsystematic training these areas would be found by trial and error, but particularly where safety controls are concerned, it is imperative to have a real awareness of the dangers of negative transfer, which is most likely to occur at critical times, or when the trainee has also to concentrate on other matters. Trainability tests have been in use for some time under the auspices of the Clothing and Allied Products ITB, for sewing machinists, and more recently, for garment examiners. Downs (1977) quotes trainability tests for a variety of jobs, including fork lift truck drivers, bricklaying, electronics, bottling, and in social skills such as interviewing a client for a mortgage with a building society. These tests are suitable for both young and older recruits and are generally regarded as more suitable for older applicants than the traditional type of selection test.

A variety of methods can be used for the appraisal of existing employees, among which are the following:

On the job coaching The training needs of many employees are determined, and often met, during the guidance which they receive from their manager in the normal course of their work, *see* Megginson and Boydell (1979).

Annual appraisal reviews Appraisal of an employee's work by his superior once a year, or as appropriate, enables a manager to take stock of his staff' strengths and weaknesses.

A survey described by Gill (1978) shows that companies now perceive the main purpose of appraisal as assessing training needs to improve current performance. Emphasis appears to have shifted away from the development of future potential. Clearly, however, both aspects can be important when assessing training needs. Of the 288 companies which replied to the survey, only 2 per cent applied appraisal to shop floor level, 45 per cent had schemes for clerical staff, and about 90 per cent appraised their managerial staff. Gill concludes that appraisal systems now seem to be an accepted part of company life.

Performance records Production and sales figures, numbers of errors or complaints in a department etc, provide informa-

84

tion about an individual's work performance. However, these figures should be interpreted with caution as they may result from circumstances outside the control of the employee.

Employee's request for training The onus for identifying training needs is not necessarily on management. In a 'sympathetic' work setting, employees will tend to take the initiative and indicate their own needs for training. *see* Delf and Smith (1978)

Job training analysis and assessment of performance play a critical role in training. They provide the basic information about what is wanted from an employee and what is wanting in his work. In the next chapter we consider how a 'learning gap' can be bridged by the design, implementation and evaluation of training programmes.

Chapter 6

Designing and Evaluating Training Programmes

Factors in the design of training programmes — the trainer and the trainee — stages in the design of a training programme — evaluation of training

FACTORS IN THE DESIGN OF TRAINING PROGRAMMES
Learning
The object of training is to assist a learner acquire the behaviour necessary for effective work performance; it is therefore essential that training officers have a clear grasp of the ways in which learning theories are applied when designing training programmes, *see* Gagne (1967), Otto and Glaser (1970).

For our purposes, effective learning can be thought of as a 'relatively permanent change of behaviour that occurs as a result of practice or experience' and there are, according to Bass and Vaughan (1966), four main requirements for such learning to take place: Drive, stimulus, response and reinforcer.

Drive or motivation: the old saying that a horse can be led to water but cannot be made to drink holds an important lesson for the trainer. People learn if they accept the need for training and are committed to it. If their motivation is weak because, for example, they doubt their ability to learn or if they are, for some reason, anti-training, then no matter how well their training is designed and implemented, its effectiveness will be limited.

Motivation is a complex concept, and it is most important to recognize that people are multi-motivated. As McGehee and Thayer (1961) point out:

similar behaviour shown by different people may result

86

from different underlying motives, and ... (the trainer) ... must expect vacillation and indecision from people in the day-to-day work situation. The mere recognition of indecision and an attempt to discover the underlying cause may suggest solutions to the problem.

Otto and Glaser (1970) suggest a useful classification of motivation factors, based on the kind of rewards which are involved in learning:

achievement motivation, for which the reward is success

anxiety, for which the reward is the avoidance of failure

approval motivation, for which the reward is approval in its many forms

curiosity, for which the reward is increased opportunity to explore the environment and be exposed to novel stimuli

acquisitiveness, for which the reward is something tangible, such as money or material benefits.

None of these classification groups should be regarded as excluding the other; for instance, both achievement and anxiety motivation are possible in the same person at the same time. All the factors, however, are influenced by the immediate experience of the learner. As motivation is a personal matter, the case for careful discussion of individual programmes with the trainee is obvious. Programmes often consist of courses for many people and it is necessary to bear all the general motivation factors in mind. For instance, achievement motivation requires that learning should be a successful experience. This has implications for the size of the learning 'steps' in relation to the target population, for timing, for the provision of ample knowledge of results to trainer and trainee, and for assistance in case of difficulty.

Approval is also concerned with knowledge of results and psychological theory suggests that it is more effective to approve and therefore reinforce correct actions than to punish and ridicule incorrect ones. Curiosity can be a very powerful motivator, as experience with small children will show. For this reason discovery methods (*see* page 91), are often very effective if they are so designed that the experience is ultimately successful.

It may be appropriate to begin a training programme by recognizing and utilizing the curiosity motive. For example, the order of instruction for school leaver trainee sewing machinists was altered when it was found that interest in an off the job induction course and in how to thread a machine was low, because the trainee's main concern was to have a go and find out what using a machine was really like. With safety precautions and machine care very much in mind, a suitable exercise was devised which allowed trainees to come straight into the department and run a sewing machine as fast as they could. Curiosity about how to control it, thread it, or about other departments or employment conditions came at later stages and the programme was designed accordingly. Obviously there can be difficulties about this approach, but curiosity can be one of the trainer's most powerful allies and it is all too easy to kill it with tedious sessions arranged according to logicality rather than to the viewpoint of the trainee. For a useful discussion of approach — avoidance aspects of learning, *see* Mager (1968).

Stimulus and response: stimulus is the signal received and interpreted by a trainee and a response is the behaviour resulting from a stimulus: these are closely related in the learning process. Through training the learner recognizes relevant stimuli and associates them with desired responses. Examples in the case of experienced staff are: the ability to recognize danger readings on an oil refinery control panel (stimulus), causing an operator to close down the plant (response), or a marketing director analysing market research findings (stimulus), which led him to change his company's sales policy (response).

Reinforcer or feedback: this is the information which the learner receives indicating the quality of his responses. It should be made available to him as quickly as possible. Knowledge of results is essential for effective learning and may come from the work itself, from the trainer, or from other trainees. For example, in an on the job coaching situation, a manager provides his staff with his assessment of their work (feedback) and so helps them improve their performance.

The way in which feedback can control performance is likened by Stammers and Patrick (1975), to the way in which a thermostat controls a system. The temperature is regulated because information from the thermostat determines the level of power input to the system.

In a similar way, an experienced operator is receiving

'stimuli' from the environment, by which he monitors and regulates his performance, or in other words, his input to the system. Sometimes this feedback is given by training simulators which act as artificial thermostats and help the trainee to monitor his performance. This monitoring is not confined to trainees, it is a constant process in all activities. For example, someone who is profoundly deaf may develop an unusual speaking voice because he cannot hear it and must monitor it in some other way, possibly by the feel of muscles in the mouth and throat. It is vital, therefore, that before any artificial feedback (provided especially for training) is removed, the trainee is made aware of exactly how, and by which sense or stimuli, an experienced worker monitors his performance. To return to the analogy, if the thermostat (ie the feedback) is removed, the temperature will be uncontrolled. It is clear that a recognition of the 'stimuli' from the environment is a very important part of learning and therefore of training. They are perceived through the five senses, the most natural sense for a learner to rely upon being sight. It is often found that an experienced worker relies upon stimuli from other senses such as hearing or kinaesthesis and training periods can be considerably shortened by giving practice in recognition of the 'stimuli' used by an experienced operator. Probably the best known example of this is the training of typists, who are taught from the beginning to find the keys by touch or kinaesthesis, rather than by sight. Since perception stimuli are central to learning, a training officer should understand the process involved in perception. Training for inspection, for instance, is largely a matter of organizing the perception to highlight certain stimuli and ignore others. For more detailed study, the reader is referred to Thomas (1962) and Wright and Taylor (1970).

A learning curve is another example of feedback and represents the rate at which learning takes place. It is plotted on a graph with the vertical axis denoting achievement, and the horizontal axis representing the time period or number of attempts made. The interpretation of a learning curve may be difficult, but it can provide general guidance to both trainer and trainee on the latter's progress.

Figure 6.1 illustrates a learning curve in which there is no output up to point 'A', since this represents the initial training period. Performance then improves until a plateau is reached at

89

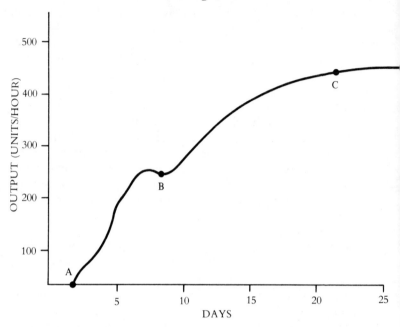

Figure 6.1
Learning curve

point 'B'. Plateaux are periods when performance does not improve, although learning may or may not be taking place. There are a variety of reasons for plateaux, such as the waning of a trainee's enthusiasm, or the unequal difficulty of learning the various stages in the training. It may also be that the trainee is beginning to learn the stimuli of an experienced operator, described above, or going from a lower to a higher order of learning, eg learning to type short words as units, instead of thinking in terms of individual letters. His progress will appear to plateau and then, as he masters the new stages, it will move upwards. Examination of plateaux common to all trainees can yield valuable information leading to adjustments and improvements in the training programme. It will be seen from figure 6.1 that the returns on time spent in training decreases after point 'C', when learning is slower. Learning curves can also be used as a basis for the comparison of different methods of training, *see* Corlett and Morcombe (1970).

THE TRAINER AND THE TRAINEE
The trainer or instructor can be thought of as a learning leader

who assists trainees by structuring learning opportunities for them and by offering guidance at appropriate times. The trainer acts as a mediator between the learner and the complexities of the job and must be sensitive to the intricacies of the work involved and to the learning difficulties facing trainees. No matter at what level the trainer operates, much of his success depends upon his technical competence and his ability to establish a good working relationship.

The approaches used by trainers to assist learning depend on the learning objectives, the trainees, and on the time and other resources available. For example, when training operatives for work having a high manual skill content but little discretion, a trainer spends much time demonstrating the precise skills involved in the job and coaching the trainees as they practice. The training programme is highly structured. On the other hand, a management trainer relies heavily on active discussion with and among the members of a course to achieve the objectives of communicating and stimulating ideas. The course members are continuously influencing their programme, which is of necessity less structured than is the case in the previous example.

Active participation is always desirable in training as long as it is planned and controlled. Planned participation, for example, is a key factor in discovery learning, which

> is a means of teaching which avoids expository instruction. The trainee is presented with tasks which engage him in the search for and selection of stimuli on how to proceed. The effectiveness of the Discovery Method depends on the design of these tasks which have two aims: to provide an intrinsic means for unassisted learning and to provide the experience upon which insight into key relationships can be developed. Department of Employment (1971).

Belbin RM (1969) quotes an example of discovery learning used in a training project at British Rail which involved the transfer of steam locomotive drivers to diesel/electric trains. Trainees were given switches, meters, miniature motors, etc and were encouraged to discover relevant electrical theory, by drawing conclusions from observations they made during practice periods. The trainers gave general guidance and were available to assist in case of difficulty.

According to Holding (1965), 'the job of a trainer is to

91

observe and analyse and to arrange to supply the right amount of the right kind of information to the learner at the right time'. Thus informally structured programmes, the trainer chooses between either giving the trainee a part of the job to practise until he is competent at doing it before going on to the next (the part method), or giving him, from the beginning, the whole job to learn (the whole method). The 'part method' has virtue in that initially the trainee learns those parts of the job which are easily learnt, leaving the difficult parts until later. On the other hand, there is some evidence to suggest that the 'whole method' is more suited to the learning needs of older workers (Belbin (1965)), and to learners of above average intelligence, such as technical or management employees.

Experiments have also shown that in learning manual skills, such as typing or assembly work, the distribution of practice sessions (distributed practice) between decreasing rest periods is generally more effective than continual practice (massed practice). The value of distributed practice also applies in the learning of theoretical material. As well as referring to some of the points above, Otto and Glaser (1970) propose a number of additional principles which are likely to be helpful to training officers and instructors.

The learner learns what he does: the implication here is that the conditions of learning should be arranged so that the trainee will make the correct responses early in the programme. First impressions are often more lasting and mistakes can be difficult to unlearn. Practice should be supervised to ensure that trainees are not learning bad habits. This generalization also has implications for discovery learning and the training officer must weigh the advantages and disadvantages in each situation.

People learn more effectively when they learn at their own pace: A training programme should be flexible enough to allow for individual differences in the speed of learning and in the rate at which information can be assimilated. This is just as important for the fast learner who may be bored, as for the slow learner who may be confused. Programmed learning or individual assignments with coaching can help to overcome this difficulty.

There are different kinds of learning and they may require different training processes: for example, in learning the skills of interviewing, a trainee needs demonstration and guided practice,

92

while the accumulation of knowledge may be achieved by directed reading or listening to lectures. No one would dispute that it would be difficult to learn how to ride a bicycle by sitting in an armchair reading about it, although knowledge so gained might possibly reduce the learning time. There is a strong case for maintaining that, although the skill in using a fire extinguisher might not be very great, since it is almost definitely going to be used in an emergency, training in safety precautions should include actual practice rather than merely being told how to use it. The different kinds of learning may, however, be much more subtle. It is an easier process to recognize stimuli than to recall them for oneself and this has implications for tests with multiple choice answers.

This principle of selecting the appropriate learning strategy takes the training officer straight to behavioural objectives, as an example may help to explain. Some electrical apprentices had to learn a coding comprising nine colours and the job required instant association of a number (1-9) with a particular colour. The behavioural objective would therefore not be met if the trainees learned the sequence of colours by heart, because each time they wanted to pair a colour and a number they would have to repeat the sequence, causing delay and allowing the possibility of error, which could have serious effects on safety. The training method which was devised was a visual presentation of well known objects associated with each colour, such as one brown penny, five green fingers. The use of vision and the association with previous knowledge enabled the trainees to learn almost instantly in the exact form in which the information was required, a green wire immediately bringing to mind the number five.

If a training objective is to change attitudes, then participative or discussion sessions may be required, or possibly the use of experiential learning. Wellens (1976) suggests: 'If you seek to teach some aspect of human behaviour, don't stand there and talk about it, cause it to happen, then you can talk about it, probe what it felt like and what is the subsequent reaction it caused.' Such an experimental approach can be very effective but if the experiential is unpleasant and the trainees fail to understand it, it can have unfortunate repercussions for the trainees and trainer. This learning is usually specific to a situation and may not transfer from one problem to another unless, as Kolb *et al* (1974) point out, we proceed through the full cycle from experience to

93

reflection about that experience, then form concepts and generalizations about that experience which we then test out in new situations, and this is bringing us back to experience.

When using the experiential method it is necessary to provide for each of these stages. Training officers may like to consider that 'learning to learn' also transfers, and that by practising this method, managers learn from their own experience on the job.

Practice in a variety of settings will increase the range of situations in which the learning can be applied: varied practice will make the trainee resistant to forgetting, so important parts of the training content should be stressed by using more than one training method.

Meaningful learning, that is learning with understanding, is more permanent and more transferable than rote learning or learning by some memorized formula: material should be presented in a form that the trainee will understand. If the new learning can be linked in some way with the learner's present knowledge, it will help him comprehend and remember it. Participative methods, such as discussion or questions, will help to ensure that this comes about.

The learner's perception of what he is learning determines how well and how quickly he will learn: this has a clear relationship with the previous principle. The way in which material is displayed is critical and the learner's attention should be drawn to important stimuli. Otto and Glaser (1970) quote the example of school children who erroneously learned that a full stop comes at the end of a line because all the examples they were shown had sentences one line long.

Transfer of learning, or the degree to which training will transfer to the actual job, is closely connected with the last two principles. Transfer of learning from one job to a new job involves a consideration of the extent to which the previous work experience relates. Transfer of learning from a former job can be positive or negative. A typist can usually learn to operate a computer terminal without difficulty because of her previous experience at typing: this is termed positive transfer. Negative transfer occurs where the trainee's previous experience is a hindrance to learning. For example, the waiter who is used to working in a guest house may find it difficult to learn the skills required of him in a four-star hotel. Negative transfer creates problems for trainees, who have to unlearn certain skills and

94

knowledge, since they tend to cling to familiar work methods and standards.

Predicting the extent to which learning is transferable is becoming increasingly important as costs of training and re-training rise, and Downs (1977) has described the use of traina-bility tests for forecasting the transferability of learning in industrial situations. Transfer of learning is a phrase which is also used to describe a trainee's ability to transfer learning he has acquired during a course to his job (see page 102).

The age factor

The younger trainee: the setting and approach to teaching in schools is usually different from that in industry, and school leavers can experience considerable difficulty in adjusting to a new kind of learning situation. Trainers must take this into account when designing programmes if young people's natural enthusiasm on starting work is to be channelled in the right direction. Young trainees usually react favourably to inter-group competition and appreciate variety in their prog-rammes. They prefer to keep within their original training groups, membership of which gives them confidence. Leav-ing school and starting work is a big step for most young people, and behaviour such as over-confidence or shyness often results from a feeling of insecurity. A patient and sup-portive trainer can do a great deal to help.

Training Adults: industrialized societies are beginning to accept that training is necessary for most employees and that, if technological change continues at the current rate, they will need training several times during their working lives. Re-training is therefore attracting considerable interest, and gui-dance in this field is available for trainers (see, for example, Belbin E (1964), Belbin E and Belbin R M (1972) Newsham (1969), Iron and Steel ITB (1970) and Bienvenue (1969).

Learning difficulties tend to increase with age, although Belbin (1965) refers to instances where 'interest, aptitude, intelligence, education, character and emotional stability prove more decisive than age itself'. Nonetheless, there are special points to be considered in designing adult training programmes as listed below.

A fixed pace of learning should not be imposed on older employees; they should be allowed to learn at their own rate, even if this means an extended training period. This

95

applies to the training of staff for manual as well as for technical or managerial work. Formal lectures, for example, should be avoided as they have a built-in pacing which inhibits learning.

The older employee usually profits from longer learning sessions and, where variety is required, it is best achieved by variations in teaching methods rather than by changes in subject matter.

If several adults are to be trained in a company, it is desirable that membership of the training group includes, as far as possible, staff of equal status and of a similar age. Adults may require considerable individual attention and support, particularly if they are being trained as a result of changes in the organization. Redundancy, for example, can produce an actual or apparent loss of status and cause the staff concerned to lack confidence in themselves, so creating a serious barrier to learning. Despite these difficulties, there is evidence that re-training is a worthwhile investment for the individual, the organization and society, *see* Hughes (1970).

STAGES IN THE DESIGN OF A TRAINING PROGRAMME

Successful training depends on the training officer's ability to work closely with line management in constructing a programme which is relevant to the needs of the employees and minimizes their learning difficulties. A training programme can be defined as:

an interpretation of the training specification in terms of units of instruction or learning, set out in chronological sequence and showing the time allowed for each', Department of Employment (1971).

This definition suggests that a training programme is always a tightly structured sequence of controlled events. In some cases it is, in others it is not, since learning objectives dictate the approach to programme design. If the objective is concerned with the development of inter-personal skills, such as, to increase a manager's awareness of group behaviour and to see himself as others see him, a loosely structured or unstructured programme is necessary, as in a T-group approach, *see* Whitaker (1965). If, however, the learning objective is concerned with the trainee acquiring, for example, a motor skill

96

such as typing, a structured learning situation with a detailed timetable is used. The latter approach to the design of training programmes is widely used in industry and commerce and involves the eight main stages illustrated in figure 6.2 below.

Figure 6.2
Stages in the design of a structured training programme

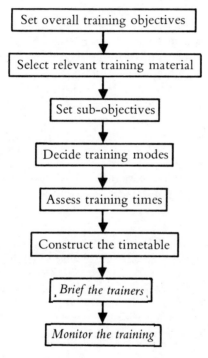

Stage 1: set the overall objectives

As we explained in chapter 5, job training analysis is necessary to produce clear objectives, expressed as far as possible, in terms of the behaviour expected of the employee on completion of training. Several references to behavioural objectives have already been made, *see* page 3. For further details *see* Mager (1962) and Davies (1971). At this stage it becomes obvious as to whether the required knowledge and skills have been analysed in sufficient detail. For instance, communication skills is too broad a description to be of much assistance; it could give rise to a wide range of behavioural objectives, for which the appropriate training sessions could include report writing and learning the morse code. On the other hand, 'ability to give accurate information about train times to all telephone enquirers' gives a very clear indication of what is needed. Behavioural objectives, therefore, are essential to the design of an effective programme.

A major factor which must also be recognized when setting objectives is the amount of time available for training.

Stage 2: Select relevant training material

Training analysis provides information about the skill and knowledge requirements, not all of which are required for inclusion in a syllabus. The training officer, in consultation with line management, determines which aspects of the job need to be emphasized in the programme, weighting them accordingly in deciding the content of the syllabus. The information selected from the analysis is then sorted into separate headings, each of which becomes one or more units of instruction.

Stage 3: set sub-objectives

Sub-objectives are then decided for every instructional stage in the programme, care being taken to include all relevant parts of the syllabus.

Stage 4: decide training modes

When the coverage of the programme has been determined, it is then necessary to decide how the objectives for each section can best be achieved, by on-the-job coaching, job rotation, external or internal course, attachment or any combination of these. The choice of a particular training mode varies with the category of employee and the available training resources. *See* later chapters.

Stage 5: assess training times

When the objectives, syllabus and training modes have been decided, the trainer assesses the time required for the individual parts of the programme. This, to some extent, is a matter of trial-and-error, but an experienced trainer usually gauges training times fairly accurately by:

consulting with those responsible for the various parts of the training
using as a guide the duration of similar programmes
taking into account the age, experience and motivation of those to be trained.

Stage 6: construct the timetable

At an early stage in designing a programme, the trainer establishes a logical sequence for its contents. A timetable is then constructed which is flexible enough to be modified, if required, without affecting the whole programme.

Stage 7: brief the trainers

This is an important stage in the design process where misunderstandings can easily arise if the objectives for every section of the programme are not fully discussed with the proposed trainers. At this stage also agreement should be reached on the training techniques to be used. The choice of techniques will be determined by the following main criteria:

Objectives: type of objectives set. (*See* pages 66 and 93).

Trainees: their age, general intelligence, present knowledge and skill, uniformity of knowledge and skill, their availability, probable attitudes and motivation, number of trainees.

Resources: time: participative methods may be more effective, but are likely to be more time-consuming.

Instructors: their capabilities and availability.

Equipment: projectors, tape recorders, syndicate rooms, etc.

Money: to pay wages of trainees, instructors, or to pay outside speakers and tutors.

Transferability of learning: should some material be presented in several different ways? (*see* page 94).

Variety: is it necessary to vary the technique to keep interest?

Time of day: it is normally best to start after lunch with a participative session and the same is true for evening work.

Appendix (ii) illustrates the main techniques used in training, what they achieve and their limitations.

Stage 8: monitor the training

Evaluation depends on appropriate controls being built into a training programme at the design stage by establishing what information is required about a learner's progress, and when this is needed. Progress is monitored in a number of ways eg output records and learning curves provide the necessary information in certain types of operative training, while a log-book is frequently used for craft and technical training.

Practical advice on the preparation of programmes has been published by a number of ITBs (*see* for example, Ceramics, Glass and Mineral Products ITB (1968c) and Paper and Paper Products ITB (1970a).

EVALUATION OF TRAINING

While it is generally accepted that there is a strong case for attempting to evaluate training, particularly in view of the very large sums of money which are spent on it, the attendant problems often appear insuperable. In fact, evaluation is one of the more difficult of the training officer's tasks, but not necessarily impossible. A useful definition of evaluation is:

> the assessment of the total value of a training system, training course or programme in social as well as financial terms . . . it attempts to measure the overall cost benefit of the course or programme and not just the achievement of its laid down objectives . . . Department of Employment (1971).

Evaluation is therefore concerned with measurement and embraces the total training situation. The significance of this statement will become clearer as we examine the questions which need to be answered in evaluating a particular training programme. These are as follows:

Why is the evaluation required?
Who is to do it?
What aspects should be evaluated, and when should this be done?
What kinds of measurement will be used?

Why is the evaluation required?
Evaluation is needed for a number of reasons:

in general terms, it enables the effectiveness of an investment in training to be appraised
it provides 'feedback' about trainees and training methods, and so can aid learning during the programme
it indicates the extent to which objectives have been met
the results of evaluation can be used to improve subsequent programmes
it provides data which can justify expenditure on training, a very significant factor as companies become more conscious of training costs.

Who is to carry out the evaluation?
Tracey (1968) makes the point that 'evaluation must be cooperative. A one-man evaluation is little better than no evaluation, regardless of who does it, how competently he does the job, or how valid his findings may be. All who are a part of the
100

process of appraisal or who are affected by it must participate in the process.' While accepting the desirability of a cooperative evaluation, day to day practice falls well short of this ideal.

The main interested parties in evaluation are, or should be, the trainee, his manager, his work group, his trainer, his company and, possibly, the relevant ITB. To some extent the criteria used in determining the value of the training will be common amongst these individuals and groups, but there may also be differences:

the training department's and the line management's expectations from training will differ if inadequate communication exists between them and mistakes are made in the content of the programme

trainees, particularly on long programmes, can be critical of training which, in the view of the trainer, is satisfactory; such differences of opinion may be due to trainees not receiving adequate feedback on their progress

training which is specific, in that it is useful only to the company that provides it, may be less highly valued by a trainee

the company's training plans will not necessarily coincide with ITB policy (*see* page 251).

What aspects of the training should be evaluated and when?
Traditionally, evaluation has meant examining the results of a training programme to determine the extent to which its objectives have been achieved. This is valid as far as it goes but a broader approach is necessary. Warr *et al* (1970) have developed a fourfold framework of training evaluation which reviews not only the results of a programme but the whole training effort, beginning with the job training analysis. This recognizes evaluation as a continuous process and not merely as a post-training activity.

Warr *et al* argue that all stages in the training cycle should be evaluated as they are carried out, focusing on four aspects of evaluation: context, input, reaction and outcomes.

'Context evaluation' is the process of deciding whether a particular problem in an organization has a training solution and, if so, of specifying training objectives.

'Input evaluation' takes place when the trainer reviews the resources available to meet the training requirement and decides how to use them to achieve his objectives. This

101

involves the use of judgement when assessing the advantages of one approach against others.

'Reaction evaluation' is obtaining information about employees' reactions to their training, so as to improve current or subsequent programmes. Information is gathered by the trainer formally from mid course and end of course reviews, from critiques on individual parts of the programme and from informal discussion. These are useful sources of information but require careful interpretation. For example, while it would be unwise to ignore the views expressed by trainees, it should also be remembered that they are not necessarily in a position to appreciate what is best for them or the organization.

'Outcome evaluation', as its name implies, measures the extent to which objectives have been achieved. This is the traditional approach to evaluation.

Three levels of 'outcome evaluation' are recognized by Warr *et al*. First, 'immediate outcomes' which are the changes in the trainee's skill and knowledge measured by appropriate tests at the end of his training, and before he starts using his newly-acquired expertise. Secondly, 'intermediate outcomes' these are the changes in the employee's job behaviour which occur when he applies newly learnt skills and knowledge to his work. It is important to distinguish between an employee having learnt a particular skill by the end of his training and his ability to apply the same skill in his work. Training can only be considered successful if job behaviour, as opposed to 'end of course behaviour', is as specified in the training objectives. Evaluation may show a success at the 'immediate outcomes' level but failure at the 'intermediate level' and there are various reasons why this might occur. For example, the trainee's manager may not encourage, or even allow the application of certain skills or techniques, as in the case of the junior manager who learnt certain O and M techniques on a course, but on returning to his company found no support for them; the trainee who finds difficulty in adapting from training to the work environment; or the work group norms which are in conflict with training objectives, ie training operatives for a higher level of output than is acceptable to the staff working in the department. Thirdly, there are the 'ultimate outcomes' of training which cause changes in the functioning of the firm, such as increased productivity at a departmental or organizational level. 'Ultimate outcomes' of training are the most difficult to measure because of the many other variables influencing them.

Hamblin (1974) provides a detailed structure for the evaluation and control of training while underlining the problems and practical difficulties which evaluation activities generate. He evaluates training at five levels and describes strategies for obtaining evaluation at each of these levels.

Level 1: reactions of trainees during training to the trainer, other trainees and external factors

Level 2: learning attained during the training period, assuming prerequisites such as basic aptitude and receptiveness on the part of the trainee

Level 3: job behaviour in the work environment at the end of the training period

Level 4: organization: the overall effects on the organization

Level 5: ultimate values: this refers to such factors as survival, profit, welfare of interested parties and social/political welfare.

What kinds of measurement will be used?
There are a number of yardsticks which can be used to evaluate training, and preference should be given to objective measurements. This is not to discount the often considerable value of subjective measurements, but their limitation should be appreciated. Jones (1970) has described the following levels of measurement which can be applied to any training effort.

The validation level: this measures the extent to which skills and knowledge objectives have been reached. Measurement is in training terms and is determined by tests, such as questionnaires, or the ability to achieve an output target. Measurements are not made in financial terms, nor are comparative methods of obtaining the same results considered.

The budgeting level of measurement: this is restricted to recording and controlling training costs and is not, as such, concerned with the success of the training.

The cost effectiveness level of measurement: this compares, in cost terms, the various training methods by which a specific training objective could be achieved. For example, a recently appointed supervisor may require training in work study techniques. This training need could be met by attachment to the company's own work study department, or by attending a full-time or a part-time course. The costs that would be incurred in these possible courses of action can be assessed to find out which of the three provides the best value for money, ie is the most cost effective.

The cost benefit level of measurement: Jones defines this as 'relating training objectives to departmental or company objectives and translating them into money terms'. Attempts are made to identify the contribution which training makes to a company's operations by measuring all costs and benefits which can be attributed to a particular training investment. This is a difficult measurement to make for the reasons discussed on page 18, but detailed cost benefit studies of training investments have been successfully completed, *see* Thomas *et al* (1969), Hall (1976) and Hughes (1970).

The measurement of the best 'mix': this measures all training costs and benefits in a company having a number of training objectives for its various staff categories, and a variety of costs of methods to achieve these objectives. This type of measurement is very complex but can in theory help optimize the total training investment of the company. In practice, it is rarely made as the necessary information on costs and benefits is usually unavailable.

Investment appraisal: here the opportunity cost of training (*see* page 20), is examined and the return from investment in training compared with that from other forms of investment. For example, a large company may investigate the pros and cons of having its own management training centre. The benefits and costs involved in such a project would first be considered on their own merits and then in comparison with alternative investment opportunities open to the company. The outcome of this appraisal may show that the investment in a training centre would yield, say, an eight per cent return on capital, but that a similar level of investment in new plant would produce a 15 per cent return. Investment appraisal is essential for a company which anticipates spending large sums of money on training but is well beyond the scope of most trainers.

The majority of training in industry and commerce takes place in a busy work setting and a rigorous scientific approach to

104

evaluation involving pre- and post-training tests, control and experimental groups, etc, although very desirable, is not practicable. However, if adequate resources are not made available for evaluation purposes, the effectiveness of training will remain unchecked. This is the dilemma which faces the training officer in attempting to evaluate training.

This dilemma can be resolved, to some extent, by adopting the following pragmatic approach to evaluation:

set clear training objectives, expressed as far as possible in behavioural terms

identify and record the major costs involved in the training

test for benefits on a random sample basis: concentrating on 'immediate outcomes' but including 'intermediate outcomes' where possible.

Together these three steps will go a long way towards helping a company maximize its benefit from investment in training. For, as Hesseling (1966) puts it, 'the main task of the trainer as evaluator is to test training effectiveness or to validate his professional claim that the selected training methods have brought about the desired result.'

Chapter 7

School and College Leavers: the Transition from Education to Work

Youth unemployment — vocational guidance — youth opportunities programme — further and higher education — induction training

YOUTH UNEMPLOYMENT

Young people represent an investment in the future. They bring energy and ideas into the business and rejuvenate an ageing work force. The movement from school to work is, at the best of times, a difficult process for many young people, but their problem is extended and intensified now that suitable jobs are scarce. The wider social effects of youth unemployment demand urgent solutions at the national level and call for a parallel response from individual companies. In the latter the training officer has, as we shall see later, an important role to play.

In 1977, 671,000 young people left full time education to look for their first jobs, and by October of that year when those who were going into full-time education or starting in industry had done so, there were still 98,600 school leavers unemployed, and the average length of unemployment for boys was 12 weeks.

Part of this youth unemployment problem was due to the economic recession but there was also a demographic cause in that the number of young people in the UK leaving full-time education and looking for their first job has been rising and will remain high until 1986, Manpower Services Commission MSC (1979). Superimposed on this demographic factor is the longer term upward movement in young people's susceptibility to unemployment, identified by the MSC (1976a). For example, the number of unemployed (aged under 20) as a proportion of total unemployed rose from 12.5 per cent in 1970 to 27.8 per cent in 1976. During the 1976 recession the increase in young people's unemployment was much higher than that for the total unemployment and their situation was much less favourable than in the last recession. The duration of unemployment of young people, though still less than for any other age range, has risen sharply.

This problem is not confined to the UK in that, for example, there has been a steady increase in youth unemployment every year since 1970 in all the major EEC countries. The question of transition from education to working life has therefore been investigated by the Commission of the European Communities (1976), which reports that:

> finding employment is only the first step, making sure of congenial and suitable employment, adjusting to it, finding satisfaction in it and learning how to progress in a career are quite as important parts of the process of transition . . . The period of economic recession and the dramatic unemployment situation affecting young people have served to highlight in starker terms the problems for each generation of young people making effective transition from education to working life, and of being sufficiently adaptable to meet changing circumstances later in life.

Some of these problems highlighted in the Commission's Report are:

need for work experience, which is particularly important to help young people compete with adults in times of unemployment

special help required for certain groups, such as girls (intensive guidance is needed for girls and their parents and teachers to combat the effects of popular beliefs about womens' opportunities, ie girls undertaking training traditionally given only to boys)

migrants who may have linguistic or social and cultural difficulties

those who are ill-prepared for work because of lack of qualifications or low motivation

the need to strengthen relationships between education and employment and the necessity of obtaining information on

107

the attitudes of young people leaving school. *See* page 111.

Training cannot strike at the root causes of unemployment, it will not solve the problem, but it can alleviate some of the consequences.

Another dimension is added to the question of youth unemployment when we consider that 'for the bulk of the population, maximum intellectual capacity in the biological sense is probably reached somewhere between the ages of 16–20,' Bromley (1975). Thus, unless some appropriate form of training is provided at the time when they are most able to take advantage of it, a considerable proportion of young people (particularly those at the lower end of the intelligence scale), may never acquire the skills needed for interesting work, and may never have the chance of reaching their full potential.

VOCATIONAL GUIDANCE

Young people start in full-time employment when they are between 16 and 20 years old, although this is not necessarily their first experience of the work situation. Some of them will have had vocational training at school in, for example, shorthand-typing, catering or machine shop practice; a few may possibly have spent a short period of time attached to a company, and many young people will have had temporary jobs at weekends and in the vacations. Among the older age groups, an increasing number of students will have followed vocational courses which included practical training in industry or commerce, sandwiched between their academic studies.

For most young people choosing a career is a difficult decision to make, and contacts with the world outside their educational institutions can be very valuable in helping them to make up their minds about the type of work they want to do. Less fortunate are the many other school and college leavers who have not had such contacts and who are uncertain about the job opportunities which exist, the training which is available and their own suitability for particular employment.

Vocational guidance is described by Vaughan (1970) as the 'means of helping people to choose work in which they will be reasonably contented and successful within the limits of their ability. The considerable expansion in this field over the last few years has been due to the increasing complexity of our educational system, the proliferation of job categories and the dissatisfaction felt by educationists, young people and employers

108

at the haphazard way in which the choice of a career is often made. In spite of this expansion, the amount of vocational guidance available to young people is still very limited.

Under the Employment and Training Act 1973, primary responsibility for placing school leavers in their first employment rests with the Careers Service of the local education authorities but young people may also use the Employment Service of the MSC. The main functions of the Careers Service are:

to work with careers guidance teachers in schools and colleges and to provide students and their parents with information on education, employment and training opportunities, also to help with the planning of careers education programmes in schools

to help young people to find suitable training and employment, and employers to find suitable workers

to offer help and advice to young people on problems connected with their settlement in employment.

Pupils have individual interviews with careers officers, supplemented by self-report questionnaires and, where necessary, school and health reports, Department of Employment (1978). Psychometric tests are sometimes used.

Considerable disquiet has been expressed about the limited facilities for vocational guidance, and while provision has gradually improved, the 'careers service is spread thinly over the school population and because of this it often has less influence on job choice than parents, relatives or friends . . !' MSC (1975). Because of the increasing demands on their services, caused by current levels of unemployment, considerable extra resources have been allocated.

The work of careers officers is made more difficult by the shortcomings of careers education in schools which, although given more attention in recent years, is still inadequate. As Hopson and Hayes (1968) have stressed, vocational guidance is specialized work and few schools have been able to obtain an adequate number of trained staff and the other resources they need to provide an efficient service for their pupils.

Apart from the guidance they may receive from their tutors, careers help for students comes from two main sources. First, universities and colleges have appointment and career advisory services to assist students find suitable employment. However,

109

the large number of students in many colleges makes it very difficult for the appointments staff to give personal attention to them all, particularly as few students think seriously about the career implications of their degrees or diplomas until they are in their final year and are faced with getting a job. At this stage such guidance as may be available is often too little and too late.

Secondly, the Professional and Executive Register run by the Department of Employment offers, for suitably qualified people over the age of 18, a similar service to that which the Youth Employment Service provides for school leavers. The initiative in seeking this help rests with the student.

YOUTH OPPORTUNITIES PROGRAMME
One of the five main aims outlined in the MSC Review and Plan (1977b) was 'to help to secure for each worker the opportunities he or she needs in order to lead a satisfactory working life'. One expression of this aim is The Youth Opportunities Programme, which was set up by the MSC in consultation with many organizations including the Confederation of British Industries and the Trades Union Congress, and which was fully implemented in September 1978. It is designed to accommodate a wide range of needs and offers courses of two main kinds:

work preparation, ie to 'prepare young people for work by helping them to decide which job they are best suited for and providing training in a range of skills from the most basic to semi-skilled operator levels'
work experience, ie to give different kinds of work experience.

The Work Preparation programme comprises assessment or introduction to employment courses, short courses to develop basic industrial skills and remedial rehabilitation or preparatory courses for disabled people, including the educationally handicapped (although in the main, the responsibility for providing remedial education lies with local education authorities).

Work Experience includes induction, planned work experience, further education (which can include social and life skills training), personal counselling and support. There are four different kinds of work experience:

work experience on employers' premises
training workshops
work experience projects

community service opportunities.

With the exception of the last item, these can be sponsored by any organization, or, in some cases, by an individual. A flat rate allowance is paid to the young people and a variety of financial contributions can be made by the MSC towards the cost of the operation.

Other measures which are complementary to the Youth Opportunities Programme are: incentive grants to support training in industry, the unified vocational preparation scheme and the community industry programme. This last programme offers a distinctive kind of assessment, employment, rehabilitation and training for some of the most seriously disadvantaged amongst the young unemployed who find it most difficult to hold down normal jobs.

Since a high level of unemployment for young people is likely to be a feature of the labour market for the forseeable future, the Youth Opportunities Programme will be needed for some time. This need is emphasized since young people are in competition with other age groups for a wide range of jobs and because there is evidence (MSC (1977a)) that employers believe the calibre of young people has deteriorated in terms of their motivation and basic education — hence older applicants for jobs tend to be given preference.

The mismatch between school curricula and employment needs is not new but its reality comes home to young people when they recognize their lack of preparedness by school for employment. There can be no immediate solution to this mismatch problem, but the gap between industry and education can be lessened in a number of ways:

some of the government sponsored measures, to which we have already referred, eg work experience, are steps in this direction

an interesting proposal by the Engineering ITB (1978b) is that the first stage of craft engineering training (which normally takes six months), take place during the last two years of compulsory schooling, with the possibility of developing an appropriate CSE examination. Williams (1978) has suggested that the scheme could be the forerunner of a large scale injection of courses related to working life into the largely academic schooling system. A discussion on the wider implications of this idea is beyond the

111

scope of this introductory book but the reader may care to reflect on the changes in educational resources, including staff, and the help and cooperation from industry which would be necessary for success

another development is the payment to 6th formers of grants scaled to encourage students to take courses related to work skills

at an international level, the Commission of the European Communities (1976) refers to 'the dialogue on the vocational dimension of education systems on the one hand, and of the employment systems on the other' and the need to sharpen the reciprocal responsibilities of education and employment systems in defining more effective methods of providing for the diverse social, educational and employment needs of young people.

Although statements such as the above are made at national and international levels and some resources allocated, the problems facing young people seeking employment will not be resolved unless companies, and often this means their training officers, are prepared to respond to the local situation. For example, most of the Youth Opportunity Schemes described above require the instigation and assistance of the training officer, who needs to be aware of the national perspective and of the implications for his own organization. Obviously the training officer is well placed to play a key part in the dialogue between education and industry. A good relationship with local schools and colleges can be of great mutual advantage; careers talks in schools, visits to industry by schoolchildren and teaching staff, or possibly work experience programmes. These activities require careful planning and cooperation but can be of considerable assistance in vocational guidance and in helping to bridge the gap between industry and education.

A gradual shift of some of the responsibility for vocational training in the future from the employer to the educational system would be more in accord with the philosophy and practice of a number of the Common Market countries. It would certainly provide a fairer chance for all school leavers as, under the present system, economic or geographic factors play a great part in determining industry-based training opportunities in any particular year, chance factors, which could affect a young person for a lifetime.

Successful change of this nature will not, however, take place merely by national statements nor by alterations in school curricula. Vocational training which does not in all important respects match the real needs of the organizations concerned can be worse than no training, because nothing is so disheartening at the outset of a career than to have to unlearn all that has been enthusiastically acquired to date. The aims of education are concerned with individual development, whilst those of industrial training are related to the acquisition of work skill, possibly demanding near perfection in certain respects. These objectives are not necessarily mutually exclusive and ideally they can complement each other, but the differences have to be recognized and accepted by both teachers and industrial trainers, *see* page 2. It is sobering but instructive to reflect upon the difficulties in obtaining transfer of learning from the early off the job training centres to the actual production line within the same organization. The important lesson is that a great deal of cooperation, agreement on teaching methods and content, and continuing coordination will be necessary before useful integration between education at school and industrial training can be achieved. Obviously, the training officer will have a key role to play.

Recruitment criteria — young people
Employers have a difficult task in trying to recruit and select the right school and college leavers for their particular business. This is usually more of a problem than selecting adult staff for when interviewing young people about to start their first permanent job, there are fewer criteria against which to assess their suitability. They rarely have a relevant job history, their ability to do the work in question is unproved, their expectations of the job are frequently inaccurate and, at times, wildly so. For such reasons as these, compared with older staff, there is often a greater risk involved in spending money training young people and some employers hold the view that the risk is not worth taking. Others minimize the chance of having square pegs in round holes or a high turnover of young staff, by deciding detailed job specifications beforehand and by using systematic methods of recruitment and selection, *see* Denerley and Plumbley (1969).

One of the basic criteria used in selecting school and college leavers is the educational attainment and background of the applicant. Qualities such as manual dexterity or personal

113

appearance can be very important in selection, but in the first instance it is normally academic attainment which tends to determine the type of work for which young people are eligible and the level at which they enter a company. Most firms set minimum standards of education (expressed in terms of examination achievements) for entry to certain jobs, such as graduates for management trainee posts, 'A' levels for potential private secretaries or 'O' levels for technician apprentices.

Aptitude tests of various kinds can also be very useful, particularly where no educational qualifications are available: these are used extensively in selecting craft trainees.

Qualifications

Young people leave full-time education with a wide range and variety of vocational and non-vocational qualifications, *see* Venables (1970). At one end of the scale are those who start work at the minimum school-leaving age without academic qualifications, while at the other are students approaching their mid-twenties who leave universities with higher degrees.

Three main categories of school and college leavers come on to the job market. First, boys and girls starting work at, or soon after, the minimum school-leaving age, with or without GCE or CSE qualifications. Secondly, 18 year olds, usually with one or more GCE advanced level or equivalent passes. Thirdly, university and college leavers, normally in their early 20s, with degrees and diplomas. There are very different employment and training opportunities open to these three categories of young people when starting work and as might be expected, the role of the training officer varies considerably in helping them. Initially, he may be involved in preparing job descriptions which assist the personnel department in drawing up a profile of the prospective employee. In some cases he may also take part in interviewing and testing candidates.

There are also variations in the degree of flexibility which the training officer has in structuring training programmes for young people. Often it is necessary for him to plan in-company training within externally imposed constraints, such as a fixed time span of training or a college's curriculum and academic year. On the other hand, the training officer usually has more flexibility in designing and running programmes for many semi-skilled jobs where training takes place entirely within the company.

114

FURTHER AND HIGHER EDUCATION

In recent years further and higher education have become integral parts of the training programmes for many school and college leavers, especially for those trained for skilled and professional employment such as trainee craftsmen, technicians, technologists or private secretaries. The term further education is generally used to denote courses which are mainly vocationally orientated and which lead to technical and professional qualifications. There is therefore some overlap between this and higher education, which refers to courses of first degree standard or above which are taken by students from about the age of 18 or over. The former Central Training Council (1966a) described the main purposes of further education as:

> to provide the knowledge and appreciation of techniques necessary to enable a trainee to do his job; to inculcate a broader understanding of relevant science and technology so that the trainee appreciates the problems of those working in associated occupations and is also better equipped to adjust to changes in the nature of his work; to widen the trainee's understanding of the society in which he lives and to develop him as a person; and to prepare suitable trainees for more advanced study leading to more highly skilled work.

These aims will not be fully achieved unless there is close cooperation between employers and the colleges concerned. Often the training officer is the main link between the college and the company management and, to be effective in this liaison role, he needs to have a working knowledge of the further and higher education systems and the contribution they can make towards his company's training programmes. This includes advice on selecting suitable candidates for particular work, recommending appropriate courses of further education, providing feedback on trainees' progress and their eligibility for more advanced work. *See* British Association for Commercial and Industrial Training (1976).

Employment and training at 16-plus

Young people leaving school with 'O' level passess in GCE or good CSE grades are mainly eligible for skilled or professional employment of one kind or another, and when starting work with good employers usually receive some training and possibly further education. Compared with their academically less

115

able schoolmates, these boys and girls have a wide range of employment and training opportunities open to them. Depending on their aptitudes, they may take up craft or technician apprenticeships or begin to learn office or commercial jobs for which formal training is necessary. Career prospects are often very important for a proportion of young people in this category and they look to their employers for the preparatory training needed to achieve their ambition. Not all school leavers are either able or motivated to prepare themselves for a career and many are satisfied to do a job which they can learn rapidly, with a minimum of formal training and further education.

The approach to training career-minded teenagers should take into account the fact that a number of them are likely to have held positions of responsibility at school. They will have been encouraged and allowed by their teachers to learn by themselves and so will be accustomed to working with the minimum of supervision. Instructors and others concerned with their training should bear these points in mind and be ready to give the trainees responsibility early on in their training and avoid excessive supervision.

Further education is included increasingly in training programmes for young people in this category. However, many employers are unable or unwilling to release their young trainees during working hours and their trainees have to study at evening classes or by taking correspondence courses. Some employers provide additional facilities within their firms to help students to prepare for their examinations.

The awards of the Business Education Council (BEC) and the Technician Education Council (TEC), are important qualifications for these young people. These have been developed from the recommendations of the Haslegrave Report (*see* chapters 9 and 12), and replace the former Ordinary and Higher National Certificates and Diplomas and certain City and Guilds courses. Both BEC and TEC are particularly mindful of the necessity to integrate employment needs and education and, for example, the courses leading to BEC awards must be designed to:

> provide rungs on the ladder for those who are aiming at professional qualification
>
> provide knowledge and skills for those planning careers in business or public administration, Business Education Council (1976).

Leavers without formal qualifications

Many boys and girls leave school believing that it can no longer offer them any relevant further education, whilst to some the opportunity to earn a wage and to be independent is too great a temptation to resist! They take unskilled or semi-skilled jobs such as labourers, machine operators, office juniors, messengers and junior shop assistants. The growing tendency for firms to recognize the value of a systematic approach to training staff for unskilled and semi-skilled work means that an increasing number of school leavers now receive some planned training when starting work. The instructor often has to contend with motivation and learning difficulties when training these young people.

While the majority of school leavers in this category find that their abilities are at least adequately employed by unskilled or semi-skilled work, there will be others whose talents are under-utilized and who ought not to have left school so soon. Instructors or supervisors will probably be the first to notice these youngsters, who stand out as being the particularly bright and capable trainees in their groups. These trainees should be given the opportunity of developing themselves by training for more skilled work.

Employment and training at 18-plus
Career prospects

Since 1945 there has been a major increase in the number of young people who go into the sixth form at school (or transfer to a college of further education) and so do not start work until they are about 18 years old. These school-leavers normally have one or more GCE 'A' level passes and leave full-time education for one of three reasons. First, their examination grades are not good enough for them to continue their studies; secondly, although qualified for a place at a university or college, they prefer to start work or, thirdly, they have been selected to follow a sandwich degree or diploma course.

These school and college leavers have spent 13 years in full-time education and a high proportion of them look for employment which offers good career prospects. Those who have already had some vocational training may get jobs immediately as, for example, junior secretaries, while others who have followed science-based courses may obtain posts in industry as trainee technicians and technologists. Still others will use their education as a general background and start a professional career in, for example, accountancy, insurance or banking.

Eighteen and nineteen year old leavers are realizing the importance of receiving a good training and rightly expect their employers to provide systematic programmes. These should be designed to take into account points such as the following: the fact that these trainees are usually well-motivated and prepared to work hard; that they tend to be self-starters; that they are very capable young people and need to be given work which challenges their abilities, and that education will probably play an important role in their training and development programmes.

It is from this group of school leavers that companies recruit young men and women with potential and sponsor them on company-based sandwich courses. These are available in a wide variety of disciplines such as mechanical and electrical engineering, business studies, chemical technology, food science and applied physics, and lead to a first degree of a university or of the Council for National Academic Awards (CNAA) or, in some cases, to a National or Higher National Diploma.

Sandwich courses are vocationally orientated and designed so that the student spends time in industry and at college before graduating. They require careful planning on the part of the training officer to ensure that the in-company part of the course is effective and in phase with the academic curriculum. Project work and job rotation through different departments and sometimes in different companies or industries are features of many sandwich courses. Projects provide a very useful learning experience for students, but a great deal of preparatory work is needed on the part of the training officer and the college lecturers in selecting and defining a project which is feasible from the company's point of view and of value to the individual trainee and to the firm. Job rotation is also a useful method of learning for students and contrasts with the traditional tour approach, although the latter is still followed by some companies.

Eighty nine per cent of CNAA sandwich course graduates obtain jobs on completion of their courses, which compares most favourably with university graduates, who traditionally show a preference for continuing in higher education on graduation. Fifty per cent of the CNAA graduates go into manufacturing industry as compared with 25 per cent of all graduates,

118

Daniel and Pugh (1975).

Most major companies and a growing number of small organizations sponsor suitably qualified 18 year old school leavers on sandwich courses in preference to employing graduates straight from full-time courses. The advantages of the former approach are that during the three or four years of the sandwich course, trainees receive formal education and practical training, and on qualifying are familiar with the sponsoring company's ways and capable of doing a job with the minimum of further training. Further, as trainees progress through their courses, their talents for particular work can be spotted and developed. Both employers and trainees are then in a strong position to select the most appropriate field for eventual employment and steps can be taken to plan, in good time, for their first job.

Day-release is used increasingly for the further education of 18 year old school and college leavers. Trainees attend college for one or more days per week to study for professional examinations in such subjects as banking, purchasing, accountancy, or for BEC or TEC qualifications in a wide range of vocational subjects. The duration and academic level of these courses vary considerably.

Employment at 20-plus
Career opportunities
Young men and women who have taken full-time or sandwich courses of higher education leading to a degree or diploma are between 20 and 22 before they start their first permanent job. Whilst some final-year students have a clear idea of the careers they will follow, others, and in particular those who have taken non-vocational courses, have considerable difficulty in deciding the kind of employment that they want to pursue.

The blame for their dilemma does not lie entirely with the students. A fundamental reason why some graduates have difficulty in finding suitable employment, whether in industry, commerce or elsewhere, is that there is little or no overall planning by national bodies of the supply of, and demand for qualified personnel. Nor, it must be said, are employers always aware of the value of the qualifications offered by graduate applicants for jobs.

Unfortunately, careers in industry or commerce have tended, in the past, to be regarded by many students, and their advisers, as second-best to university research, the civil service or teaching, and concern has often been expressed about the need to attract more graduates into business. Many companies, especially large ones, offer graduates excellent training opportunities and promotion prospects, and this has helped to create a better image of commercial and industrial organizations; it has shown that they can offer graduate careers which compare well with some of the traditional fields of employment for highly educated young men and women.

Recruiting graduates is one problem: keeping them is another. Lester (1970) examined the problems of graduates entering industry and found that their most frequent complaint was that their talents and capabilities were not being fully used. This and later surveys suggest that in general companies have not yet mastered the art of employing graduates effectively.

Rogers and Williams (1970) divide the pattern of demand for graduate employees into three periods: the pre-1950 era, when graduates tended to be recruited for the public service and the armed forces; the 50s when hostility to graduates as theorists diminished, and enlightened employers, particularly the larger companies, recruited their 'crown princes'; and the 60s, when graduates were being accepted generally and in brisk demand the decade of the 'taut' and brief training programme. To this must be added a fourth period of the seventies characterized by a buyers' market.

The rapid growth in the number of young people obtaining degrees and diplomas has not been matched by a parallel increase in the number of jobs of the kind which graduates had come to expect. This has created serious difficulties at a personal level, with new graduates having to come to terms with the hard fact that a degree is no longer a passport to success nor even a guarantee of employment.

The Department of Employment (1974) has predicted that the number of highly qualified people (with first degrees and equivalent qualifications) will grow by one million between 1971 and 1986. At the same time there will be a slower growth in the kind of jobs they have traditionally held. The evidence points to a change in the pattern of graduate employment but there may well be problems in helping them find job satisfaction and to feel that their talents are being utilized.

The employment and training opportunities in industry and commerce which are open to graduates depend on a number of factors, including the discipline they have studied, their person-
120

ality and interests, and the job market. There are, however, basically three categories of new graduates seeking employment: those with qualifications which are vocational, semi-vocational, or non-vocational.

Graduates with vocational qualifications

Students who have successfully completed vocational courses in subjects such as production engineering, computer technology, industrial design or business studies have qualifications which are relevant to specific fields of employment. They have acquired sufficient skills and knowledge during their courses to be able to do a responsible job after only a few weeks of induction and job familiarization training, particularly if they have followed a sandwich course.

However, many vocational first degrees and national diplomas provide students with a broad-based education and relatively little specialization. As a result, a graduate in, say, business studies who specialized in accountancy in his degree course is not a qualified accountant. Similarly, a mechanical engineering graduate is not immediately eligible for membership of his professional body. These students may be exempted from certain professional examinations, but to qualify for membership they will have to study further and gain relevant practical experiences at work. The early part of their employment is, in effect, further training, being the practical experience needed by the graduate seeking a professional qualification.

Not all vocationally trained students take up the career for which they have been prepared at college, owing to inadequate advice in selecting a career at 18 or earlier and because some students at the end of their courses do not want to use their subjects in their work. Improved careers guidance would reduce this loss of highly-trained people, although some wastage is inevitable.

Graduates with semi-vocational qualifications

These students have certain expertise of potential use to a company, but they need to acquire commercial or technological skills before they can be gainfully employed. Examples include graduates in physics, chemistry or pharmacy being prepared for technical sales or research and development positions: in English for journalism and advertising, and in foreign languages for export-import business, or overseas travel agency work.

121

Assuming that these graduates have the appropriate personality, drive and other qualities required by an employer, they will need training to induct them into the company, to provide them with a general background to the industry or the field of commerce, and to enable them to acquire the business or technological knowledge and expertise they need for their work. This expertise may be in manufacturing technology, selling, or in other fields, and is developed during in-company or external courses or a mixture of both. On-the-job training and practical work experience is a major part of their training. Training programmes for these graduates vary in length: six to eight months is an average time, and they are thus much longer than those for graduates with vocational degrees or diplomas.

Graduates with non-vocational qualifications
Students who have studied subjects such as classics, history, or politics find that the currency of their qualifications in the commercial job market is very limited, as they cannot offer an industrial or commercial employer any technical skills or knowledge which he can profitably use. Their degrees indicate academic ability, but this by itself is not enough to obtain employment, since employers will only be willing to provide the necessarily lengthy job training (of a year or more) if this investment seems prudent.

A greater number of graduates in non-vocational subjects are recognizing that they need to improve their qualifications by studying for the membership examinations of professional bodies such as the Institute of Personnel Management or of one of the Accountancy bodies. Others may read for a higher degree on a day-release basis in, say, operational research or manpower studies.

INDUCTION TRAINING

The main aims of induction training are to welcome new employees into the organization or department, and to ensure that they understand certain basic information about the job. Thus induction is the one type of training necessary for all 'trainees'; whether young or old, whether they are newcomers to the company or have changed their work within the organization. This training need has been recognized by training boards which recommend that induction training should be made available at all levels in industry. *See*, for example, Cotton and Textiles ITB (1970a).

122

Induction is necessary for both personal and economic reasons, in that as well as the social benefits it gives to new employees, it also aims to reduce labour turnover and to enable new starters to reach an efficient standard of performance more quickly.

Induction should be seen not merely as an activity arranged by the training officer, although this of itself can be helpful, but as an overall managerial responsibility. Many induction needs are concerned with the immediate working environment and therefore a most important part is played in the induction by the supervisor and those working in the vicinity. For these reasons, induction must be regarded as an integral part of the organization's training plan and its importance should be stressed in the training given to all employees and especially to managers and supervisors.

Recent legislation in, for example, the fields of safety and of industrial relations has caused companies to review the content and effectiveness of their induction arrangements and these reviews have led to two major conclusions.

First, an awareness that the traditional induction course which all employees attend disregards the particular needs of special groups of employees such as the school leaver, immigrants, the disabled, or adults being re-trained for new jobs. Whilst such staff will share some common induction needs, their induction programmes must reflect the differences as well, and as a result will vary in both content and duration from one category to another.

Secondly, companies recognize that the wider induction objectives cannot be achieved in an initial short course of training. This position is illustrated in the context of school leavers by the following quotation from the MSC study on the Vocational Preparation for Young People (1975), but also applies to other categories:

> But such evidence as there is about the reaction of young people themselves to the induction training they receive suggests that the limited form recommended by ITBs does not go far enough. What is needed rather is a personnel policy specifically for young entrants which recognizes the special problems they face in the transition to the new environment of adult working life, at a time when they are also experiencing the personal problems of growing up. Such a policy would reflect awareness of the teaching methods in use now-

adays in schools, the common attitudes of young people towards work and the community; their ideals and expectations; the difficulties faced by young people in growing up; in adapting to working life, in working with older people, and in understanding and accepting the discipline of the workplace. Particular attention would also be given to trying to see that those close to the entrants, particularly their supervisors and workmates, were able to guide them in their development both as individuals and as capable members of the working community, and that the young people themselves know where they can go to get advice, whenever they need it.

The following list indicates the points which may need to be covered during the induction period, *see* also Marks (1974).

Conditions of employment: the contract of employment; payment procedures; holiday agreements; Factories Act; absence and sickness procedures; meal and tea breaks; disciplinary procedures

Welfare: pension and sickness schemes; welfare and social activities; medical services

The organization: foundation and growth; products; standards; market; who's who; future of the organization

Introduction to workplace: meeting the supervisor and fellow employees; geography of department (eg canteen, toilets); the job

Safety: hazard areas; fire alarm procedure; fire points and exits; no-smoking areas; first aid and accident procedures; safety rules; security arrangements; safety committees

Training arrangements: person(s) responsible for training; content of training programme; further education; company facilities

Pay system: how to read a pay slip; overtime and incentive payments; pension schemes; income tax and other deductions

Trade unions and staff associations: the role of trade unions; grievance procedures.

As we have seen, the content and approach to induction training should be planned around the needs of the trainee. In some cases a few hours' induction is adequate but in others it may last for several weeks. It is preferable to split the content of longer induction programmes into several sections, providing the trainee with information as he needs it. As an extreme instance,

124

a school leaver is unlikely to be interested in details of the pension scheme the minute he has arrived in the organization. His first concerns are likely to be what his supervisor and co-workers will be like and whether he will be able to do the job. The importance of timing in the presentation of induction information, is well made by Van Gelder (1967), whose work is a valuable practical guide to anyone planning induction training.

Chapter 8

Operative Training

Operatives — the justification for operative training —
characteristics of operative jobs — operatives' training
programmes — further education

OPERATIVES
The term operative or operator refers to:

> work people directly concerned with production or service in
> a wide range of industries and occupations, possessing vary-
> ing degrees of skill and knowledge which is usually of a
> narrower range and capable of a lesser degree of adaptation
> than that of a craftsman . . . . Department of Employment
> (1971)

The range of operative (sometimes referred to as semi-skilled)
jobs is considerable and includes in the industrial context sewing machinists, packers, assemblers, and process plant
operators, and in the commercial sector, telephonists, certain
shop assistants and some clerical workers. In this chapter we
describe a systematic approach to the training of industrial
operatives; the training of their commercial counterparts is
discussed in chapters 9 and 10.

Operatives are an essential part of the workforce of every
manufacturing industry and are often its largest single group of
employees: nearly half of the labour force in the engineering
industry, for example, comes within this category. The importance of the operative labour force in industry was among the
reasons why ITBs made operative training a high priority in
preparing their recommendations for companies (see Iron and
Steel ITB (1966) Engineering ITB (1967)). Another reason for
this priority was that in 1964 operative training was well understood, since the principles of systematic training were originally applied to operative programmes based on job training
126

analysis (*see* Seymour (1954)). However, it is only fair to add that the successful use of these techniques in operative training led in some cases to some techniques being misapplied to other levels of training (*see* chapter 5).

THE JUSTIFICATION FOR OPERATIVE TRAINING
To many people, operative work appears to be the easiest to learn and the simplest to do. This may be true of certain jobs but it is a quite inaccurate view as far as others are concerned. Some operative jobs, as we shall see, although classified as semi-skilled, require a very high degree of expertise, and it is mainly with these that we are concerned in this chapter. For an illustration of the training of operatives for less exacting occupations *see* the Training Within Industry (TWI) approach described by the Ceramics, Glass and Mineral Products ITB (1968b) *see also* chapter 5.

There are a number of reasons why companies train their operatives:

operative training is usually the least contentious form of training: it does not generate the resistance often felt when, for example, initiating training for managers. It is therefore a good and safe starting point for a company to begin a systematic approach to its training

results can often be more easily measured in operative than in any other field of training: reduced learning times, decreased scrap levels and increased utilization of plant, for example, are all factors which can be measured. Companies are likely to be most interested in the early stages in training which can be shown in financial terms to be profitable. *See* Talbot and Ellis (1969)

many operative jobs are specific to an industry and at times to an individual company. Employers have little opportunity of recruiting ready-trained operatives in the open market, and have, therefore, to train their own.

Much operative work is boring: it provides only limited opportunities for job satisfaction and pay levels (excluding bonuses and overtime) are often low. It is not surprising, therefore, that it is amongst operative grades that companies tend to have their highest labour turnover. Training can help with this problem in two ways: first, it can bring new recruits up to experienced workers' standard (EWS) in the shortest possible time, which means that they can earn bonus and on money grounds at least are not deterred from staying with the firm. Secondly by keeping learning times to a minimum, a recruit is more effective sooner, and unless he leaves during or just after his training, the cost of training is more than offset by his work output. In situations where there is a high turnover of operatives the case for training is very strong, since the costs are relatively low compared with those of recruitment and selection. *See* Jones and Moxham (1969), Carpet ITB (1967).

CHARACTERISTICS OF OPERATIVE JOBS
In spite of the wide variety of operative occupations, most share the following characteristics.

Short learning times
Training programmes for operative jobs vary in length but generally last a matter of weeks rather than months, and are therefore much shorter than those for technician trainees, for example, which may be measured in years. The reason for this difference is that the operative normally has to acquire a high degree of skill but in a very limited field and for restricted application. This contrasts with the training programme of a trainee technician or craftsman who has to acquire a much broader range of skills and apply them in many different situations.

Standard training programmes
Operative jobs are largely prescribed, in the sense that little variation is allowed or possible in the work methods used by different operatives doing similar work. As a result, operative training programmes tend to be standardized rather than tailor-made for the individual. Training manuals can, therefore, be prepared for operative jobs and used repeatedly as long as the job content remains unchanged.

Limited knowledge content
Operative jobs generally depend on the use of manual skills, the practice of which requires a restricted range of technical knowledge. However, the knowledge necessary for competent performance may at times be detailed, although limited in range.

Significant manual skill content
Operative jobs, as we have seen, usually require considerable manual skill and in certain occupations, such as short-cycle
128

assembly work and sewing machining, a very high degree of manual dexterity is essential.

Minimal education
Academic qualifications are unnecessary for the majority of operative jobs, since the type of work involved calls for physical rather than mental skills. There are exceptions to this rule, however, such as the process plant operative, whose general standard of education has to be sufficiently high to have a working knowledge of the process he is controlling.

Wellens (1979) illustrates a practical approach to the areas of manual craft and physical skills and argues the case for the application of existing knowledge about training. He views job performance as having not only knowledge and skill requirements (with requisite planning, perceptual, sensori-motor and procedural skills), but also includes interactive skills requiring personal motivation dependent on personal relationships.

On and off the job training
Although there were some very good operator training schemes prior to 1964, the most common 'training' practice was the haphazard one of putting the newcomer with an experienced worker, who was expected to instruct while actually doing the job. With increased emphasis on the use of job analysis and the benefits of systematic training, this method of Sitting with Nellie, fell into disrepute. ITBs required off the job training centres to minimize interference with production, to provide a learning situation away from the day-to-day pressures of work, and to avoid the risk of accidents through the misuse of plant. *See* Paper and Paper Products ITB (1971a). Where exacting expertise has to be acquired, such as the basic training for some types of sewing machining, this is still regarded as the best method of training, but difficulties can be experienced in the transfer of learning to the production line. For example, a new supervisor on the section, production pressure, having to work an unfamiliar machine or using real materials instead of simulators, can have an adverse effect on the trainee.

In certain instances there has been a trend towards what Wellens (1979) describes as: 'an on the job type of training carried out, not by full time professional trainers but by skilled operators who are in reality part-time semi-skilled trainers'. He

129

terms this sitting next to the New Nellie, and gives interesting examples where the background work has been done by training boards who have produced training packages specially designed for operator instructors. The TWI operator instructor course is also in line with this development.

OPERATIVES' TRAINING PROGRAMMES
Training programmes for operatives are similar to those for other categories of employee in that they are based on an analysis of the job which the trainee has to learn and on his need for training (see chapter 5).

To accommodate the wide variety of operative jobs, many different types of programmes have been developed, but in most cases they consist of three stages: induction, basic off the job training, and planned on the job training. Some idea of the types of programme for operatives can be gained from the following examples, illustrating jobs involving respectively a high degree of manual dexterity, and the operation of complex machinery. For further details see Seymour (1966).

Training sewing machinists
Programmes for this occupation normally consist of three stages, King (1964).

Stage 1: induction
Traditionally, operatives received little or no induction training, but the benefits derived from helping newcomers to adjust to their working environment are as we have seen now more widely recognized, and in a growing number of companies suitable induction schemes have been designed for new operatives (see page 122)

Stage 2: basic training
This enables a trainee to learn the knowledge and skills required before she attempts to apply them to the job. Basic training for a trainee sewing machinist consists initially of three types of exercises interspersed with rest periods: exercises to prepare the trainee to use the sewing machine by learning its parts and how to select the required needle positions; exercises to acquire skill in the feeding of material into the machine, sewing straight lines and arcs; and further exercises to extend the above skills. Time and quantity targets are supplied to the trainee for all exercises.

The trainee next performs short, simple exercises on production work and is given tasks of increasing difficulty until she attains skill at experienced worker's standard on short runs.

Stage 3: stamina development
This takes place initially off the job, as the trainee extends her experience of short runs and gradually develops her capacity to maintain output targets for longer and continuous periods of time. When she can maintain EWS under production conditions, she is transferred to the factory, and there builds up her stamina until she achieves EWS over a complete working day.

The length of the training programme depends on the difficulty of the job, the flexibility required and the trainee's learning ability. For a detailed example of the training programme for a similar operative job, *see* Knitting, Lace and Net ITB (1970a).

Training an operator to work complicated plant

Many operatives have to be trained to run sophisticated plant, such as that used in paper-making, packaging and in chemical processing. Moreover, in some cases a trainee has to learn more than one job, if several staff are required to operate the plant and if a new employee is expected to learn each job before he is regarded as fully trained.

Training programmes for this type of operative work vary in content and duration depending on the particular plant, and typically consist of:

Induction, which covers points discussed on page 122
Basic training, this consists of instruction on the function of the different parts of the plant and the sequences to follow in starting and stopping it under normal conditions; emergency procedures; safe working practices; common operating faults and action to be taken to correct them; quality standards and inspection procedures; cleaning and possibly routine maintenance.

It is preferable for at least part of this stage of training to take place off the job in a suitable learning environment away from the hazards and noise of the workplace. Off the job training enables the instructor to use certain training aids to help the trainee understand the processes that he will be controlling and help him learn essential skills. Diagrams and models of the plant

131

can be very helpful, while if controls are complex, initial training can take place on a simulator. A mock-up control panel
manipulated by the instructor to display normal and abnormal
settings is a valuable training aid in these circumstances. For
certain process operative jobs, a trainee may be required to
follow a course of further education.

Planned experience, this stage of the training takes place on the
job under the guidance of an instructor. Its aim is to enable the
trainee to operate the plant under everyday work conditions.
Initially the trainee uses the skills and knowledge he has learnt
during basic training to carry out routine work procedures, and
when these have been perfected, he tackles non-standard operations. In this way the trainee gradually accepts full responsibility for operating the plant.

For further details of training operatives for these kinds of
occupation *see* Crossman (1960), the Paper and Paper Products
ITB (1970b) and, for an example of the training of young
operatives for process work, the Ceramics, Glass and Mineral
Products ITB (1971).

FURTHER EDUCATION
As mentioned previously, parts of certain operative jobs can
best be learnt by a trainee's attendance (usually on a part-time
basis) at a college of further education. These courses are
designed to complement the more practical side of an operative's in-company training and, at the same time, provide
national standards of attainment. The following City and
Guilds of London Institute's courses indicate some of the occupations concerned: chemical plant operatives; glass process
operatives and coal preparation.

The inclusion of further education in operative training programmes has developed over the last 20 years, but on a limited
scale. The change has been restricted to a small but important
category of operative jobs which can be described as having a
significant technician/supervision content. Typically, these jobs
involve tasks which require an operative to make technical
decisions in controlling a particular process. The decisions may
be routine and programmed in the form of procedures, but are
critical to the operation, and the margin for error is often very
small. It is therefore important that trainees learning this type of
job have an appropriate understanding of the technology
involved and its implications for their work.
132

Chapter 9

Office Training

Developments in office work — training for the office
— examples of training programmes — the future

This chapter outlines an approach to the training of office
workers, such as punch-card machine operators, clerks employed on routine work, copy and audio typists, private secretaries and the important group of sub-professional employees
in senior clerical, office technician or similar positions.

DEVELOPMENTS IN OFFICE WORK

Prior to the passing of the Industrial Training Act in 1964 and
particularly before the last war, it was unusual for office staff to
receive training. The main reasons for this were the high level of
unemployment and the limited opportunities for education
beyond the minimum school leaving age. This enabled companies to over-select new office staff and to employ intelligent
boys and girls who today go into the sixth form or possibly to
college, but were then very glad of the opportunity to start their
careers as office juniors. These school leavers were bright
enough to pick up the skills and knowledge that they needed not
only for their first office job but also for subsequent more senior
posts. In cases where specific office skills or knowledge were a
prerequisite for employment, young people were expected to
train themselves at their own expense before a company would
engage them. The onus was on the individual employee to
attend evening classes or to take a correspondence course where
formal qualifications were required.

During the current high levels of youth unemployment
many of these brighter school leavers are still available for office
work but, because they have stayed longer at school and taken
higher qualifications, their career aspirations have been raised.

133

At the same time many office jobs have been de-skilled and employers often find they have a flood of applications for the few skilful jobs, such as executive secretary, and a dearth of interest in the less skilled jobs such as punch operators. A different perspective, however, is that of the employers (quoted in the Manpower Services Commission's survey (1977a) *see* page 111), who expressed the belief that the basic education of school leavers has deteriorated. In particular young peoples' inadequate skills in the '3 Rs' causes problems in office work.

Since the last war there have been a number of far-reaching changes in office employment with a consequential impact on related training. From a national point of view, office staff have become a much larger sector of the working population. There are well over three million people employed in offices who together account for approximately 12.8 per cent of all workers in the country. These employees therefore play an increasingly important role in the economy and employers in both the public and private sectors will inevitably be looking closely at ways of improving the productivity of their office staff. Training and development will provide part of the answer.

Today the spectrum of office work is much wider than it was before the war and includes many new jobs of a semi-skilled nature and others of a technical or quasi-professional character. One expression of this change is that certain jobs which used to be very important numerically now comprise a minority group within many offices. For example, typists, shorthand-typists and secretaries are now outnumbered by other office workers, and particularly by those concerned with accountancy, *see* Wise (1970).

The employment of semi-skilled office workers has been made possible by the revolution in office methods which had been accelerated by earlier shortages of clerical staff of pre-war calibre. The widespread use of office equipment, such as addressing machines, duplicators, and photocopiers; the introduction of computerized accounting and other records; and more recently the advent of microprocessors have transformed the character of work carried out in many offices. In some cases these changes have de-skilled traditional office jobs and created a demand for staff to do work which is similar to that of semi-skilled factory operatives, for example, preparing punch cards or tapes, or assisting in running a large computer installation.

134

Changes in systems usually involve retraining and attitudinal aspects must not be overlooked, particularly where the staff are to be taught skills that appear to them to be of a lower level than those required for their original jobs. For example, introducing a computerized system requires a substantial outlay and full benefit will not be gained unless the training assists in the development of favourable attitudes at all levels in the office hierarchy, from management to operator.

There are also training implications stemming from the changes which have taken place at the other end of the commercial and clerical skill spectrum. The development of management services such as production planning, organization and methods, personnel, computers, and cost accountancy, has created demands for specialist ancillary staff to work under the direction of the functional manager. In-company training, supported in some cases by further education, is the most efficient method of ensuring that these staff acquire the necessary expertise.

Another important development which has affected most offices, and particularly those in major cities, is the change of attitude which many office staff have towards their employers. This has shown itself in a number of ways, such as the growth in the membership of white collar unions, and not least in the increased turnover of office staff. In pre-war days there was a high degree of labour stability in offices, and it was not uncommon for staff to spend much, if not all, of their working lives with the one employer. As Singer (1977) has pointed out, 'In this situation the pressure to train fast and train well is not a major one.' Today the pattern of office employment is very different. Even in times of high unemployment, the demand for certain staff such as shorthand-typists, general clerks or telephonists, frequently exceeds the supply (particularly in large conurbations) and a high labour turnover results. In these circumstances companies are often forced to employ a lower standard of recruit than is really appropriate. Training then assumes a critical role because of the urgent need for new staff, whether permanent or temporaries from agencies, to be trained as rapidly as possible, and also because, compared with their pre-war counterparts, recruits are often less able to train themselves.

Apart from this continuous but short-term office training, companies can have a hidden training need stemming from the

135

unstable office employment situation which has characterized offices since the end of the last war. In some companies an analysis of the age distribution of the senior office staff reveals an ageing work force caused by a failure to attract and retain younger staff. Often the implications of this situation have not been apparent because companies have been able to rely on a core of able and loyal staff recruited soon after the last war when jobs were scarce. But these employees who grew up with their jobs to hold key positions such as senior wages clerk, typing pool supervisor, or chief sales correspondence clerk, are now approaching retirement and often have no one to succeed them. A related problem in offices with high labour turnover (40 per cent per annum is not uncommon), is that senior staff have to do routine work and cannot concentrate on their managerial function.

Surprisingly, industrial and commercial concerns have been slow to react to these training needs. Indeed, there is little evidence to suggest that adult clerical staff are being trained in their companies in any significant numbers, while according to a survey by the Central Training Council (1966c), it was rare for young people starting office jobs to be trained. The survey showed that no more than eight per cent of office staff under the age of twenty-one were following a formal training programme, and only about seven per cent were being released from work to attend a course of further education.

The former Central Training Council (1968a, 1968b) and a number of ITB's, eg Engineering ITB (1969a), Knitting, Lace and Net ITB (1970b), Ship Building ITB (1979), have issued recommendations for a variety of clerical and commercial staff and have shown how training can be applied to these employees. However, these proposals and recommendations have not been widely adopted and office training still lags well behind that for other staff. There are a number of reasons for this:

  a feature of the original CTCs proposals for new entrants to office work included a full-time basic course for school leavers, but this was in advance of its time and unacceptable to employers, so the scheme failed

  ITBs did not make office training a top priority in their early grant arrangements, and the lead it was hoped would be given to clerical training by the proposed training board for banking, insurance and financial institutions did not materialize most companies lacked expertise in this area where traditionally there was no in-house training, and as a result failed to appreciate that systematic methods could help solve problems caused by the changing pattern of office employment.

As a recent development, however, the Training Opportunities (TOPS) schemes (*see* chapter 15) have expanded very rapidly in the field of clerical and commercial occupations, and the Training Services Division is attempting to raise standards of adult clerical training. An Office Training Centre opened in 1977, is developing new methods of training *see* Manpower Services Commission (1977b).

TRAINING FOR THE OFFICE

This requires, as in other areas of staff development: the active interest and support of management, the identification of the training needs of the commercial or clerical staff in question, the design of appropriate training programmes based on analysis, in-company courses and planned experience (being supported, where necessary, by further education) and records of individual trainee's progress being kept for evaluation etc.

The training of office workers will no doubt be stimulated by the various pressures for change described above, but the form of the resultant training will be different from that which is traditionally associated with this sector of employees.

In the past, as Walker (1970) has pointed out, such formal training as there was for office work usually had two closely related characteristics. First, its implicit aim was to develop those skills common to all jobs in a particular category. Secondly, because virtually all formal, as opposed to unplanned office training, took place off the job, it did not, and indeed could not, accommodate the special features and differences of the individual jobs to which the trainees were to be appointed.

The standard training which would-be junior secretaries usually receive even today provides a good example of this traditional approach. Typically, trainees learn common secretarial skills, shorthand and other associated office tasks, in a college or an off the job training centre, but only rarely are they taught the particular office systems and procedures which they must know before they can do their future jobs efficiently. In other words, although there is much more to a junior secretary's job than being able to take dictation and to type letters, it is only in these latter tasks that they receive training. It follows that however

137

effective the common skills training may be, it can only meet part of the trainee's requirements, so the remainder is usually acquired by experience, or more accurately, by trial and error! What is missing from this common skills approach to training office staff is that programmes are not based on an analysis of the particular jobs for which the individuals are being prepared. Such an analysis is essential to take into account the training requirement for common skills, and to investigate the specific job knowledge which the individual trainee must have. If this information is not available O and M studies are necessary and only when this has been done is it possible for training objectives to be set and a suitable programme prepared. This emphasizes the need for close liaison between the training and other management services departments such as O and M, systems and computers.

It will be appreciated from the above that training programmes for office staff should invariably include on the job instruction. This is of two kinds. First, and most important, is the assistance trainees receive from their own office supervisor. The latter is the company's expert on the specific work for which he or she is responsible and is therefore potentially the most suitable person to help the trainee to learn the job. However, supervisors are not necessarily adept at coaching new staff and may themselves need some training as instructors before much progress can be made with on the job training of their staff.

The second kind of on the job instruction is self-instruction. Office procedures which appear to be complicated when explained verbally to someone who is unfamiliar with the technical language and systems within an an office, become easier to grasp if made available to trainees in a manual form, expressed as a flow chart or possibly as an algorithm. Where appropriate, planned job rotation within an office or company can be used to give a trainee the opportunity to learn procedures or office systems, and Thompson (1968) has described a successful application of a do-it-yourself approach to the training of secretarial and other office staff.

Training for office staff can take many forms and depends on such variables as: the age, ability and past experience of the trainee the degree of difficulty of the work, whether training is job or career orientated, and the level of responsibility involved. However, apart from college leavers whose training has been discussed in chapter 7, a company has two broad categories of

138

staff requiring commercial or clerical training: adults and school leavers.

Training adults

It is necessary to retrain existing office staff for a number of reasons, such as changing the order procedures in a sales office, transferring from a manual to a computer-based accounting system, or starting an export department. It is impossible to describe here the wide variety of training programmes necessary in such circumstances, but it is worth stressing that adults who are expected to tackle unfamiliar or complicated new work may find it difficult to adjust to the change, *see* chapter 6. Special care is also necessary when designing training programmes for adults coming into office work for the first time, or, as in the case of many married women, returning to it after a long break. The latter are an important source of manpower and the Department of Employment and Productivity (1970) has examined the problems associated with their entry or re-entry to office employment. One of these problems is that since training is not available to utilize the potential of these staff, they are often employed on the more junior and less highly skilled office jobs. This practice has led to the anomaly that nearly half the office boys and office girls are now adults! Apart from the fact that this is expensive, since adults are paid the adult and not junior person's rate, it is highly desirable that the work talents of these staff are developed for their own and their employer's benefit. Many such staff have had a limited education, but their lack of qualifications is often an index of past social conditions and not of their potential abilities for office work.

Married women returning to employment after bringing up a family form an important source of recruits for the office and training them can be a good investment for a company. They are usually keen to start new careers or to return to their old ones, and at 35 or 40 they have a potential of twenty or more years of service to offer an employer. If they like their work and general conditions of employment, they usually want to stay with the company and there is evidence that married women office staff are far less likely to change their jobs than was commonly assumed, *see* Hunt (1968). This is also reflected in their low absence rate.

Married women (or widows) returning to office work will, apart from induction training, probably need help to bring their

139

rusty skills up to par. They have to learn the relevant office procedures and how to operate 'modern' equipment, since photocopiers, electric typewriters and computer terminals may be unfamiliar to staff returning to work after a break of fifteen or so years. For other adult women, starting work in an office is breaking new ground, and they need basic training to acquire the appropriate job skills and knowledge.

Training school leavers

The growing and unsatisfied demand for office staff, the shorter working hours, the usually more attractive physical environment, the higher status of office workers compared with other employees (although much less significant than it was in the past), have all combined to make office jobs popular among school leavers.

Some girl school leavers have had training in office skills such as shorthand or typing and so can start jobs immediately as junior shorthand or copy typists. However, most school leavers who want to work in an office and have had no previous vocational training are often unaware of the variety of jobs open to them. The type of work these young people can do and the training they are likely to receive depend largely on their educational background. Those with limited or no paper qualifications are eligible only for semi-skilled office jobs requiring limited training such as machine operators or office juniors, while young people with GCE O or A levels or the equivalent usually hope for employment in skilled or professional work and their training is correspondingly more extensive.

EXAMPLES OF TRAINING PROGRAMMES

Administrative and professional trainees

For the reasons discussed earlier, it has been unusual for companies to provide formal training programmes for school leavers aspiring to administrative or professional posts, although training practice in this field varies widely from company to company.

It was not until 1957 that the Association of British Chambers of Commerce (ABCC) launched a National Commercial Apprenticeship scheme. The Association recognized the need to provide training for bright young staff who would in time take over important administrative or professional positions in
140

the office, and so pioneered a new scheme of training. Initially, this provided a five year training for 16 year olds and a three year programme for school leavers with A levels – later modified to four and two years respectively. A company wishing to join the scheme had to submit its proposed training programmes to the Association for approval and had to agree to release the trainees for at least one day per week to study for an appropriate business qualification at a college of further education.

Writing five years after the apprenticeship scheme started, Tonkinson (1962) reported disappointing progress. At that time very few companies had responded to the ABCC's initiative and since then the picture has not improved. Although the scheme itself was not the success that had been anticipated, it nonetheless helped to highlight the need to train young office staff.

One of the main reasons for the failure of the ABCC's scheme was that it did not accommodate the changing patterns of office work and employment discussed at the beginning of this chapter. For example many of the bright 16 and 18 year olds, for whom the scheme was originally intended, no longer come into business direct from school but instead go to university or college. The reservoir of potential administrative and professional talent among school leavers is therefore very much smaller than it was in pre-war days and so companies are looking more to graduates for future section leaders and office managers.

This is not to say that young people starting work with GCE O or A levels have little to offer a company; on the contrary, although they may not be of graduate ability and their promotion ceilings are generally lower, they nonetheless have considerable potential. Some will qualify professionally and others, given appropriate training and planned experience, can be prepared over a period of years for important office technician or sub-professional posts working in support of functional managers. A chief credit control clerk, a personnel assistant in charge of wage administration, a work measurement assistant in a work study department, are examples of such office staff assisting respectively, the financial controller, the personnel manager and the production manager.

However, while 16 or 18 year old school leavers might eventually develop the ability to be promoted to this level of responsibility, they start work much lower down the ladder and in practice many receive no formal training. The programmes for those who are trained systematically usually take one of two forms, traineeships or direct job training, *see* below.

In selecting school leavers, companies look for applicants who are interested in office work and who have good educational backgrounds. This usually means four or more GCE O levels, including English and mathematics, or one or two A level passes, or their equivalents. Administrative and professional trainees need a broader introduction to the company and its constituent parts than other new office staff since their work requires them to have a wider understanding of the work of the company. A longer induction period also gives the trainee the opportunity to assess the kind of work in which he or she would like to specialize.

Traineeships

Some companies have a policy of recruiting well-educated school leavers and giving them an extended training in different aspects of the business before appointing them to a specific job. These extended programmes are similar in principle to those provided for graduate management trainees. They are, however, not so advanced and last longer - four years or more for 16 year olds, and at least two years for A level entrants, compared with up to 18 months for a graduate. The duration of training varies with the ability of the trainees and the availability of suitable jobs to which they can be appointed. A typical programme consists of the following:

Basic office skills training
This teaches the trainees standard business terms and any special terminology which they need to know eg how to write business letters and memoranda, the use of the telephone, office equipment and filing systems.

General office training
Having mastered the above skills, they are shown, or encouraged to find out for themselves, how an office works by identifying its purpose, organization structure, systems and controls. Planned job rotation through a number of departments gives the trainees a general understanding of the office and other business activities of the company, and a more detailed skill and knowledge in one or two administrative tasks. This enables

142

trainees to accept responsibility for doing a job of work and at the same time prepares them for subsequent specialist training. As Bingham (1968) has pointed out, much of the success of this approach depends on the training officer or other manager in charge of the training.

Specialist training
Having successfully completed basic and general training, the employer and trainee select a particular area of work in which the latter can specialize, and a suitable programme is then prepared and followed. This may be in accountancy, personnel, production, or other functions and is supported by a matching course of further education.

Associated further education
In 1969, the Haslegrave Committee on Technician Courses and Examinations concluded that although the term technician was traditionally applied to the technical sector only, there is a wide range of occupations in the business sector to which this term can also be applied. They recommended the setting up of the Business Education Council (BEC) and this was formed in 1974, to 'plan, administer and keep under review the establishment of a unified national system of non-degree courses for people whose occupations fall within the broad area of business or public administration', *see* Business Education Council (1976). BEC courses are designed to provide rungs on the ladder towards professional qualifications and to provide trainees with knowledge and skills appropriate to their work. Four central themes are integrated into all BEC awards; money, people, a familiarity with numbers and technology, and ability to express oneself clearly.

The courses are of three levels:

General or first level awards which are suitable for trainees starting work at 16. There are no academic entry requirements. All the BEC courses are modular in design and the general awards include core areas of study such as communications, human relations, organizational structures and environment, office services and clerical skills, as well as option modules.

National awards are for students who have attained credit standard in BEC first level awards, or the required number of GCE O level passes. The subjects studied include

English language, communications, human relations, accounting, quantitative methods, law and structure of business organization.

Higher national awards. These courses have an entry qualification of BEC National Award, or a required number of GCE A and O level qualifications or the equivalent. Many of the subjects are similar to those in the lower level courses, but studied to a higher standard. They include the environmental framework within which business operates, resource analysis and allocation, quantitative methods, technological environment, and option modules.

Students can study for the awards on a full-time, part-time, block release or sandwich basis and, if successful, they can obtain some exemptions from the examinations of appropriate professional bodies eg Accountancy, Purchasing, Personnel Management.

Direct job training

The second, and probably more common, form of training teenagers for responsible office work is typified by a company which employs school leavers at 16 or 18 and trains them for a specific job. Only if they do well in their first posts are they subsequently considered for transfer or promotion to more responsible work. They may then be given additional training and further education. This approach assumes that young people are best developed not by being classed as trainees and given special attention, but by treating them as any other employees. They are given the training necessary for a particular job but have to prove themselves worthy of further responsibility and training before it is offered to them.

The approach has this to be said in its favour; it gives the school leaver an opportunity to start a worthwhile job after a short training period and so avoids some of the frustration which can arise when trainees are moving rapidly from job to job, and from one department to another, on a long training programme. It also avoids the distinction between the favoured trainees and other employees by giving equal opportunity to all staff, finally it provides more information about an employee's capacity to succeed in doing a job rather than his ability to learn about many jobs superficially. This is a particularly important point because it is difficult to decide whether a 16 or 18 year old school leaver is going to make the grade until he or she has actually proved him or herself, not as a bright trainee, but as a capable employee. This approach needs to be supported by a staff appraisal system.

Training school leavers for shorthand-typist or junior secretarial posts

Because of the shortage of good secretaries, some companies recruit well-educated school leavers of between 16 and 18 and train them for secretarial posts. These recruits have usually had no previous training in office work, but have several GCE O level passes including English (or equivalent CSE) and perhaps an occasional A level grade. A training programme includes the following

Induction this achieves the aims set out on page 122

Basic training this has the objective of enabling the trainees to
gain competence at routine office tasks such as filing, use of
the telephone, and post-room work. During basic training
they also start learning shorthand and typing by working
initially for the examinations of the Royal Society of Arts.
The length of the basic training course varies according to the
age and abilities of the trainees but normally lasts for at least a
year. The training takes place partly in the company's own
training centre, if available, partly in a college of further
education, and partly by working on the job, under supervision, in different offices.

It is important that a detailed programme be agreed and published in advance, so that in moving from one office or section to another, the trainees and those responsible for them are aware of the work to be covered and of the preparation to be made.

Planned experience having completed basic training, the trainees
will have sufficient knowledge of general office work, adequate shorthand and typewriting skills and, an important
point, the confidence to act as junior secretaries. The next part
of training consists of learning how to apply the common
skills they have acquired to particular jobs. To do this they
must learn the specific procedures and systems in the office,
be helped by their boss and by the other methods mentioned
on page 137. They are then attached as junior secretaries to
different offices in turn. In each case the attachment is planned
so that the trainees gain useful experience and have the opportunity to tackle progressively more senior work.

145

This planned experience training lasts for a year or more, depending on the complexity of the work involved, the interest of the trainees and their ability.

Many trainees are content to stop training as soon as practicable and are satisfied to do junior secretarial work. Others, with more ambition and ability, continue to train for higher shorthand and typewriting speeds and study to acquire a more detailed knowledge of secretarial practice. They may also study for the Private Secretaries' Certificate of the London Chamber of Commerce and subsequently, if successful, for the Diploma.

Training of office machine operators

Most of the machines which are commonly found in offices are simple to use and staff need only a minimum of training to be able to operate them. This applies, for example, to franking machines and most photo-copiers, but trainees need to acquire special skills and knowledge to work a computer terminal, an accounting, calculating or punched card machine.

The type and duration of systematic training programmes for office machine operators varies from one machine to another and depends on the aptitude of the trainee. In general the following elements are included in the programmes for school leavers:

Induction

This a very important part of the training for school leavers and aims to help them settle into their jobs by bridging the gap between school and work, *see* chapter 7.

Basic office training

This gives the trainee a broad introduction to the work of the office to show how the job fits into the overall picture. Basic training for machine operators concentrates on the important functions of the different staff or sections in the office and avoids detailed explanations and technical language more likely to confuse than help the trainee. Basic training takes place in parallel with skill training, *see* below. This is particularly desirable if the range or complexity of work in the office is such that it is difficult for the trainee to grasp. It also serves as a break in the skill training session.

Skill training

A trainee has to acquire a high degree of manual dexterity to
146

operate keyboard machines, such as typewriters or calculators, and to be capable of producing accurate work over a working day. Manual skill training can take place on the job under supervision, in a company training centre or at a college. Some machine manufacturers also provide training schools in which their clients' employees can be trained.

The pattern of this training is essentially no different from that described in chapter 8. The trainee initially learns the necessary hand and finger movements by following basic exercises and then develops stamina by practising them for successively longer periods. The knowledge content of the work and the relevant procedures are learnt between skill training sessions.

Task training
After achieving an acceptable level of skill at working a particular machine, the trainee starts to learn some of the easier tasks which will form part of the job on completion of training. Depending on the machine, these could be preparing uncomplicated wages cards, working out simple discounts on calculating machines, or audio typing routine letters. As greater dexterity and confidence is acquired, the trainee is taught the correct procedures for dealing with all standard and non-standard work associated with the job in order to be able to do the work of an experienced operator by the end of the training.

The time required for a trainee machine operator to reach experienced worker's standard varies from a few days to several months, depending on the degree of difficulty experienced in learning the necessary manual skill and the related paper work procedures. Three and a half months is an average training time for a punch machine operator, *see* Chemical and Allied Products ITB (1970c).

Further education
Trainees recruited from school specifically to operate office machines would be eligible for a course leading to the appropriate BEC award as described above.

THE FUTURE
For the various reasons discussed at the beginning of this chapter, office training will increasingly figure as a priority item in company training plans. Moreover, training in this field is likely to increase because it is an area where the advent of micro-

processors will make a major impact. In short, office training today is in much the same position as semi-skilled factory training was two decades ago.

Chapter 10

Sales Training

Retail sales staff — training requirements — implementing the training — training the sales representative — an
outline programme

In a competitive economy the prosperity and indeed survival of
a commercial or industrial company ultimately depends on its
ability to sell its services or products. Selling is one of the key
activities in every business, and the training of sales personnel
requires a high priority in every company's plans. This chapter
reviews two aspects of sales training; the training of retail sales
staff and of sales representatives.

RETAIL SALES STAFF
The present position
Businesses providing goods or services to domestic consumers
have adopted different selling strategies such as wholesaling,
mail order and door-to-door selling, but most people buy from
retail outlets. Retailing is, therefore, one of the most important
methods of distribution and ranks as one of the country's major
industries.

In the United Kingdom there are over half a million retail
establishments including sole traders, large department stores,
chains of shops and supermarkets. Small outlets predominate
with four-fifths of Britain's shops employing fewer than four
people — a fragmented structure which has had a profound
effect on training for all retail occupations including that of sales
staff. The major retail organizations have developed systematic
training since they are large enough to employ training
specialists and have sufficient personnel under training to war-
rant the provision of off the job training facilities. However, it is
difficult to estimate how much training takes place in small
establishments because much of it is ad hoc one-to-one instruction and coaching.

149

There are a number of features which have tended to retard the development of systematic schemes in the retail industry. First, retailing suffers from the same training difficulties which characterize all industries dominated by small businesses. An owner-manager (and his two or three employees) can often benefit from training but usually lack the expertise and other training resources enjoyed by larger enterprises. Even if the owner is convinced of the value of training and can afford to finance it, it is difficult for him or his staff to be released for off the job instruction without interfering with trading. In many cases these problems can be overcome with the help of ITB advisers or by forming a consortium of small companies to operate a group training scheme (*see* page 27). The Distributive ITB, which covers training in some four hundred thousand firms, has reported considerable success with informal groupings originally co-ordinated by a board training adviser, often obtaining help from colleges of further education, as well as appropriate staff from the organizations concerned.

Secondly, the spread of training and vocational education in retailing has not been helped by the diversity of businesses within the industry. The motor vehicle, the food and the clothing trades, for example, have little in common with each other, and have understandably made varying progress in adopting systematic training. One result of this uneven and unco-ordinated development was that prior to 1950 there was no specific further education for young people in retailing, *see* Bloodworth (1969).

Thirdly, despite increased unionization, retailing is still regarded as a Cinderella industry because of its generally less attractive conditions of employment compared with most office and factory jobs. Low wages, the hours of work and particularly Saturday opening tend to dissuade adults and many of the more able school leavers from considering retailing as a worthwhile employment. As a result the industry has more than its fair share of marginally suitable recruits. A substandard level of recruitment is reflected in the high turnover of sales staff. This in turn has strongly discouraged shopowners or managers from investing in the training of employees who are likely to leave. The circle is vicious and not easily broken. Similar difficulties arise in the training of part-time and seasonal staff, particularly if they are hurriedly recruited at busy trading periods. Their training is, however, equally important as the
150

customer does not differentiate between these categories of staff.

A high staff turnover is a problem which some firms in all industries have to face but in retailing the problem is particularly acute and high labour turnover figures are common. Whilst systematic training can alleviate the effects of labour turnover among sales assistants by minimizing the time needed to bring new employees up to experienced workers' standard, treating the symptoms of a labour turnover problem is costly and is justified only if the cause, ie unsatisfactory selection, cannot itself be cured.

Some retailers tackle their labour turnover problem by improving conditions of employment as a first step in recruiting more suitable staff. They find that the costs involved in paying competitive salaries, providing training and offering shorter hours can be more than offset by the reduced labour turnover and the increased sales achieved. The importance of effective selection in this context was highlighted by the National Economic Development Office (1968).

It is not enough to improve conditions of employment. Raising the quality of staff recruited by the shop or store often calls for changes in the work itself. As part of their policy to attract and retain better staff some retail stores have examined the content of existing jobs and where possible have made them more interesting and satisfying. One method of doing this has been to give a sales assistant the responsibility for not only selling a particular line but also for maintaining stock levels and for reordering when appropriate. This policy requires more versatile staff and this in turn means the management must take into account the greater number of tasks in which employees require training.

Career and promotion policies also have to be examined if, in the longer term, the business is to benefit from improved recruitment. With greater ability often comes greater ambition, and some of the more able sales staff will look for promotion. A business must have a positive policy on staff development if it is to increase and retain the talent among its staff. This involves reviewing work performance and, where appropriate, giving employees the opportunity to gain relevant experience and further training in preparation for more responsible jobs. This approach cannot apply to small shops or to part-time staff except in a very limited way, but it is feasible in large stores or in retail chains where there are opportunities for promotion and transfers within the business, (*see* Hurley, 1971).

Thus at times, the success of sales training is dependent on substantial changes being made in the business's manpower policy and practice. Small retail concerns with the owner-manager anxious to ensure succession, require a less sophisticated approach than larger companies, but the same principles apply. There is, however, no real evidence that these changes are taking place and a flat career structure with limited opportunities for sales assistants persists (*see* National Economic Development Council, 1974). It may be partly as a result of this that there has been some diminution of skill requirements and a lack of success in attracting sales assistants with managerial potential.

Developments, such as supermarkets and self-service stores, have highlighted the necessity to consider not only the objectives of the enterprise, but also where its entrepreneurial skill really lies. This may be mainly in competitive buying and display of goods to make them attractive to the customer, as in a supermarket, or it may be in face-to-face selling skills which could include the giving of specialist information and advice, as in the case of selling expensive photographic equipment. It may be in the skills of telephone selling, or in the expert compilation of a catalogue to make the goods attractive. This is not to deny that there are likely to be training needs in all these areas since it is the depth of knowledge and skills which is often affected, not necessarily the range. A successful scheme will be based on the actual needs and standards of each job.

TRAINING REQUIREMENTS
The training required will vary widely from one business to another, depending on such variables as the following:

The size of the shop: assistants in small businesses are usually required to carry out a much wider range of tasks than their counterparts in a larger store. In the latter an assistant may be employed on selling duties alone, while an assistant in a small shop as well as selling has to help with receiving and unpacking merchandise, pricing, displaying, stock-keeping and buying

The type of merchandise sold: the sales approach appropriate in a slow selling department such as furniture is very different from that required in a quick selling department such as grocery. Different types of selling have their own characteristic skills and knowledge and this must be recognized in any training

The selling method associated with the business: is the assistant briefed to maximize sales in the short run by hard selling, even at the expense of losing customers who react adversely to this approach? Or, is the policy to help develop a reputation for quality service and to build up a regular clientele? Whatever the sales method, it must be communicated to trainees so that they can identify themselves with it and project it in their approach to selling.

Bearing in mind these variables, training in retail selling can be illustrated by considering some of the skills and knowledge trainee sales staff need to acquire. These two facets are treated separately although they are in practice interrelated and interdependent.

Selling skills

A trainee sales assistant must develop a number of different skills of which the most important is learning to sell. There is, of course, a great difference between serving and selling, as Williams (1969) puts it, 'Serving customers all day long is not an easy task. Selling to them all day long is very much more difficult.'

Selling is a highly skilled activity and calls for a positive approach on the part of the shop assistant. This can take many different forms and depends on the merchandise, the assistant's personality and natural selling style, the selling situation or environment and company policy. A fundamental part of the stock-in trade of all successful sales staff is their competence in interpersonal or face-to-face relationships. The repertoire of interpersonal skills employed in selling is considerable. At the beginning of a sale, rapport with the customers must be established. This is the ability to greet them in such a way as to show a willingness to assist without setting up sales resistance by appearing to be overbearing. A successful start to a sale prepares the ground for the main sales effort.

The experienced sales assistant builds on this initial relationship and is skilful at perceiving customers' requirements and deciding how best these can be met. This involves being a good listener, being patient, tactful, articulate and confident, handling objections, demonstrating merchandise and stimulating interest in its qualities. Throughout the sale, but particularly at this stage, the assistant must be sensitive to the customer's reaction and be flexible enough to adjust the approach accordingly.

Skill is also needed to know how and when to close the sale. The sales assistant must ensure that the customer's requirements have been met, generate goodwill to encourage the customer to return, and (often important) sell, where possible, the more profitable lines.

Sales trainees often require training in related tasks such as: telephone sales, writing business letters, displaying and demonstrating merchandise, wrapping customers' purchases, using a till, and other trade-specific skills such as measuring a customer for clothing or footwear, or assessing weight in a greengrocer's or butcher's shop.

Job knowledge

In addition to the terms and general conditions of employment and other information given to new staff in an induction programme, there are three main areas of knowledge which a trainee sales assistant must learn: knowledge of the shop's merchandise, sales procedures and commercial policy.

A sales assistant must always know the selling points of the merchandise and this is particularly important in the case of new or high priced products which are less likely to sell themselves. Staff can be helped to learn about their stock in many different ways: by reading trade publications and product information sheets, by attending courses run by manufacturers, or by the store buyers explaining their reasons for buying the goods in the first place!

Depending on the commodity, knowledge of merchandise includes: quality, physical characteristics (such as size, durability and colour range) comparable alternatives, guarantees and servicing, the price and availability of the merchandise from suppliers and its location in the shop. Other important details are special offers, promotions or discounts offered by the shop.

The sales trainee needs to know the various procedures to follow in carrying out tasks such as: the paper work involved in preparing bills for cash, cheque and credit customers, dealing with complaints, ordering stock, knowing what action to take when suppliers deliver their goods to the shop, safety and fire procedures, the information required and the methods to·be followed when stocktaking. The use of computerized stock and financial control systems makes it important for trainees to understand the necessity for dealing promptly and efficiently with paperwork, stock cards and tickets.

In the area of commercial policy, a trainee needs information on the types of customer which the shop wishes to attract, the sales approach which should be adopted and whether to assist customers by ordering goods not normally held in stock. As is the case with other types of work, relevant legisation has important training implications. These include the Trade Descriptions Act, the Supply of Goods (Implied Terms) Act, the law concerning consumer credit, and health and safety. It is worth noting that in addition to their responsibilities concerning the health and safety of their employees, retail organizations have similar considerations regarding their customers. Learning all this information is no easy task for a newcomer and the sales trainer should introduce only the more important details at the beginning of the training.

Job knowledge is clearly an important element in training sales staff, but as Herzberg (1964) has stressed:

training which is satisfied with the acquirement of knowledge stops in the middle. . . the need to gain knowledge and, therefore, the will to acquire it is self-evident for newcomers. However. . . if one realizes that knowledge can be taught but attitude cannot be made to order, it is clear where the emphasis of training must be: on the creation of the right attitude, in the development of people after the routine knowledge has been acquired.

The right attitude or work behaviour (as defined by the shop manager) should be evident in the way in which the assistant eventually performs and to achieve this, certain points need to be stressed during training. The trainee must be encouraged to maintain an appropriate standard of dress, to develop a manner helpful to customers, consistent in standard yet flexible in style, and be encouraged to follow a systematic approach to work, since selling is more efficient if it is planned. Other important points to stress are care of stock, in order to reduce losses from theft and damage, and the need to be profit conscious.

This part of sales training is achieved by:

explaining to trainees why a particular approach is necessary, rather than simply demanding it

155

managers and senior staff setting a good example in their own work attitudes and not expecting a higher standard from trainees than they themselves are seen to practise

ensuring that trainees are aware of their progress – this means encouraging them with praise and correcting faults as soon as possible.

Trainees will be more likely to develop a satisfactory approach to their job if they know what they are expected to do, why it is necessary, and how successful they are at doing it.

IMPLEMENTING THE TRAINING

Large retail companies are well equipped for training. They employ specialist training staff and have an off the job training centre, part of which is constructed to simulate a shop, where trainees can learn and practise selling. Role playing, *see* appendix 2, in the shop with instructors and other trainees acting as customers is an effective sales training technique, particularly if trainees' attempts are video taped and subsequently analysed with them.

Valuable as off the job training is when learning basic selling skills in avoiding interference with trading and in cutting overall training times, it must be supported by planned experience in a real selling situation. Here again the larger companies have the advantage over smaller ones in having sales trainers available behind the counter to assist trainees.

Sales training in large stores is not regarded as a once-and-for-all event because such companies are well aware that sales assistants do not remain successful simply by completing initial training. Further training will be necessary in such areas as improving sales performance, learning about new merchandise or store reorganization. Some businesses meet these needs by holding regular store training sessions, usually held in the morning when the store is opened later than usual.

A somewhat different approach is required to meet the needs of staff working in a chain of small shops. It may be possible to run courses centrally, although this depends on the numbers of employees needing the same course at the same time, the geographical spread of the shops and the feasibility of trainees travelling to a centre. Even if it is practicable to run courses centrally, on the job training will still be very important, with responsibility for it resting with the branch manager. The latter may be

156

assisted by a peripatetic training officer or instructor who goes from branch to branch to give individual training sessions to one or two trainees at a time. Some companies have training manuals for their branch managers, specifying the help they should give to trainees.

Programmed learning is also used by chains of shops and other retailers, and is a particularly effective way of providing basic instruction where there are small numbers of trainees in any one shop. A good illustration of its use is in training part-time staff employed for Saturday work. Using the text, a trainee learns the technical aspects of the merchandise and its main selling points, the paperwork procedures and the basic steps in selling. This saves the supervisor's time on a busy selling day, since the newcomers can learn substantial parts of their jobs by themselves. Self-instruction does not totally replace face-to-face tutoring by a trainer, but it does enable trainees to learn at their own speed and with the minimum of help. The text also serves as a guide to which reference can be made at any time during training. For a detailed example of a programme designed for trainee cash register operators in a supermarket, *see* Denny (1970).

In small, independent shops, training resources are limited and it is unusual for training to be formalized. Virtually all instruction takes place on the job, and is highly successful if the shopkeeper is a good trainer. As well as instructional skills, those of coaching and appraisal are vital in the face-to-face situation. There are no problems of transferring trainees from a training area, the ratio of tutors to trainees is one-to-one, and from the start trainees are involved in the business and feel that they are doing a worthwhile job. However in 'sitting-next-to-Nelly' training, everything hinges on the ability of the trainer.

Further education

An element in retail training programmes not so far mentioned is the further education available to support in-company training. The retail industry is a large employer of young people with approximately 15 per cent of all boy and 26 per cent of all girl school leavers (41,000 and 61,500 respectively per annum) starting work in the distributive trades, *see* Department of Employment (1975), and many of them join retail businesses on the sales side.

For school leavers who do not wish to attend formal courses at colleges of further education, the Distributive ITB runs unified vocational preparation courses. The Board has also designed modular training schemes for sales assistants, with the aim of providing basic trade knowledge. These include at least four modules of general occupational knowledge and skill, such as induction, basic training, basic selling techniques and display and merchandising, and at least one module which is product based, mounted in cooperation with the relevant trade association. The training includes organization-based exercises supported by off the job sessions, and the trainees are required to keep workbooks. At the end of the course a certificate is issued, and the achievement is recorded by the appropriate trade association.

There are two main types of further education leading to qualifications in distribution: the general and the trade courses. For the former, students can prepare for three levels of BEC awards at colleges of further education, *see* page 143. The students would choose option modules specific to the distribution industry.

Alongside these general vocational courses, are various trade courses which provide specific technical training and are sponsored by numerous trade bodies such as the Institute of Meat, the National Institute of Hardware and the Photographic Dealers Association. For details of both general and trade courses in distribution *see* the Distributive ITB current literature.

The following programme illustrates the main features of the systematic approach to training a junior sales assistant. For other examples, including those for career sales staff, *see* Williams (1969) and the recommendations of various ITBs, for example, Road Transport ITB (1968) and the Electricity Supply ITB (1968a).

An outline training programme for a junior sales assistant
Induction
The newcomer to retailing has much to learn, but job training is easier if the trainee is first helped to adjust to the adult work environment. In a small shop, induction is necessarily informal and merges into basic training, but it should nonetheless be systematic. In larger establishments induction normally takes place off the job.

Induction provides the first opportunity for the employer to
158

set the standard and pace both for the training and for the subsequent work. It is therefore essential to stress those aspects of the job which are particularly important as, for example, good grooming and a high standard of personal hygiene for young people starting work in a food shop. First impressions are important and a well run induction programme will help create the right work attitudes in the trainees.

Basic training
Selling skills are acquired by doing rather than by watching or listening to others so the sooner the newcomer breaks the ice and starts to deal with customers the better. However, some preparation is needed and initially the trainee can be given simple tasks to perform which are ancillary to selling, such as tidying or checking stock. This involves the trainee in the operation of the shop and gives a sense of achievement as well as the opportunity of learning about the merchandise. In this way, and by receiving additional instruction as needed, the new-comer acquires a sound knowledge of the stock. It is, however, important that if liable to be approached by a customer wanting to make a purchase, the trainee will be able to cope.

The next stage is to understudy experienced sales staff, who explain the various steps in systematic selling. As ability and confidence grow, the trainee starts selling, working initially under the guidance of an instructor. Success and failure at selling are discussed and advice given for future attempts.

Development training
The purpose of this stage is two-fold. First, to enable the trainee to consolidate and perfect the fundamental skills acquired in basic training, and second, to give the opportunity to gain planned experience in handling non-routine and more difficult work. These two aims are achieved largely by continuing the on the job coaching described above with the assistant being set challenging but realistic sales targets, which are gradually increased as progress and competence permit.

In parallel with this development the trainee is helped to extend product knowledge and selling skills. Typically this involves specialising in a particular aspect of the merchandise, using point of sale and other display material, dealing with customers' complaints, learning to sell to more than one cus-tomer at the same time, and perfecting skill at introductory selling ie promoting extra sales.

The duration of basic and development training varies from a few weeks up to two years, depending on the type of business and the calibre of the trainees. It is important to record progress by observation and other checks throughout the training.

Further education

Trainees should be encouraged to take appropriate courses of study (see page 157) for the following reasons: to supplement on-the-job training by learning those aspects of the trade which cannot easily be acquired within the company, to obtain recognised vocational qualifications and to improve their general standard of education.

Many ITBs, including the Distributive ITB, require as an important levy criterion a written training policy which includes allowing day release to all staff under 18 wishing to attend courses of further education. Despite this, relatively few retail staff attend further education vocational courses.

TRAINING THE SALES REPRESENTATIVE

It is scarcely necessary to argue the case for having competent and well-trained sales representatives for these are the employees who obtain business for a company and on whose expertise and success so much depends. It is not surprising therefore, that many large companies had appointed sales training officers long before the Industrial Training Act of 1964 and as a result have well-established sales training schemes.

The trainee, the product and the buyer are the three main variables which determine the type of sales training programme for representatives.

The trainee

Training programmes are required for a variety of staff including:

new employees with no previous selling experience or knowledge of the company's products

existing staff with knowledge of the company's products, but no selling background

existing salesmen who are being prepared for more responsible positions, and

representatives being given refresher training in such areas as advanced selling techniques, new company products or marketing plans.

160

Moreover, programmes are designed to cover the training requirements of different types of sales staff such as conventional commercial travellers, product demonstrators, technical sales representatives, and senior sales staff with specific responsibilities for major customers.

The product

While there is an element of truth in the saying that a good salesman can sell anything it is important to recognise that the transfer of selling skills from one type of product to another is normally limited. Training can help increase a representative's versatility, but success in one field of selling is no guarantee of similar success in another.

Differences in the type of market, advertising support, the product's technical characteristics, and the type of buyer, all call for different selling strategies and tactics and in turn demand specific expertise in the salesman. In the consumer product field, the job skills and knowledge needed to sell low priced items such as soap products or frozen foods, are different from those required by the manufacturer's representatives selling tractors or haute couture garments. The skills and knowledge needed by representatives selling invisible products such as insurance, or industrial products such as machine tools, or the tens of thousands of raw materials used by industry, will again vary. In particular, many industrial representatives require a high degree of technical knowledge of both the products and the manufacturing processes in which they are used and this must be emphasized in their training.

The buyer

Training programmes must help representatives develop the appropriate approach needed to sell to the particular buyers they will meet. Examples are: owners of small businesses, various levels of professionally-trained buyers in larger organisations, technically qualified people such as engineers, physicians, architects, and chemists, representatives of government departments, and agents responsible for negotiating multi-million pound contracts.

Export selling is an area of urgent national importance and specialized training of representatives is needed not only in the language and possibly in regulations and documentation, but also in the culture, customs and special needs of the countries

161

concerned. For further information on this topic *see* the Central Training Council (1968b) and the British Institute of Management (1975). In industry and commerce there are many possible combinations of salesman, product and buyer so it is essential that a job training analysis (*see* chapter 5) is carried out to identify the specific tasks and associated standard of performance which a particular salesman is expected to achieve.

AN OUTLINE PROGRAMME

The following programme indicates the typical skills and knowledge required by trainee representatives. It should be regarded only as a general guide for training in this field and for further details *see* Jeffries and Duxfield (1969) and the training recommendations of the Chemical and Allied Products ITB (1969b), the Petroleum ITB (1970) and the Cotton and Allied Textiles ITB (1970b).

Induction training
During this stage the objective described on page 122 should be met.

Basic training
This provides the trainee with the following:

Training in how to sell the company's products. This key objective is partly met by training in selling skills similar to that described earlier in this chapter in the context of retailing, but there are important differences. A sales representative has to seek out customers as well as maintain existing ones and he therefore needs guidance as to the amount of time and energy that he should spend on these different tasks. He also needs advice on how to obtain new customers and what volume of new business he is expected to achieve. Another important task in which a trainee representative needs help is in planning calls so as to achieve an optimum coverage of his territory. This includes the use of market intelligence, setting work priorities, and instruction in planning journey cycles. The value and importance of a planned approach to each individual sales call must be stressed with, as far as possible, the trainee representative having a clear selling strategy with specific objectives to achieve before he arranges an appointment with a customer.

162

A precise knowledge of the company's current and proposed products. This includes: prices and the authority, if any, to vary them, product specification, availability, company marketing policies, sales promotions and advertising support.

Details of the market in which he will be selling. This includes: the company's position in the market and its strengths and weaknesses, major competitors and their strengths and weaknesses, important and prestige customers, market trends.

Information on the company's sales organization and its relationships with other parts of the organization in so far as they affect the representative's job. For example: the activities of technical sales, production, accounts and transport departments should be explained and the salesman introduced to the staff in these departments with whom he will be in contact. Basic training also specifies the paperwork and other procedures to be followed when communicating with the office. For example writing customer and other reports, obtaining credit ratings of proposed customers, placing orders, legal implications, dealing with complaints, invoicing and credit arrangements, production dates and delivery schedules.

One important point to be stressed during this part of the training is that the representative must learn to work as a member of a team. His success in the field is dependent on the cooperation and help of other employees in the company.

Basic training usually takes place in the company and in the field. Much of the factual information which a trainee representative must learn is best acquired from discussions, visits, and meetings in the company and from reading material. Initial training in selling skills also takes place in the company, using where appropriate, role-playing exercises, for example, in work planning. The representative is given practical experience in selling as soon as possible during basic training. Specific performance objectives are set before each customer call and the degree of success evaluated after the sales interview. The sales manager or trainer must be present during the sale and allow the trainee to handle the interview with the customer in his own way and without interference.

163

Wilson (1970) has recommended the following sequence for what he calls the 'kerbside conference' or post mortem coaching session that should take place immediately after a sales interview during field training:

> as appropriate, show appreciation of the trainee's selling skills
> help him to identify his own weaknesses in the sales interview
> if necessary, but as a last resort, specify any of his shortcomings which he does not recognize in himself
> ensure he really accepts the deficiencies and is motivated to correct them
> instruct and rehearse the trainee in how to correct his deficiencies
> agree specific follow-up action with him by setting targets for improvement
> summarize the content of the discussion to ensure that he has a balanced understanding of his performance.

Wilson stresses that 'the kerbside conference will only be successful if the manager concentrates on specific deficiencies, identifies particular actions to be achieved within defined time periods, and achieves maximum participation from the salesman'.

Development training
This final part of a programme for a new representative has three main objectives: to consolidate the skills and knowledge learnt during basic training, to raise the trainee's level of performance to that expected of an experienced salesman and to develop the representative's potential ability still further, by broadening his experience.

Development training takes place on the job as outlined above, but appraisal of a representative's performance may indicate the need for other kinds of training, such as working with a senior representative, attending relevant sales conferences or training courses.

Steps must be taken to ensure that development training is effectively implemented since it is all too easy for training to be given a low priority once the representative has started selling. Each representative's post-basic training is coordinated within a forward training plan determined by the sales manager and reviewed in the light of the representative's progress. Although necessarily flexible, the plan specifies such details as: the objec-
164

tives of any refresher and advance training course which the new salesman attends during his first year or so with the company, when these courses should be attended, who is responsible for initiating the arrangements and the dates when interim reports are required on the representative's progress.

In this country, salesmanship does not usually enjoy as high a status as many other occupations in industry and commerce. This is because the expertise involved in selling is frequently undervalued and too many salesmen are amateurs. They have learned their job in a haphazard manner and this shows in their performance. Training can improve the efficiency of sales staff and so help this very important business activity to achieve the professional recognition which it properly deserves.

Chapter 11

Craft Training

The development of craft training — a systematic
approach to craft training — factors influencing training
programmes — the module approach — developments

A craft apprenticeship, or the opportunity to learn a skilled
trade, is one of many careers open to young people starting
work under the age of 17. For boys it is numerically the most
important class of employment. In 1974, 43 per cent of all boys
entering employment for the first time went into apprenticeships, (an increase of 7 per cent since 1964). In the same year
only 6 per cent of girls entered this form of training, *see* Manpower Services Commission (1975).

Craft apprenticeships are available in a wide variety of trades,
as almost every industry employs craftsmen. Typical craftsmen
are motor vehicle mechanics, bricklayers, plumbers, chefs,
welders and there are many others. In the past, apprenticeships
for girls have been in such areas as hairdressing and the needle
trades, although there are indications that they are beginning to
take an interest in some of the types of craft training traditionally associated with boys.

A craftsman has been defined as a 'skilled worker in a particular occupation, trade or craft who is able to apply a wide range
of skills and a high degree of knowledge to basically non-
repetitive work with a minimum of direction and supervision',
see Department of Employment (1971). The word craft, however, has no uniform meaning in industry and it is applied to
describe the broad range of work between semi-skilled and
technician levels. An example of a less highly skilled craftsman is
a house-painter, whose work is of similar difficulty to certain of
the more exacting semi-skilled jobs such as sewing machinist,
while at the other extreme are craftsmen such as pattern makers,
166

whose work has more in common with that of technicians.

THE DEVELOPMENT OF CRAFT TRAINING

Formal craft apprenticeships in this country date back to the reign of Elizabeth I, when the medieval guild system was given legal standing by the 1563 Statute of Artificers. The time-honoured method of training young people to become craftsmen was, and still is, through an apprenticeship and in its original form the apprentice learned his trade by working with a master craftsman for a number of years, and eventually became a skilled man in his own right. This on the job method of training was successful in the pre-industrial revolution era, when master craftsmen personally supervised their apprentices' training, and took pride in handing down their craft skills to the younger generation. In today's terms, this was 'sitting-by-Nelly' training at its best.

The method of training craftsmen that was appropriate to the sixteenth century could not be expected to meet the craft training needs of a modern industrial society. Yet, as Wellens (1963) has shown, the traditional pattern of craft training survived, almost unaltered, up to the early 1960s. At that time, according to Wellens, an apprenticeship had six main characteristics:

1 It is, with very few exceptions, of five years duration, whether the trade is a simple one such as house-painting or a complex one such as cabinet making.
2 There is no certification of the qualified craft worker at the end of the apprenticeship — all who enter the system at one end emerge from the other victorious and equal. So far as can be ascertained, it is the only training course of its importance in the country with no failure hazard.
3 There are rigid age limits above and below — a condition relieved by certain escape clauses which are only very rarely applied. Even in those cases where later admissions are permitted, the relaxation is normally for one year, possibly two in exceptional cases, never more. This applies to young men with half a century of working life to offer society. The escape clauses can be requested or granted by an employer in association with the union, but no boy can claim them of right.
4 It is not *necessary* to follow an academic or theoretical course alongside the practical training in order to become accepted as a qualified adult worker.

167

5 There is no national control of apprenticeship, nor any supervisory authority, and therefore no agreed standards and no inspection.

6 Training is invariably uni-craft. A boy cannot aim to become both a carpenter and a bricklayer, he must choose a single craft.

In spite of anomalies and inadequacies in the old apprenticeship system, some craft training in the early 1960s was of a very high standard, as was evidenced by the United Kingdom's successes in the international apprenticeship competitions. Although constrained by externally imposed restrictions (such as the fixed duration of the apprenticeships and their limitation to single crafts) some employers provided excellent training schemes for their craft trainees.

The majority of apprentices were less fortunate. They did not follow training programmes, but were placed with craftsmen who were not necessarily able or willing to teach them. This was a particular problem if a craftsman was employed on a payment-by-results basis, as he tended to lose pay if he spent too much time teaching apprentices. To make matters worse, indifferent or poor on the job training was often the only form of instruction that an apprentice received because, prior to the late 1950s, release to attend classes in a college of further education during working hours was not usually encouraged or permitted. Apprentices were regarded as a cheap source of labour, available to do the unpopular jobs (hence the 'teaboy' image) and their training frequently took second place to the demands of production.

Nonetheless, both good and mediocre craftsmen were produced by the old system of apprenticeship and their employment opportunities varied considerably. The best young craftsmen usually had no difficulty in obtaining suitable jobs, the others found that if they were offered employment in craft departments, they were allocated the less demanding type of work, and their pay was correspondingly lower. This *laissez-faire* method of providing a flow of skilled craftsmen into the economy was inadequate and unsuited to the economic social and technological conditions of the mid twentieth century and pressures to reform it came from different sources.

The Carr Committee Report (1958) *see* page 237, set up to recommend how the post-war bulge of school leavers could be given appropriate training to enable them to be absorbed into industry, was critical of the then existing apprenticeship arrangements. Significantly, the membership of the Carr committee included trade unionists and, as Williams (1963) pointed out, 'This was the first occasion on which representatives of the trade unions signed a public document expressing disapproval of the inflexible and restrictive characteristics of apprenticeship schemes'. Williams was a strong protagonist for the reform of craft training. By analysing the weaknesses in the contemporary arrangements she showed how, in many respects, our approach to training for skilled trades compared unfavourably with those adopted in continental Europe.

Informed members in government circles, enlightened employers and educationists were also aware of the need to bring the system of training apprentices up to date and, as mentioned in chapter 15, this was one of the main issues which led to the passing of the Industrial Training Act in 1964.

The reform of the apprenticeship arrangements in this country could not be achieved overnight. Apart from introducing a systematic approach to the training of potential craftsmen, there were many problems to which solutions could only be found by negotiation and agreement between employers and trade unions. These were described in the Donovan Report (1968), and included: industry's unwillingness to provide opportunities for women to be trained for craft work, the need for flexibility in providing the skilled workers needed by new technologies, and the difficulties faced by adult craft trainees (trained at government training — now skill — centres), in gaining recognition as craftsmen from union officials and time-served skilled men. On this last point *see* Hall and Miller (1970).

Substantial progress has been made in streamlining the approach to training craft apprentices, largely as a result of the Industrial Training Act. One of the first priorities which a number of ITBs set themselves was to investigate the training needs of potential craftsmen and to publish craft training recommendations to help improve the quality of training. The present position is that through their grant policies, ITBs have gone a long way to guaranteeing that most school leavers taking up apprenticeships receive a thorough training in their craft.

A SYSTEMATIC APPROACH TO CRAFT TRAINING
The craft training recommendations issued by ITBs have been designed to suit the particular conditions of their industries and

169

so vary in their content and emphasis. ITBs working with employers, trade union representatives and educationists, have built their recommendations on the following premises:

all training for skill is systematically derived and taught
initial training is broadly conceived
further education is an integral part of a young trainee's course.

The craft training recommendations of the Engineering ITB provide a model illustration of the application of these points. This Board, which is responsible for a large number of differing craft apprenticeships, investigated, on a national scale, the training needs of craftsmen in the engineering industry. As a result of these investigations, the Engineering ITB (1968a) developed the following eight principles as the basis of its craft training recommendations. These principles, which express the approach of most ITBs towards craft training and the current best training practice, if compared with the defects in the traditional system cited by Wellens above, indicate the extent of the reform that has been achieved.

1 *Flexibility*

The system requires that trained craftsmen shall be able to adapt to technological and other changes. This implies that the training must be broadly based, and also that craftsmen are equipped with a range of specialist skills which they can use in a flexible way. It is also implicit that whilst all craftsmen must have a minimum level of attainment, some will develop further to meet the requirements both of industry and the individual.

2 *Length of training*

The length of training shall be based on what has to be taught and on the rate of learning of the individual, subject to sufficient time being allowed to acquire maturity. This means that there will be an incentive to become qualified as quickly as possible.

3 *Standards of craftsmanship*

Standards of performance of craftmanship will be set and will be recognized by certification when they have been reached.

4 *Assessment*

The attainment of approved standards will be measured by a system of tests. The tests will take place at intervals throughout the period of training, and will be used together with training records and log books as the basis of the award of certificates of craftsmanship

5 *Further development*
There will be an opportunity for all craftsmen to acquire further knowledge and to add to their skills in accordance with industry's requirements. It is to be expected that whilst the initial training as a craftsman could be as short as three years, most craftsmen will need to return to the training system at intervals throughout their careers to learn new skills and to be brought up to date.

6 *Instruction*
Formal instruction of trainees in practical skills will be given by skilled people who have been trained in the techniques of instruction. Full advantage is also to be taken of modern teaching aids such as programmed learning devices, instruction manuals, and audio-visual systems.

7 *Further education*
Throughout the period of training, release will be given on full pay for attendance at a college of further education for a matching course of studies. Release will be at least for one day per week during the college session (or for the equivalent in block release) and those trainees who can benefit should be allowed to continue their studies after formal training is completed. Craftsmen of the future must have a sound background of theoretical understanding as well as a high standard of practical ability.

8 *Status of craftsmen*
The new system will identify the craftsmen and enhance their status by requiring approved programmes of training, recognized standards of performance, certification and registration.

Apprentice training programmes

These vary from one industry to another, and for details of specific trades the reader is referred to the craft training recommendations published by the various ITBs, for example, the Joint Committee for Training in the Foundry Industry (1966) and the Paper and Paper Products ITB (1971b). Later in this chapter the recommendations of the Engineering ITB are considered in some detail since this Board has the greatest number of craftsmen within its scope.

171

FACTORS INFLUENCING CRAFT TRAINING PROGRAMMES

Tradition in the industry

Employers and employees usually have established views on what is an appropriate form of training for craft trainees and while these views may be susceptible to some change, they nevertheless determine the broad pattern of training acceptable to the industry. For example, inter-craft disputes may arise if a training programme includes tasks which traditionally belong to another trade.

The time factor

The period of time devoted to craft training, normally about four years, is determined by what is acceptable to both the employer and employee representatives and, being the subject of negotiation, does not necessarily relate to the actual training time required. As training becomes more systematic, the tendency is for training requirements to be fulfilled in a shorter time. For example the Hotel and Catering ITB (1971) developed a craft course in Food Service which lasts for six months.

Balance of content

Research by the Engineering ITB (1971b), has shown that there had been a tendency in some craft training programmes to give undue attention to manual rather than diagnostic and planning skills. The application of these findings should result in some cases in less emphasis being placed on manual skill development and this will alter the nature and perhaps the duration of training programmes.

The need for recognized standards

Increasingly employers' associations, examining bodies and ITBs are expecting companies to meet national standards as a condition for recognition of their programmes. ITBs are also acting as centres for the registration and certification of craft trainees. These developments raise difficulties for some trainers, not least of which is that of compromising between nationally set standards and those required by individual companies, see also Singer (1970).

The need for off the job training

The risk of accidents and the non-availability of production
172

equipment for instruction purposes in the workplace make it advisable for basic craft training to take place off the job.

High incidence of on the job training
Since much craft training must take place on the job, there is a continual risk of it being subordinated to the demands of production. There is, therefore, a need for constant supervision of on the job training.

Selection of craft apprentices
Criteria for selection differ widely. The normal age for entry into an apprenticeship is 16 irrespective of the craft, but the minimum educational requirements vary between crafts and from one employer to another. In general, as the number of would-be apprentices exceeds the apprenticeships available, employers tend to select school leavers preparing for CSE or, in some cases, for GCE O levels. Care is needed to avoid setting too high an educational standard which would lead to the recruitment of potential technicians, not craftsmen.

It is important to have an effective method of selecting young people for apprenticeships, bearing in mind the investment that will be made in them during what may be up to four years of training. In addition to formal interviews, head teacher's comments and the report of the careers officer, many companies use selection tests. For engineering apprentices, the selection procedures typically include test papers in simple arithmetic and general knowledge and a mechanical aptitude test, *see* Beverstock (1968).

The successful applicants for an apprenticeship, their parents and employer, normally sign an indenture form, which details the legal obligations of the various parties, but does not usually state or attempt to define the training to be followed by the apprentice craftsman.

THE MODULE APPROACH
Soon after its formation, the Engineeing ITB, in conjunction with engineering employers and educationists carried out detailed analyses of many hundreds of tasks which craftsmen in different engineering trades are required to perform. The purpose of the analyses was to find out the precise skills, knowledge, experience and further education necessary to complete these tasks satisfactorily and to use this information to produce

a comprehensive system of training for apprentices in the industry. The data collected by the Engineering ITB was grouped into a number of units such as grinding, oxy-acetylene welding and vehicle painting, each covering a specific area of skill. Each unit is called a module and this gave rise to the modular approach to training. Module training has been defined as:

A type of training based on the concept of building up skills and knowledge in units as needed by the individual. Each module is based on a skill or group of skills which analysis shows to be a viable unit in the job situation and has a training element, an experience element and, where appropriate, a further education element. The satisfactory completion of a series of modules usually denotes a recognized level of qualification and the satisfactory completion of further modules may lead to a higher level of qualification. The duration of a module varies according to its contents, see Department of Employment (1971).

For each of its modules, the Engineering ITB (1968a) provides:

- a skill specification indicating the range of skill to be developed during training and the standards to be reached at its completion
- a training specification setting out the details of the training to be given
- an instruction manual indicating methods of developing each element of skill contained in the training schedule
- a set of sample performance tests which are to be completed successfully during the progress of the training
- a recommendation for further education
- a log book in which the trainee records the training received.

A module can therefore be thought of as a training package containing the information which a company requires to train its apprentices in a specific skill. Depending on the company's needs and the trainees' aptitudes, the appropriate modules are selected as the basis for the training programme. If it is more appropriate, a company develops its own modules.

It is important to note that the Engineering ITB does not specify how long the trainee should spend learning a module, as this depends on the ability of the individual concerned. Normally, however, trainees take approximately six months to complete one module and then need a further period of time, which
174

again varies with the individual, to acquire the necessary experience to perfect the skill. So far, the Board has published some 70 modules and others will be made available as new skills evolve and it becomes necessary to teach them to young or adult trainees. One of the basic principles underlying the module system is that craftsmen can keep themselves up to date and avoid skill obsolescence by learning appropriate modules of training, as necessary, at any time during their working lives.

The structure of an engineering craft training programme

The recommended training of an engineering apprentice lasts for a minimum of three years and consists of three stages, each supported by a course of related further education. The stages are:

basic training (off the job)
the first period of modular training (off, or on the job), plus planned experience
the second period of modular training (off, or on the job), again with planned experience.

In practice, two modules may be run concurrently and the planned experience may take place either during or after the module training. To be recognized by the ITB as qualified craftsmen, trainees must normally have completed at least two modules of training.

Basic training
This lasts for one year and takes place off the job in one of the following: a company's own training school, a group training centre, an Engineering ITB craft training centre or at a college of further education. The aims of basic training are to introduce the school leaver to industry and to provide him with initial training in a broad set of basic engineering skills, so giving him the opportunity to learn about engineering in general, before choosing a particular craft. The Engineering ITB consider that by giving potential craftsmen a wide base to their initial training, they will be the better prepared for any retraining needs later in life. Basic training also aims to teach safe and effective working practices, to integrate theoretical and practical work and to give the trainees the guidance of skilled craftsmen, who are also proficient instructors.

Trainee craftsmen spend their first three months on an induction course and are introduced gradually to the tempo of industrial life. During this period they begin to learn how to use simple hand and machine tools, and to apply their newly acquired skills.

On satisfactory completion of the induction course, the apprentices begin a six month programme during which they extend their knowledge and skill in using basic workshop machines. All trainees learn machine shop skills common to a number of differing crafts, but not necessarily the ones they will subsequently use in their first jobs as craftsmen. This practical training takes place at the same time as the trainees are learning the theoretical background to their craft at college.

For the last three months of their first year at work, the trainees begin to learn the specific skills of the craft in which they will be specializing. This gives them the opportunity to practise and gain confidence in applying their recently acquired skills and knowledge to work within their chosen craft.

Module training
By the end of the first year of their programme trainees have a general appreciation of engineering craft practices and are ready to begin module training. The trainees and their employers jointly decide the particular craft in which they will be specializing, and the appropriate modules of training are selected.

There is no fixed duration for this second stage, but it normally lasts for approximately a year. During this period the trainees complete what is called a Stage 2 module and gain experience at applying the skill and knowledge learnt during the module. Their training takes place either on or off the job, and is controlled by a qualified instructor, working to a planned programme. Both trainees and instructors have copies of this programme and of the appropriate instruction manuals.

Throughout their training, the apprentices are required to keep log books of their work and to record their progress. The latter is judged by the results of performance tests which they take during the module and in the post-module experience period. They also have to pass a final test under production conditions to ensure that they can achieve the required quality and quantity of work, within a specified time, before they are eligible to begin the third stage of training.

The third stage also lasts for approximately a year, during

which the apprentices work through a further module of training and acquire relevant practical experience. At the beginning of this stage, they and their employers have another choice to make and one possibility is for the trainees to take a stage 3 module. This provides for advanced training in a specific field, but can only be taken if an appropriate stage 2 module has already been completed. This choice would produce a craftsman with a very specialized, if somewhat narrow, range of skills. An alternative option is for the trainee to take a second stage 2 module, which would produce a craftsman with a wider range of skills.

Trainees who have completed their basic and modular training, and have satisfactorily passed the appropriate performance tests, are eligible (if at least 19 years old) to receive an Engineering ITB certificate of engineering craftsmanship. The certificate indicates which modules the craftsman has completed and is evidence that the holder has reached a national standard of craft skill in those work areas, *see* Lawrence (1970) for an early review of the module system.

This brief account of engineering craft training illustrates the important advances that have been made in providing systematic preparation for craft occupations in one industry, but similar progress has been made by other ITBs in restructuring their craft training to meet present day needs. ITBs, such as the Road Transport ITB (1978), have adopted a system similar to that of the Engineering ITB, so the module approach has become a model for areas of other craft training.

Further education for craft trainees

Further education is an essential element of craft programmes and aims to continue the broad education which the trainees received at school and to prepare them for the appropriate City and Guilds of London Institute's craft examinations.

City and Guild craft courses last for three or four years and may be taken by attending day or block release classes at a college of further education. At the end of the first two years of the course the apprentice takes the part I examination, which is set either by the City and Guilds, or by one of the Regional Examining Boards. The part II (final) examination is usually taken in the final year of the apprenticeship. The syllabuses of City and Guilds courses are designed to relate, where possible, to the trainee's progress through the apprenticeship.

DEVELOPMENTS

As mentioned in chapter 7, important and very far reaching discussion proposals have been put forward by the Engineering ITB (1978b). The Board suggests that the first six months off the job training could be carried out by schools or the further education system through suitably developed CSE, GCE or equivalent courses, which would have some learning objectives directly related to the world of work. The first year of the apprenticeship could then concentrate on off the job modular training, and the second year would be on the job modular training. The apprenticeship could then be completed not according to the length of time taken, but on attainment of the necessary standards, when a certificate of craftsmanship and the appropriate craft rate of pay would be awarded. Some trainees could achieve this status by the age of 18, although not before. It would also enable young people who stayed on at school after the minimum school leaving age to obtain credit for the relevant job related examinations in engineering, which they had taken at school.

It is argued that the Engineering ITB's proposals would help to increase the supply of craftsmen and that they would foster closer links between education and industry. Seeing the practical application of school work to employment might increase the motivation of schoolchildren to learn subjects like mathematics, in which many craft trainees have to receive remedial education (see Engineering ITB (1977) and Engineering ITB and Shell Centre for Mathematical Education (1978)). It is also hoped that motivation would be maintained during the apprenticeship as certification and appropriate pay would be linked to achievement of standards. A further anticipated advantage is greater flexibility in the use of skills in order to meet technological and other changes.

The Engineering ITB's proposal has provoked considerable discussion during which certain reservations have been expressed. For example, an apprentice's physical and mental maturation can proceed at a slower rate than his/her technical progress and reducing the apprenticeship to two years may get the two processes out of phase, see Shepherd (1978) British Association for Commercial and Industrial Education (1979).

Technological change has meant that many people are doing very skilled jobs of high responsibility for which there are no apprenticeships and Parkin (1978) suggests that perhaps we
178

have a greater need for a thorough examination of the occupational structures of our society than for a review of existing apprenticeships. He maintains that mechanistically defined skills are not enough and that in our enthusiasm to analyse them, we have tended to lose the main value of apprenticeship as a vehicle for 'creating the self-motivated, constantly learning craftsman'. The apprentice often emerged as a very mature adult with the capacity to go on developing and we must 'define the purpose of apprenticeship in terms of the overall behaviour and approach of a journeyman'.

The old apprenticeship system was certainly out of tune with modern times and sorely in need of revision. Developments, particularly the Engineering ITB modular approach, have gone a long way towards improving craft training in this country. However although much necessary consideration has been given to the weaknesses of the old apprenticeship system, very little attention has been paid to its strength and, as we pointed out at the beginning of this chapter, it did produce some very fine craftsmen. The current developments in craft training appear to have many advantages but they have yet to stand the test of time.

In many trades, technology has had a considerable impact on the craftsman's job and a progressive tendency to de-skill his work. Whilst this can bring problems of reduced job satisfaction and motivation for the craftsman, it also highlights the growing importance of technicians in our society. Their training is considered in the next chapter.

Chapter 12

Technician Training

The technician population — defining the technician —
the characteristics of technician work — systematic training programmes — educating the technician

Technicians perform a wide variety of important jobs in industry, commerce and the public services, and are numerically a
very significant proportion of our skilled manpower. As we
shall see later, it is difficult to define what jobs or parts of jobs
are of technician level and it is, therefore, impossible to state
with certainty how many technicians there are in this country.
One estimate has put the figure as high as one in six of the
working population, or some four million people, *see* Association of Teachers in Technical Institutions (1970). The term
includes all employees who, in the broadest sense of the word,
are engaged in technician-type work, not only those in scientific
and engineering jobs.

THE TECHNICIAN POPULATION
Before looking at the nature and variety of work carried out by
technicians, two further general comments on technician manpower statistics are appropriate. First, because of technological
and other developments, the number of technicians in certain
categories is increasing rapidly. For example, according to the
Committee on Manpower Resources for Science and Technology (1965) there were, in the sectors surveyed, 622,000 technicians and other technical supporting staff. By 1968 this figure
had risen to 710,000 an increase of over 14 per cent on the 1965
total, *see* the Haslegrave Report (1969). Although evidence is
not readily available, there is every reason to believe that a
similar pattern of growth is taking place in other technician
areas.
180

Secondly, while the total number of technicians is important, of greater significance is the ratio of technicians to technologists and other professional staff who depend on supporting technical personnel. Jackson (1969) in reviewing the stock of engineering and technological manpower in this country, concluded that the present annual output of qualified technical supporting staff is inadequate in this very important sector of the economy. In 1968, for example, the overall ratio of ordinary technicians to graduates in engineering and technology was 5.10 to 1, while the comparable figure for qualified higher technicians, ie technicians immediately below technologist level (sometimes termed technician engineers), was only 1.90 to 1. Moreover, as might be expected, these average figures conceal very unsatisfactory ratios in certain branches of engineering and technology.

The implications of this shortage of supporting technical staff are particularly serious in the United Kingdom, with its economy so dependent on technology-based industries. The remedy lies in more resources being allocated at national and company levels for systematic training and vocational education for technicians.

DEFINING THE TECHNICIAN
There is a great variety of technician-level jobs, ranging from higher technicians who, as we have seen, work in direct support of professional staff, to technical operatives whose jobs are close to those of semi-skilled employees. Between these two extremes is a wide spectrum of technician jobs including : radio and television servicing staff, laboratory technicians of various kinds (such as those working on product development or quality control), refrigeration technicians, computer programmers, draughtsmen, hospital technicians, electrical estimators, work study engineers and many others.

This diversity of job types is one of the main reasons why a generally accepted definition of a technician has proved difficult to produce. But it is not the sole reason. The role and function of technicians depend on variables such as technical developments, the size of the firm and styles of management in organizations. Moreover the concept of a technician as a separate category of skilled manpower, with specific educational and training needs, has emerged only relatively recently and has still to gain recognition in many quarters. In some industries, such as engineering

181

and chemicals, the technician function is well-established, in many others it has not evolved sufficiently to be regarded as a separate category.

The position and work of the technician in the manufacturing organization (the industrial technician) is well illustrated by the definition adopted by the Committee on Manpower Resources for Science and Technology (1965), *see* also Moss (1971):

> Technicians and other technical supporting staff occupy a position between that of the qualified scientist, engineer or technologist on the one hand, and the skilled foreman or craftsman or operative on the other. Their education and specialized skills enable them to exercise technical judgement. By this is meant an understanding, by reference to general principles, of the reasons for and the purposes of their work, rather than a reliance solely on established practices or accumulated skills.

This definition, however, is not readily applicable to the growing numbers of staff employed in the business sector of the economy, few of whom are called technicians, but whose jobs are in fact comparable (making allowance for the different work environment) to those of industrial technicians. The non-industrial technician has been defined in the Haslegrave Committee's report (1969) as:

> one who has acquired detailed knowledge and skills in one specialist field, or knowledge and skill to a lesser degree in more than one specialist field; is required to exercise judgement, in the sense of both diagnosis and appraisal, and initiative in his work; is frequently called upon to supervise the work of others; and has an appreciation of the environment beyond the immediate limits of his duties.

This definition includes many office staff who are specialists in a particular aspect of business and whose work involves more than a routine responsibility. Examples are employees concerned with data processing, or vehicle scheduling in a large transport department, or shipping in an export department. However it seems unlikely that the term technician will be extended to include these non-industrial staff, in spite of the similarities between their functions and those of technicians employed in industrial jobs.

182

THE CHARACTERISTICS OF TECHNICIAN WORK

Since there is a wide range of technician-type jobs, it is more helpful for our purposes to consider in some detail the general skills and knowledge which technicians use in their work, and then to illustrate the specific expertise involved in a number of cases.

The results of the Engineering ITB's (1969b) analysis of the work of technician engineers is particularly useful in this context. The Board found that, to a greater or lesser degree, all technician engineers, in whatever branch of the engineering industry they may be working, demonstrate the following six main abilities:

> the ability to use and communicate information
>
> the ability to measure or make use of measurements which involve a variety of tools or instruments
>
> the ability to choose materials and components and understand the processing of materials
>
> the ability to understand manufacturing activities and the general commercial organization and practice of their companies
>
> diagnostic ability
>
> the ability to organize (but not necessarily supervise) and give direction to the work of others.

Although referring specifically to technician engineers, this list is relevant to other technician-type jobs, as can be seen from the following examples:

Electrical estimator (electrical) technician
The main job of an electrical estimator working, for example, on a new building development, is to obtain information about the wiring layout, positioning of electrical equipment, including the number and loading of outlets from the architect's (the technologist's) plans, and to provide an estimate of the materials, labour and equipment that will be required. When approval is given, he produces detailed instructions for the site foreman and his staff (craftsmen) advising them of any special features of the job and, where necessary, modifications required. He also gives technical advice to prospective clients and to the manager in charge of the building site (the site agent).

Assistant work study (technician) engineer
Such staff employed in a work study department often have the

title engineer but are in reality technicians as defined above. An assistant work study engineer advises management on the contribution that method study and work measurement techniques can make in helping to ensure the economic use of an organization's resources. He works mainly with first line supervisors and their subordinates and carries out investigations aimed at increasing productivity by, for example, changing plant layout, improving work methods and/or introducing financial incentives. He examines the cost and other implications of his recommendations and if they are approved he may assist in their implementation.

Roles of the technician

Three distinct roles emerge from the above examples. First, the technician is essentially a practitioner with an expert knowledge of certain techniques, which he applies in a variety of work situations. These techniques require the exercise of mental and sometimes manual skills.

Secondly, the technician takes decisions on matters of considerable complexity. In the course of his work, he makes decisions which may require the use of considerable discretion and if this is misapplied it can be costly for his employer. The implications of this particular facet of a technician's work for the training officer have been succinctly expressed by the Foundry Industry Training Committee (1969):

> The training of a technician is a continuous process, not necessarily confined to his specialist function. It should take into account both his role in the organization and the influence his decisions can have on the operation of the business, in particular on cost control, quality control, production control and other parts of the technician's job which overlap into the function of management.

Thirdly, the technician has an advisory role in that he provides management with technical information or recommends specific courses of action which influence their decisions. For example, a work study engineer, called in to investigate a complaint from a shop steward about alleged tight bonus times, analyses the query and recommends that the times remain unaltered or are reviewed, in either situation backing his case with the necessary evidence. Management's reply to the shop steward takes into consideration the technical advice received

184

from the work study engineer.

Recruitment to technician jobs
The majority of men and women currently employed as technicians were probably not recruited as such. They have either developed with their jobs or alternatively have previously worked with technicians and this experience has enabled them to transfer to technician work, with only limited retraining. The source of many technicians is illustrated by the small percentage of them who have passed relevant vocational examinations. French (1970) quotes the results of a survey of technician manpower carried out in 1960, which revealed that some 69 per cent of the existing technician force in this country had no relevant educational qualification, while a survey of technicians employed in engineering and technology-based industries completed in 1968, found that 62 per cent of this group of technical supporting manpower possessed no nationally recognized academic qualifications, *see* Committee on Manpower Resources for Science and Technology (1968).

Increasing numbers of potential technicians are now recruited from school and college leavers with relevant GCE at O or A level or equivalent CSE grades. This form of entry is termed *ab initio,* and selection is normally based on the following: job specification, school examination results, head teacher's report and interviews at which selection tests may be used. Trainee technicians in certain instances may also be recruited from young people employed in the company in another capacity who have demonstrated that they have the potential to become technicians. Examples are the 'end-on' entry of employees who have recently completed a craft course, and who are able and willing to tackle the more responsible and theoretical work carried out by technicians, or from adults who have the ability to be trained as technicians. *See* Engineering ITB (1971a) for examples of training programmes for adult, craft and *ab initio* entrants.

SYSTEMATIC TRAINING PROGRAMMES
Technician training programmes depend on the age, qualifications and experience of the trainees. In the case of adult trainee technicians, and to a lesser extent young staff transferring from other training schemes, individual programmes are necessary to accommodate their previous experience. Training for *ab initio*

185

entrants to technician careers also varies greatly, as will be seen from the examples later in this chapter. Of particular interest is the modular approach developed for potential industrial technicians and recommended by a number of ITBs, *see* Engineering ITB (1969b) and Knitting, Lace and Net ITB (1971). An illustration of this approach is shown in diagrammatic form in Fig 12.1 below.

Figure 12.1

Training of technicians in foundries
Example: methods technician

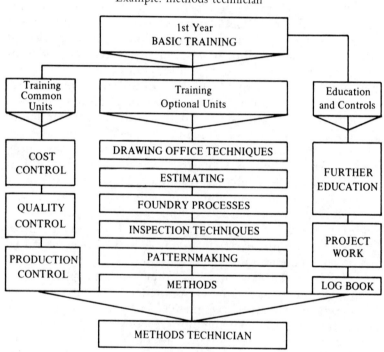

The diagram illustrates the integration of common and optional units, together with an appropriate course of further education. Project work and log books provide controls which help to measure the effectiveness of the training given and its co-ordination with the educational syllabus. The system provides for additional units of training to be undertaken as and when need arises.

Reproduced with permission of the Foundry Industry Training Committee

It refers to a programme for a trainee methods technician in the foundry industry. A methods technician is responsible, within defined limits, for deciding the most appropriate method by which a particular casting should be made in a foundry. He takes into account the production resources available to the company and decides or recommends how these can best be used to achieve a technically and commercially satisfactory product.

The recommended programme for industrial technicians consists of basic training which includes induction, common unit or general training, optional unit or specialist training and appropriate further education. A similar pattern is suggested for both higher technician trainees (18 year olds with relevant GCE A level or equivalent qualifications) and ordinary technician trainees (16 year olds with relevant GCE O level or equivalent qualifications). In both cases the training programme extends over approximately four years.

Basic training
This introduces trainees to the role and function of a technician, enables them to acquire the basic skills and knowledge, and helps them understand the principles underlying the techniques and procedures that they will be learning. It usually lasts for a year and takes place off the job. Although this programme is similar, in some respects, to the first year off the job training of craft trainees, the content and emphasis are different. Technician's basic training aims to develop diagnostic rather than manipulative skills, and to encourage the trainees to perceive future jobs in a broader context. Stress is laid on the importance of accuracy when making technical judgements and on the implications that a technician's decisions have elsewhere in the company. While undergoing basic training, the trainees also begin an appropriate course of further education, which they follow throughout practical training (*see* page 191).

General, or common unit training
On successful completion of the basic course, the trainee technicians begin this second phase of their programme, during which they learn the common or general skills and knowledge needed by all employees in the particular technician occupation. For example, the Engineering ITB (1969b) recommends that all trainee technician engineers, irrespective of the particular field in which they will be specializing, should cover the following in their general training: design appreciation, manufacturing prac-

187

tice, commercial matters, control techniques and communication. The ITB gives examples of the suggested contents of general training programmes but stresses that these must always be related to the needs of the trainees and of their companies. General training takes place both on, and off the job.

Specialist training
This final phase is also known as objective or optional training and during it the trainees acquire the specific skills and knowledge required for effective performance as a qualified technician in a particular job within the company. The content of the specialist training programme depends directly on the training analysis of a specific job. A detailed programme is prepared from the analysis, stating what the trainees learn at various stages in their training, what methods of instruction will be used and who will be responsible for ensuring that the training is properly carried out.

As we have mentioned above, technician jobs require the use of considerable discretion and this important facet of their work is reflected in their specialist training. The trainees are given specific work tasks (of appropriate difficulty for which they will be held personally accountable), to help them learn how to act responsibly in exercising discretion. Projects or special assignments, carefully matched in difficulty to the trainees developing ability, are a very useful training device for this purpose. In addition, if properly controlled, they can help the trainees in other ways:

they learn to act independently
they relate the theoretical aspects of their training to real problems
their practical work reinforces the need to know relevant technical knowledge thoroughly
they learn to develop the inter-personal skills necessary to work effectively with others.

This last point is particularly important for many technicians, whose effectiveness is reduced if they lack the ability to establish good working relationships with other employees. It should be remembered that when technicians act (as they frequently do) in an advisory capacity, they have no line authority! In addition to helping the trainees, projects are useful to the company and help evaluate the trainees' ability to work under pressure.

188

A training programme for *ab initio* industrial technicians takes up to four years, and this introduces potential control problems for the training officer and line management. These difficulties can be minimized by:

  detailed training programmes being prepared and given to all concerned, and amended in the light of the trainees' progress

  the trainees being required, as necessary, to keep work log books, the contents of which are discussed regularly with their trainers

  the trainees and their trainers producing reports on specific aspects of the training which provide feedback for motivation and control purposes.

Educating and training technicians
—further examples

There is, as we have seen, a wide variety of technician jobs, and the examples briefly discussed earlier in this chapter are now used to illustrate different approaches to technician's education and training.

Electrical estimator

Trainee estimators in the past were recruited either from craftsmen-electricians who had shown potential in their City and Guilds craft course, or from those who had successfully completed the City and Guilds Electrical Technician's course. Nowadays, entrants to this work are, increasingly, young people who have left school at 18-plus with relevant passes at GCE A level, and who will follow a TEC Higher Certificate or Higher Diploma course in electrical engineering, with appropriate options.

Since a considerable part of the estimator's job is concerned with the interpretation of drawings and the calculation of material and labour requirements, on the job training is normally in the form of planned placement in sections of the organization such as stores, drawing office and site offices. This is similar to on the job training for craft electrician apprentices, the main difference being that greater consideration is given to making and interpreting drawings, and to project work, which develops the trainee's skill in calculating quantities and in costing contracts.

Projects are also used to develop trainees' diagnostic ability,

189

for example, by asking them to examine and report on unsuccessful contract tenders. The trainees usually spend some time learning relevant craft skills in the earlier part of their training, not to become skilled craftsmen, but to be able to recognize the different qualities of work which they will subsequently be inspecting. The trainees are given the opportunity to practise these skills on building sites and so learn to appreciate some of the problems of working under site conditions, such as the effects of adverse weather and the difficulties of co-ordinating site work.

In addition, the trainees' programmes include relevant sales and office experience, so that they understand the pressures and problems encountered in each phase of a contract, from the initial customer enquiry, through the contracting procedure, to the implementation and after-sales servicing of the contract. For this part of their training, the trainees work under the close supervision of experienced estimators who act as their trainer, report progress and modify the programmes as job conditions and learning requirements change.

Assistant work study engineer
There is no single route into this type of technician work and therefore no training programme which is universally applicable. Many potential work study specialists are recruited 'sideways' from other departments or companies and have some, perhaps considerable, experience of business, while others join straight from school or college. Individual training programmes are needed to meet these differing training requirements.

Training in the theoretical aspects of work study are usually catered for by external courses, which last from four to 10 weeks on a full-time basis and cover such topics as: method study, work measurement, incentives, problems in the application of work study techniques, the structuring and presentation of reports and practical in-company projects. Another approach is for the trainee to study for the Technician's Certificate of the Institute of Management Services usually on a part-time basis.

On the job training consists of in-company projects carried out under the guidance of a senior work study engineer, and includes exercises such as: the investigation of existing and proposed time standards, examination of specific jobs to ascertain how costs can be reduced, investigation of line management or trade union complaints, and planning work flow pat-
190

terns or machine layouts. During this period, trainees are seconded to other departments in the company such as the quality control and the cost offices, to learn at first hand the implications of a work study engineer's decisions to other parts of the organization. They are given increasing responsibility for specific work study jobs so that by the end of training they are able to carry out any task expected of an assistant work study engineer working in that company.

EDUCATING THE TECHNICIAN

When the Haslegrave Committee reported in 1969, there were two major groups of further education courses available for technicians. First the City and Guilds of London Institute Technician courses, which catered for those whose aptitude was practical rather than strongly theoretical, and secondly the National Diploma and Certificate courses, which were more academically biased and which were organized under the auspices of the DES.

Since the 1870s, the City and Guilds of London Institute (CGLI) has organized a number of education courses which, although not called technician courses, were in fact meeting the educational needs of certain categories of technician. In the mid 1940s, the CGLI first established courses specifically for technicians, such as those for Telecommunications Technicians and Motor Vehicle Technicians.

The variety and numbers of CGLI technician courses gradually increased during the 1950s and expanded dramatically following the implementation of the recommendations of the 1961 White Paper, *Better opportunities in technical education*. The number of recipients of higher grade Technician Certificates grew from approximately 8000 in 1960 to more than 30,000 in 1968, and the numbers have since continued to increase but at a slower rate.

The National Certificate and Diploma scheme was inaugurated in 1921, and for many years was used, with varying effectiveness, as an educational ladder by both technicians and technologists. Potential technologist students, with appropriate National Certificate or Diploma qualifications, were able to gain exemption or partial exemption from the membership examinations of engineering and other professional institu-

191

tions. As the entry standards of these professions were progressively raised, particularly in the years following the last war, the levels of National Certificate and Diploma courses had to be correspondingly raised to keep open this well-established route to professional membership. While this was desirable for the technologist it had an adverse effect on technician students, many of whom were unable to cope with courses which were becoming more academic and less related to their needs. The seriousness of the position was expressed by the 70 per cent, or higher, failure rate of technician students following ONC and HNC courses in the late 1950s.

Following the Haslegrave recommendations, a Technician Education Council (TEC) was established in March 1973 and a Business Education Council (BEC) was set up in May 1974. The two councils aim to be complementary and have comparable roles and objectives within their own spheres. We shall consider here the role of the TEC, see also Technician Education Council (1974) and for similar information about BEC, see page 143 and the Business Education Council Policy Statement (1976). The terms of reference of TEC are:

> .... the development of policies for schemes of technical education for persons at all levels of technician occupations in industry and elsewhere. To this end it will, as proposed in the Haslegrave Report, plan, administer and keep under review the development of a unified national system of courses for such people and will devise or approve suitable courses, establish and assess standards of performance, and award certificates and diplomas as appropriate.

The following TEC qualifications are awarded: Certificate, Higher Certificate and Diploma and Higher Diploma (all of which can be obtained by part time or full time study). It is hoped that they will be nationally and internationally recognized, and to this end The council has consulted the professional bodies concerned, as well as ITBs' industry, teachers' organizations and the main validating bodies in further education. TEC aims to provide rungs on vocational ladders with its qualifications giving appropriate exemption from the examinations or entry requirements of relevant professional bodies.

Colleges have the opportunity in cooperation with industry, to plan and operate their own programmes, while the role of the TEC is to produce guidelines within which courses and exami-
192

nations leading to its awards are conducted. Flexibility is a basic feature of TEC courses so that schemes can be quickly adapted to the changing needs of industry and of students. Depending on their school achievements, students enter technician courses at different starting points. This is possible since course structures are built on units, and credit is given for qualifications already gained, for example, a Certificate can be converted to a Diploma by adding more units.

At the time TEC was constituted, there were approximately 90 Joint Committees and CGLI Committees concerned with some 300 different technician awards, involving about a quarter of a million students. The development of a unified system is a major task and will be phased over a number of years. The TEC provisions have been subject to considerable criticisms, but employers will not be in a position to compare the old and the new systems of training technicians until the mid 1980s when substantial numbers of TEC trained technicians will be working in industry.

Problem areas

The pace at which the technician function has evolved in recent years has created a number of problems, which have yet to be satisfactorily resolved. For example, employers have often been slow to appreciate and recognize the increasing value of their technical staff, as is witnessed by the growth of strong technician unions, while in some industries there is evidence that the absence of a clearly defined status for technicians has contributed to difficulties which companies have experienced in recruiting and retaining these staff.

The Engineering ITB (1978a) draws attention to the fact that technician engineers hold a wide range of key jobs, including supervisor, junior manager, and some senior manager appointments in such fields as sales, marketing, purchasing and management services. This makes the task of manpower planning very difficult. The ITB emphasises the importance of maintaining an adequate supply of well trained and able people, but the engineering industry has traditionally relied upon apprentice intake 'to produce its new stock of technician engineers through training and further education'. This cannot continue, however, as the educational attainments of new recruits to company apprentice schemes are changing, as is the pattern of further education for potential technicians. The

Board also points out that large numbers of suitably qualified girls are leaving school each year and it is currently sponsoring an experimental scheme of training for young women to 'demonstrate their suitability for employment as technicians'.

High priority is being given to developing technician TOPS training (Manpower Services Commission 1977b), and courses are available for technicians in electronics, computer maintenance and construction. The range of these courses is to be extended.

Chapter 13

Technologist Training

Defining the technologist — technologist manpower —
educating and training the technologist — matching
education and training

The increasing complexity of industrial and commercial systems, the rapid acceleration in the introduction and application
of specialized techniques, and the continual pressures for innovation and development have all contributed to the demand for
more and better trained technologists. It is no exaggeration to
state that the UK's ability to use its resources effectively
depends to a large extent on its capacity and willingness to train
and utilize its technological manpower.

DEFINING THE TECHNOLOGIST
The work of the technologist, like that of the technician, is
diverse and therefore difficult to define with any precision. The
approach adopted by the Department of Employment (1971)
stresses the importance of the level of education which technologists require, and defines them as 'persons engaged on or
being trained for, technical work for which the normal qualification is a university degree in science or technology and/or
membership of an appropriate professional institution. . . .'
  Although this definition emphasizes the educational/profes-
sional background of technologists and does not mention other
characteristics of their work, it is nevertheless helpful in that it
provides a general picture of the group of employees under
discussion. The term technologist, used in the sense of highly
educated specialists concerned with the application of scientific
principles and methods to work situations, includes jobs such as
computer technologists, professional engineers, and research
chemists, as well as other professional people, such as architects

195

who are not normally thought of as technologists but whose work is in this category. In addition to educational qualifications, there are other important characteristics of technologists' work. First, they apply scientific method in a work context in that they have to resolve production, research or development problems, often requiring originality of thought and sound technical judgement, within the financial and other constraints set by the company. Secondly they must have a broad scientific approach plus expertise in their specialisation to contribute to inter-disciplinary teamwork. Social and managerial skills are crucial. Thirdly, although technologists are likely to be among the most highly qualified (academically) of a company's staff, their education has not necessarily prepared them for specific employment.

Typically, graduate trainee technologists require a period of in-company training before they can be given their first permanent post of responsibility. This puts them on a par with graduate management trainees as in both cases their training is essentially long-term. The parallel is also apt in that trainee technologists have to learn to work at management level. On completion of their training, they may or may not be in charge of people, but they will be responsible for other resources and for making decisions which will affect the profitability of their companies.

TECHNOLOGIST MANPOWER

According to the 1971 census data, there are some 200,000 engineers and approximately 200,000 scientists in this country, making a total of about 400,000 technologists (broadly defined). This represents a 20 per cent increase since 1966. Many are employed in the civil service, teaching, local government, the armed forces and other professions, so the number of technologists working in industry and commerce is small compared with the critical contribution which they make to the economy.

The Engineering ITB (1978a) points out that whilst its industry employs some 33,000 technologists, a similar number of its 120,000 managers have previously worked as professional engineers or scientists. The industry has therefore to try to develop a manpower policy which takes account of the career paths of engineers and compensates for the loss of technologists who move from professional to managerial posts. As it is likely that this situation occurs in other industries, it would appear that estimating total numbers of technologists and planning future requirements is a very difficult task.

The growing awareness of the valuable and distinctive role of the technologist led in the 1960s to a number of investigations into the supply and utilization of the country's technological manpower. Three reports, (*see* also page 204), those of Jones (1967), Dainton (1968) and Swan (1968) are of relevance to companies employing technologists. All three highlighted serious problems and made recommendations which it was in industry's own interest to help implement.

In 1967, the Jones Report examined the problem of numbers of young scientists and technologists leaving this country to work overseas, notably in North America. The brain drain, as it was called, represented a significant loss to the economy of highly qualified personnel. Among the reasons given for the inability of UK industry to attract and retain these technologists, was its failure to provide challenging opportunities competitive with those abroad. For new graduates, a general antipathy to working in industry was too frequently reinforced by the unattractive training schemes and promotion prospects which UK companies were prepared to offer them, while for those interested in a career in industrial research, the facilities available in this country in many cases were not comparable with those in North America.

The North American brain drain problem was alleviated by the difficulties which the United States economy encountered with the cut-back in its aerospace and other technology-based industries. These developments lessened the opportunities for our technologists contemplating emigrating to North America but one problem was replaced by another. The attractive employment opportunities in oil-rich and in EEC countries continue to exacerbate the shortage of technologists (and technicians) in the UK.

The Dainton Report, (1968) followed an inquiry into the flow of GCE A level and equivalent candidates in science and technology entering higher education, and found that since 1960, the proportion of school-leavers specializing in science and mathematics had fallen in relation to other subjects. The impact of this trend on the supply of potential technologists is indicated in the decline of entrants into science and technology faculties, as a proportion of the total, from 45.9 per cent of admissions in 1962 to 40.6 per cent in 1966. This swing away from science disciplines at sub-university level was highlighted as being potentially harmful to our economy since, 'it is from the science stream in our secondary schools that we obtain most of our doctors, dentists, scientists, technologists and engineers'. The report recommended that certain changes were necessary to achieve the desired flow of young people into technical careers. It suggested, for example, excessive specialization at the school level should be reduced, the quality of science teaching should be improved, and young people should be introduced to the importance of science and technology in society in imaginative ways, such as by the structuring of technology-biased projects for sixth formers.

The Swann Report (1968) examined the flow into employment of newly-qualified scientists, engineers and technologists. While the annual output of this category increased from approximately 10,000 in 1961/62 to an estimated 24,000 in 1971/72, the Report drew attention to the unsatisfactory situation in industry (and in schools) caused by too few of the *best* graduates entering these sectors. For example, 72 per cent of graduates with first class honours degrees in science subjects returned to university work and only 9 per cent went into industry on graduating. A much higher proportion of newly-qualified technologists entered industry (45 per cent), but these also showed an increasing trend towards higher education and research.

The Swann Report recommended, *inter alia*, that

industry should vigorously recruit persons qualified in science, engineering and technology, especially the ablest graduates in these fields, should see that they are fully and effectively employed, and that attractive and challenging careers are open to them.

It also recommended that educational bodies should play their part in developing technologist manpower by increasing the provision of shorter periods of post-graduate and post-experience study, in addition to higher degree programmes.

A more recent survey by the Engineering ITB (1978a) shows that nearly two thirds of the professional engineers employed in industry are in research, development or design and only about one fifth in production. Despite the movement of individuals across functional boundaries, *see* page 196, the manufacturing function continues to be starved of graduate talent. This point is reinforced by the Institution of Production Engineers (1978) which claims that the needs of British manufacturing industry for chartered engineers are falling short by as much as 50 to 80 per cent, and that the education system is:

not capable of fulfilling the needs of British industry in providing professionally qualified chartered and technician engineers in the area of manufacturing management and technology - one of the key areas of wealth creation.

The implication of this shortfall is very serious, in that the Institution predicts that three million more UK jobs could disappear by the end of the century, unless industry can absorb new manufacturing technology efficiently and quickly.

One step taken by the Engineering ITB (1978a) to encourage graduates into manufacturing industry is the introduction of special fellowships in manufacturing management. *See* also Crisp (1978). In addition, in 1976 the Science Research Council initiated a 'teaching factory' scheme, analogous to the teaching hospital. The scheme extends to a number of companies each of which collaborates with a local university or polytechnic department of production engineering *see* Wild (1979). The best postgraduate students are seconded to carry out projects for the company in such areas as redesigning products for more efficient manufacture and introducing advanced manufacturing methods. The cost is borne equally by the Department of Industry and the SRC, and the latter expects that by 1982-3 the Government will be providing about two million pounds a year for its teaching companies.

A further suggestion for increasing the supply of qualified engineers is made by the Women's Engineering Society (1978) which points out that whilst Britain has one woman in every 500 engineers, France has one in 33, Scandinavia one in 10, and Eastern Europe and Russia one in 3. It urges that local education authorities should ensure that girls can take appropriate subjects at school, that careers advice is available, and that special encouragement is given to girls to join engineering courses in polytechnics and universities. The CBI (1978) also points regretfully to the small number of women engineers, and suggests that this,'largely reflects the pattern of GCE O and A level choice in the school'.

Recruitment of technologists

Employers are concerned with three main types of entrant to

technological posts. First, the qualified technologist, with work experience in that capacity elsewhere and whose training requirements are normally minimal. Secondly, 18 to 19 year old school leavers with relevant GCE A levels (or equivalent), joining the company as trainee technologists on a sponsored education and training (sandwich) programme. Thirdly new graduates in technological disciplines, who join the company after completing a full-time degree course. There was, until recently, a fourth and numerically very important source of technologists: men and women who had worked in technician-level jobs, and who were able to obtain corporate membership of certain professional institutions by gaining endorsements to their Higher National Certificates or Diplomas. As noted in the previous chapter, this route to technologist status is now closed, but the Institution of Production Engineers (1978) and the Technical and Supervisory Staff Association (1978) has advocated a qualification route of part-time study which allows for advancement from one level to another, ie from craft apprentice through to chartered engineer.

The pattern of training for these three types of recruit varies. The experienced technologist requires induction and only limited job training, but in the other two cases extensive training programmes are needed. The form that these take depends on the knowledge and skill which the job holders must acquire, the kind of career for which they are being prepared, and the manner in which their academic work and practical training are co-ordinated.

EDUCATING AND TRAINING THE TECHNOLOGIST

Traditionally, technologist trainees were not effectively catered for in industry, frequently recruited without a prior detailed study of organizational or job requirements and they were often promised unrealistic opportunities which in all too short a time led to disillusionment on their part and on that of their employers. Potential technologists were usually trained by mere exposure to a series of job situations (the so-called tour), in which they had neither role nor responsibility, a situation which led to frustration and a consequent high labour turnover. These conditions gave support to the view held by some employers that trainee technologists constitute an expensive and potentially troublesome category of employee who tend, in terms of remuneration and responsibility, to demand too much too

200

soon. In contrast a number of ITBs, for example the Engineering ITB (1968b), Electricity Supply ITB (1968b) and the Foundry Industry Training Committee (1966), have issued recommendations on technologists' training, to help companies avoid some of the difficulties which arise when employing young, highly qualified but inexperienced specialists.

There are many approaches to training technologists, with different industries and companies tackling the problem in their own ways. However, a successful outcome of training, in this field as in others, depends on a systematic approach. It is also important that the programmes for trainee technologists are discussed and agreed with them and that the support of the departments in which they will train has been secured. The contribution that technologists can make to their company's operations is as much dependent on their ability to argue their case and implement their decisions as on their technical ability. Thus, if when in training, they are tucked away in a backwater and neither encouraged nor allowed to use their expertise to the full, or if their personal development is restricted because no one has planned possible career paths for them, then the longer term benefits of their training (and these are the ones that really matter to the company), will be in jeopardy.

Educating and training technology students on sandwich courses

A significant landmark in the development of technological education in this country was the formation in 1955 (by the then Ministry of Education) of the National Council for Technological Awards (NCTA). The NCTA created and administered the Diploma in Technology awards which were equivalent in standard to an honours degree of a British university. The various Diploma in Technology courses were all sandwich courses. They included periods of industrial training which were just as much part of the course as the academic study, see Johoda (1963) for an account of the early NCTA Diplomas. The Diploma in Technology became the prototype for later sandwich courses in technological and other disciplines developed by the Council for National Academic Awards (CNAA). The CNAA was established by Royal Charter in 1964 with power to award degrees, diplomas and certificates: it absorbed the activities of the NCTA.

CNAA and university sandwich courses in technology are

either 'thick' or 'thin' programmes: the former typically consists of one year in industry, three years at college or university, while a common form for a thin sandwich course is four years with alternating six month periods in industry and in education. The principle underlying sandwich courses is that the students learn both the theoretical and the applied aspects of their subject at the same time. As a result, they require less job training on graduating than a graduate from a full-time course, even taking into account the fact that the degree course is at least a year longer. It is further argued that the quality of the theoretical work in a sandwich course is enhanced by the opportunities which the student has to test and apply his knowledge in the real work situation as the course progresses.

Students following sandwich courses are either industry or college based. In the former they are employed by the company which sponsors them on the course, and their industrial training is arranged by their employer in consultation with the college. College based students are not sponsored by an employer and their industrial training is organised by the college in conjunction with companies which cooperate in providing training places. The rapid growth in the numbers of sandwich course students has not been matched by a similar increase in training places available in industry and commerce and this poses considerable problems for college-based students and their tutors.

Considerable care must be taken to ensure that the in-company training parts of a sandwich course are purposefully arranged. The company and the college tutors are jointly responsible for seeing that the periods spent in industry are valuable learning experiences for trainee technologists and it is significant that there is a trend to include an assessment of practical training as part of final examinations, see also Chemical and Allied Products ITB (1971). However the Engineering ITB (1978a) has suggested that sandwich courses have not developed to their full potential, and that they possibly have not attracted the more able student as measured by GCE A level performance. Thick sandwich courses, in particular, have been criticised because of poor attempts made to relate work experience with the academic content of the course. The Engineering ITB in conjunction with Aston University, has developed a more effectively integrated course of practical engineering training (covering engineering practice, design appreciation etc) which students take as part of their course.

202

Training graduate entrants

Graduates from full-time courses still form an important source of technologists, in spite of the development of sandwich courses. The young men and women who start work as trainee technologists on completion of their undergraduate studies have in most cases followed a three year full-time degree course. They are therefore, 21 or 22 years old. Students who have taken higher degrees on a full-time basis may be up to 25 when starting their first job. The latter also follow a similar training programme to recruits with only first degrees.

It is understandable that graduate trainees tend to regard the obtaining of a degree as marking the end of their education, and as being much more significant than it really is. They have usually had to work hard to pass examinations and their degree represents the achievement of an objective which has dominated their thinking and energies for years. Many of them have given insufficient thought to the kinds of jobs they will do after graduating, and are not fully aware that their academic qualification is only a partial preparation for work. One of the objectives of a training programme for graduate trainees is, therefore, to persuade them that before they can be gainfully employed they still have much to learn.

The fact that these recruits have spent most of their lives in educational institutions poses a number of problems to an employer which do not arise, at least to the same extent, in the case of the sandwich student. These have been summarized by the Chemical and Allied Products ITB (1969a).

> In effecting the change from university to industry, . . . the graduate has to be reorientated on a number of basic issues. In the university, the graduate works alone and, in many cases, arranges his or her own timetable. Work is directed towards personal objectives within the basic discipline in a relatively static organization and communication is primarily with those of similar background, intellect and discipline. In industry, however, the graduate works in a team, towards company objectives, within an expanding and changing organization. Work is in an inter-disciplinary situation and there is a need to communicate effectively with people of different backgrounds and intellects. Decisions must be taken not solely on the basis of that which is of intellectual interest, but within the constraints of time, money, objectives and, most of all, the foibles of human beings. Perhaps

203

for the first time, the graduate has to realise that in making decisions, people are often swayed by emotional or other reasons quite unconnected with the sheer logic of the situation which hitherto he or she may have considered to be the governing factor. Whether the graduate works in research, production or design, there must be an appreciation that the total exercise is not complete until the final product has been sold at a profit in a competitive environment.

Reorientation on these issues forms a fundamental part of the training programme for trainee technologists. In addition, they have to learn the technical knowledge and skills relevant to their future work in the company and understand the structure and characteristics of the organisation in which they are employed. It will be seen that some of the above are training and others educational objectives in the sense that we have described these terms in Chapter 1.

MATCHING EDUCATION AND TRAINING

The Committee on Manpower Resources for Science and Technology, recognizing that trainee graduate technologists require both training and further education, examined these requirements in the case of graduate engineers and subsequently produced two reports (the Bosworth Reports): *Education and Training requirements for the Electrical and Mechanical Manufacturing Industries* (1966) and *Graduate training in Manufacturing Technology* (1970). These reports recommended a pattern of education and training which can be adapted to meet the needs of both undergraduate and graduate trainee technologists in these fields. This pattern is referred to as a 'matching section' of education and training and its purpose is to bridge the gap between the supply of potential technologists leaving colleges and universities, and industry's need for effective technological manpower. The matching section recommended for the graduate entering electrical or mechanical manufacturing industry on graduation is shown diagrammatically in figure 13.1 on page 205. The aim is to provide trainees with stimulating and rigorous programmes which would help both to attract more young people of high ability to technological careers in design and manufacturing and effectively to convert new graduates into technologists capable of holding responsible jobs in industry.

The illustrated matching section, shown in figure 13.1 consists of six stages and covers the main educational and training

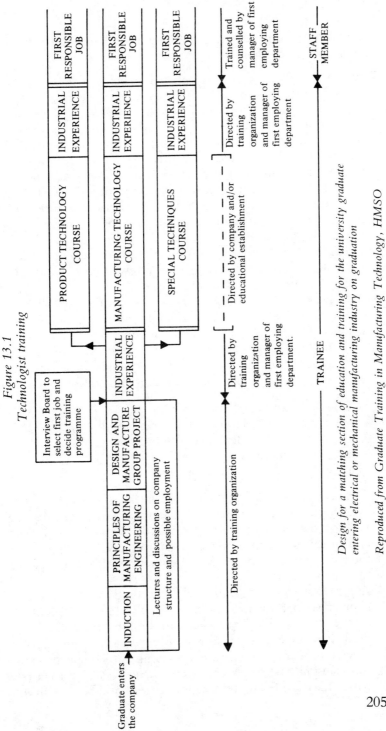

Figure 13.1
Technologist training

Design for a matching section of education and training for the university graduate entering electrical or mechanical manufacturing industry on graduation

Reproduced from Graduate Training in Manufacturing Technology, HMSO

requirements from induction to the point where the graduate trainees are given their first job. These are as follows:

1 *Induction training:* this varies in length from a few days to several weeks, and may be distributed over several months, depending on circumstances (see page 122).
2 *A course in the principles of manufacturing engineering:* during this trainees learn the basic principles involved in this field of engineering. The course is a potted version of an industrial technician's training. The course covers an appreciation (not workshop practice or skill acquisition) of manufacturing techniques, properties of materials, systems and an introduction to the work organization and its management. This stage, Bosworth suggests, should be covered in twelve weeks, with reduction or complete omission where trainees have already covered this ground elsewhere, for example, during sandwich course training.
3 *A design and manufacture group project:* a group of graduates is set a task to complete within certain time and resource constraints. They must learn how to 'organise themselves, delegate activities, apportion time, money and skills — in fact, manage a technical-machine-human complex'. The learning value of such projects can be substantial if they:

> are related to actual problems
> have specific objectives and are realistically costed
> are carried out under normal work conditions
> are completed in a given time
> are acted upon by management.

The project also takes about twelve weeks and, like the rest of the programme, is carried out under conditions of pressure with 'persistent themes of time and cost throughout'. At the end of this stage the trainees are interviewed to determine their first job and to decide the content of the remainder of their programme.
4 *A period of industrial experience:* this needs to be carefully planned so that the trainees learn about and become involved in the day to day stress situations of business life. The graduates must have responsibility for achieving specific objectives if this stage in their training is to be purposeful.
5 *Attendance on a relevant specialised technology course:* the course, which may last for up to nine months, should be specifically

directed towards preparing graduates for their first job. The technical content of the course therefore depends on the field of technology in which the trainees will be specializing. It also gives instruction in the organization and the management activities necessary for manufacture. The first Bosworth Report recommended that these specialized technology courses should be devised and mounted at a limited number of centres, jointly by educational establishments and by one or more industrial organizations. Courses in a variety of technologies have since been successfully launched.

6 *The final stage in the matching section training educational programme:* this is a further period of industrial experience, again geared to preparing the graduates for specific jobs. The duration of this industrial period is elastic and depends on the needs of the trainee and a suitable job becoming available in the company.

The Reports stress that the principles underlying the matching section approach to training and educating technologists are capable of flexible application, subject to the overriding consideration that the various components are planned and assembled as a composite whole, relating to the trainee's first job and to his longer term career. The matching section approach can, therefore, be adopted for sandwich course students in these disciplines.

The Engineering ITB (1968b) has published recommendations for the training of professional engineers based on the matching section approach, and give a number of examples of training programmes for both sandwich and graduate trainee engineers. For further examples of training programmes, *see* Chemical and Allied Products ITB (1969a).

Company tutor
The role of the company tutor is of particular importance in training technologists, and should be a manager who appreciates the trainee's learning problems and who has the authority to see that the training is correctly implemented. The tutor's main responsibilities are: to work, in close cooperation with the relevant managers in structuring the training programme, to ensure that the training meets the actual needs of both the organization and the trainee and to monitor the training to see that it is sufficiently flexible to allow for reasonable changes in, for example, organizational requirements or rates of

learning. This involves agreeing with departmental managers the detailed arrangements for the planned placement, assisting in the structuring of in-company projects, ensuring that a system of feedback is both established and utilized, and weak spots, if any, are rectified.

The tutor co-ordinates and oversees all aspects of the training activity so that in-company work, private study and formal education are integrated, as far as is possible. Tutorial activities also require the keeping of records of in-company and external training, and making regular assessments of the trainee's progress. The recording of progress may be achieved, at least partially, by trainees keeping log books, which they complete and discuss regularly with the departmental manager and their tutor. The log book approach helps to provide continuity, acts as a record of progress, and supplies feedback to the training department when both the trainees and the training scheme are being appraised and the results of the programme evaluated.

Other methods of monitoring and controlling trainee technologists' work include obtaining assessments on the progress and success of project work from the line managers concerned, and requiring the trainees to submit detailed reports on various aspects of their training as the basis for discussion and action.

The systematic training of technologists is a relatively new activity for many organisations. Much analytical work is needed to produce efficient training programmes for specific technologists' jobs, and this needs to be supported by experimentation in approaches to this type of training. Moreover, these developments should not only concentrate on the young graduate. The CBI (1978) has called for an 'examination of the need for re-training and updating courses for those who remain in the technical stream, in order to maintain their value in times of changing technology and thus increase the effectiveness of the total stock of engineers'. The necessity for qualified engineers regularly to update and extend their theoretical knowledge is also made by the Technical and Supervisory Staff Association (1978) which suggests, in addition, that as a first very urgent priority, the thousands of professional and technician engineers who are without a first degree or its equivalent, should be given the chance to improve and update their qualifications.

Technologists are normally highly specialized in a particular sphere and this is both their strength and their weakness.

Commercial, political and technological changes make specialists particularly vulnerable to redundancy and create conditions in which their valuable expertise cannot be used. Training has a critical role to play here.

Chapter 14

Management Training

The manager's role — developments in management
training and education — managerial jobs and training —
an approach to management training and development
— training and developing the manager — management
education

THE MANAGER'S ROLE

In this chapter we use the term manager in its broad sense to
mean those who are responsible for the work of others and
those at that level but without direct responsibility for staff. It
includes owner-managers of small businesses, first-line supervisors, middle and senior executives holding line and/or staff
jobs in larger organizations, and working directors.

There are probably more than 1.5 million managers in the
UK and this number is increasing and is likely to continue to
grow. Wheatcroft (1970), for example, has predicted that:

> as the standard of education of those employed rises and as
> the technical apparatus for carrying out routine jobs
> increases, the percentage of those people who are classified as
> managers will inevitably increase.

To the 1.5 million managers should be added for our purposes a
further 1.25 million people, such as professional staff and supervisors, who come within our broader definition of the manager
outlined above. There are therefore nearly three million people
with responsibilities at management level in this country.

Managers are key people in any business because the way in
which they use resources in their section, department or company directly affects the efficiency of the organization. Probably
the most important resource for the majority of managers is the
people for whom they are responsible. Managers are leaders of
employees, they plan, organize, motivate and control staff and

are responsible for developing and applying their skills for the benefit of the company. Alongside their internal company role and responsibilities, managers, and particularly senior managers, need to be aware of the wider social consequences of their actions. Cherrington (1970) has examined this broader view of the manager's function and has pointed to, for example, the problems of pollution and the sense of public responsibility which 'requires enterprises to assess their activities in terms of environmental damage beyond what the law lays down'. Thus, the role of managers can be briefly expressed as meeting, as far as possible, the requirements of their employer, their staff and those of society and to achieve these objectives, managers need skills and knowledge which have to be learnt.

As elsewhere in this book, we use the word training to mean improving managers' performance in their current jobs, and development to mean preparing them for a future job in which they will have greater responsibilities. A further distinction is sometimes made between *manager* development and *management* development. The former is concerned with improving the abilities of individual managers for their next job, the latter starts from the premise that successful management of a business depends to a large extent on team-work. The purpose of management development is to build and maintain a management team. It co-ordinates the results of manager development in the context of company objectives.

DEVELOPMENTS IN MANAGEMENT TRAINING AND EDUCATION

In chapter 2, we argued that training is an investment in human resources, and that the returns on the investment can be considerable. This argument applies with particular force to managers. Their sphere of influence at work is greater than that of other staff, so the benefits of having well-trained managers are likely to be felt over much, if not the whole, of an organization. This multiplier effect makes a strong case for a high priority to be given to management relative to other areas of training, but although some companies have paid a great deal of attention to training and developing their managers, many others have not.

An indication of the paucity of management education and training in the UK was given by Rose (1970), who estimated that in 1968 less than eight per cent of all managers attended a week's (or longer) post experience or post graduate course.

Moreover, Mant (1970) reported that most managers who attended courses were high flyers who were destined for, or had already obtained, top jobs, and so he concluded that the bulk of British managers received very little formal training.

Attendance at external courses is, however, only one facet of management development and is not a dependable measure of total activity especially in view of the recent trend for companies to do more of their own training, or to arrange for courses tailored specially for their organisation, *see* Training Services Agency (1977b). It is important to remember that unless learning from courses (or any other means) is encouraged and reinforced in the working situation, little, if any, benefit is gained.

A more recent study sponsored by the Manpower Services Commission (1978c) showed that 25 per cent of the establishments investigated offered no management training, and in small firms with less than 100 employees the figure was 56 per cent. The initiative to take a course lies mainly with the managers themselves, although few of them had access to relevant information. Only one quarter of the 361,000 managers interviewed had received any training in the previous year, while in most of the companies involved, learning by trial and error was considered to be the most important part of a manager's education.

The British Institute of Management survey by Melrose-Woodman (1978) shows that the average UK manager is male, aged 46 to 55, has a grammar school background followed by some form of higher education, started work at 17, became a manager at 25 to 35 and works in the private manufacturing sector, probably in quite a large firm. The survey also illustrates the impact of changes in education and social environment over the last 40 years since there are now distinct differences between the educational achievement of older and younger management, a point which should not be overlooked by those responsible for management development. Fifteen per cent of the total sample had attended a business school full-time, 44 per cent of the graduates and those with professional qualifications had studied business management as their main subject, 36 per cent had the Diploma in Management Studies and, in every case, the figures are higher for younger managers. The number of managers starting work in a technical post is increasing, one third of the 25 to 35 age group had technical experience. It may well be
212

that education from without, may gradually change in-company attitudes, and although in absolute terms the amount of management education and training in this country is still small, the progress made in the last two decades has been aptly termed a revolution.

There were six main reasons for this increased investment in management education and training in this country:

1 A greater number of employers came to accept the need for, and the value of, training and educating their managers as the experience gained by progressive companies in this field spread to others.

2 Since the last war a number of factors combined to make a manager's job more difficult than in the past and so increased the need for management training. The growth in the size of organizations and the development of specialist management functions and techniques played their part, but the most significant developments stemmed from the changed state of the labour market in the post-war years. In contrast to the 1920s and 30s, the employment scene was characterised by a general shortage of labour, by a major growth in the power of white and blue-collar unions and by changes in many employees' attitudes to work and authority. These developments posed fundamental problems to industry and commerce and led companies to question the effectiveness of the traditional approach to managing staff. It became increasingly clear that these changes in the labour market had to be matched by equally fundamental changes in the role and function of managers. The necessity to prepare managers for their new role was being recognized.

3 The impact of legislation, such as the Trade Union and Labour Relations Act, the Employment Protection Act and the Health and Safety at Work Act, has accelerated this change in management attitudes, and has made job-related industrial relations training a 'must' for every manager, *see* page 37. Moreover, giving trade union representatives the legal right to time off with pay for appropriate training, increases the necessity for giving relevant training to managers, if the latter are not to find themselves with union stewards who are better informed than they are.

4 At about the same time as progressive companies were reviewing their approach to managing staff, assistance

213

became available from behavioural scientists. Organization theorists contributed towards an improved understanding of the behaviour of organizations, *see* Pugh *et al* (1971), Woodward (1965), the work of writers such as Maslow (1954) and Herzberg (1975) did much to develop motivation theory, while analysis of the effectiveness of managerial styles by McGregor (1960), Blake and Mouton (1964), Reddin (1970) and others, shifted the emphasis for effective management away from (in McGregor's terms) the authoritarian 'theory X' approach to the participative leadership style associated with 'theory Y' managers.

5 Another factor behind the growth in management training is the tendency for young people with ability to stay on longer at school, to obtain qualifications and then to have high career aspirations. There has been a corresponding decline in the number of those starting work at 16 with potential managerial abilities, formerly industry's traditional source of managers and supervisors. The problem of finding an alternative source has not yet been resolved but has stimulated considerable investment in junior management training. Interestingly, similar problems have arisen within the trade union ranks, ie finding enough people on the shop floor with ability to rise to responsible positions within the union. Another effect of extended education is the increase in the number of highly educated people employed in industry and commerce. In the 1950s few graduate-level entrants had followed courses designed for careers in business and so companies had to undertake the necessary conversion training and education. Understandably, employers began to ask why the UK's education system was not providing undergraduate and postgraduate courses in business studies similar to those which were well established in other countries, notably in the USA.

The demand for business graduates was a major factor in the setting up of the London and the Manchester Business Schools in 1965, and in the rapid development of Higher National Diploma, Certificate and degree courses in Business Studies in the 1960s. Since the early 1970s the employment of Business Studies graduates has had important effects on management training since existing management training programmes were inappropriate for these entrants, a new approach had to be developed and this stimulated a rise in the quality of management training generally.

214

The less well-educated managers in a company tended to view the influx of potential high-flyers as a threat to security and promotion, and turned to training as a means of improving themselves and their prospects. Companies, too, became more aware of the need to provide training for their existing managers and began to accept the responsibility to ensure that this training took place.

6 Recently, the ITBs have played an important part in stimulating management training and education and the Manpower Services Commission (1977b) declared this area of training a national priority.

The growth of management training and development can be attributed in the main to the above factors. Together they have been responsible for helping to create a more favourable attitude towards achieving a new level of activity in this field.

MANAGERIAL JOBS AND TRAINING
It is helpful to consider some of the characteristics of managers' jobs and the implications that these have for training.

Uniqueness
A characteristic feature of managers' jobs is that they are all different, indeed Thurley and Hamblin (1963) reported marked differences in the work of junior shift managers ostensibly doing the same job. This uniqueness results from such factors as the size of the company, the dominant managerial style, the type of work involved, the personality and approach of the job-holder, the history of the job in the firm and the opportunities and constraints in the manager's environment.

All occupations are to some extent affected by these variables, but none more so than management. Managers, as Jacques (1967) demonstrated, have longer 'time spans of discretion' and fewer 'prescribed tasks' than other employees. They have to deal continuously with new problems and they often have to make decisions in situations which are neither black nor white. Thus managers need a flexible approach to their work and this has the following training implications:

Every managerial job must be recognized as unique. For example, the training officer working for a company with six area sales managers should not regard them as all doing the same job. While the six jobs will have some common

215

features, they will also have differences and each one must be considered separately for training purposes.

Because managers' jobs can to some extent be determined by the job-holders, their training must develop them as people, in addition to improving their knowledge and skills at handling technical or other aspects of their work.

The uniqueness of managers' jobs means that their own managers are, at times, in the best position to do the training. Attendance at a course can meet common training needs, which a manager may share with others, but if training and development are to be effective, there is no substitute for on the job coaching by senior executives. The latter alone know their managers' work in detail, can assess performance and, where appropriate, use normal work situations as learning opportunities to develop their managers, *see* Singer (1979).

Work variety

Another characteristic of a manager's work is that it is varied and can change in content or in emphasis over short periods of time. While some tasks may be repeated on a monthly or annual cycle, many managers spend much of their time doing non-repetitive work and the training implications of this are important. As we have seen in chapter 5, approaches to the analysis of managerial jobs must take into account the dynamic and complex work involved and so a comprehensive job training analysis is an expensive and unnecessary exercise. What is normally needed is a selective analysis which identifies the key objective of the job and then examines in detail only those tasks which are critical to effective performance and in which the managers must not fail. This approach is embodied in a 'key results area' analysis of the type associated with Management by Objectives, Humble (1973). Alternatively a problem-centred approach is appropriate.

It is inevitable that the dynamic nature of managers' jobs soon makes job specifications obsolete. Thus managers' jobs need regular re-definition and management training should be a continuing process and not a once and for all event on appointment.

Work fragmentation

A manager is usually a busy person, with a pattern of work

216

consisting of short and long duration activities which are themselves broken by interruptions. Work fragmentation is a serious problem for a manager. The size of the problem was indicated by Stewart (1970), who examined the frequency of variations in the activities and contacts of managers and found that they had on average one period alone each day of half an hour or longer, broken by fleeting contacts (telephone calls and personal lasting less than five minutes) and one such period every other day that was undisturbed.

Fragmentation of work makes it more difficult, and while the nature of certain jobs may impose a fragmented work pattern on a manager, the job-holder is often not without blame! Managers may need help in improving the way in which they use their time, and here their own manager has a vital training role.

Inter-personal skills
Managers normally spend much of their time with other people. Those studied by Stewart, for example, spent on average two-thirds of their working day with individuals or groups of people. If this is typical of most managers, then it follows that they should be highly competent in inter-personal skills such as persuading, negotiating, giving clear instructions, being good listeners, working as a member of a team and chairing meetings. Few managers would regard themselves as highly competent in all these tasks and therefore improving inter-personal skills is a continuing training requirement. For a review of developments in the approaches to improving inter-personal skills *see* Rackham *et al* (1971) and Honey (1976).

Until recently, the demands of a manager's job have been considered only in terms of requirements in professional, technical or organizational knowledge and experience, and this is the information that normally appears in a job specification. Stewart (1975), however, has analyzed the behavioural demands (and particularly the interpersonal relationships), characterizing the jobs of different types of managers and has proposed the following three main categories:

internal, which includes jobs which have no contact with people outside the organization.
internal/external, for jobs primarily concerned with relationships within the organization, but having some external contacts

external, where dealing with people outside the organization is the main characteristic of the job.

Within these three main categories, jobs can be grouped according to whether the job holders are in charge of many people and have contacts radiating out to different levels, or whether it is necessary for them to spend more time with people at the same level than with subordinates. Each of these categories requires different forms of inter-personal skill and Stewart suggests that when considering selection and career development, too much attention has been paid to functional level in the hierarchy and to specialist knowledge and not enough to the behavioural demands of the job. A manager can be well equipped for promotion or transfer to a particular job in terms of the first two criteria, but unprepared for the third.

Managerial style
Every organization has its own distinctive work atmosphere created by the relationships which exist between its various members and strongly influenced by the dominant style of management. The latter can take many forms and is expressed in the behaviour of managers towards, for example, status, authority, consultation, trade unions and control systems. From a training point of view the dominant managerial style in a company (or a department) largely determines the scope and objectives for management and other employee training and development. For example, a company run by an autocratic management typically has training programmes for operatives, craftsmen and possibly supervisors, but limited provision for middle and senior management.

Management training and development programmes aim to change managers' behaviour by encouraging them to question their roles and functions, to consider such topics as delegation of authority and the use of initiative, and make plans to apply their findings to their own jobs. The aim is to produce managers who are self starters and able to work effectively with the minimum of direction; qualities which are anathema to an autocratic top management but which are highly prized in a company with a theory Y management. Hence successful manager training and development must be compatible with the management's values and expectations. While it may be considered necessary to modify the latter this takes time, and training objectives must be carefully chosen bearing this in mind.

218

The experience factor
Because of their uniqueness and complexity, managerial jobs are usually difficult to learn. Part of this difficulty lies in managers trying to learn what their jobs consist of, a problem aggravated by changes in emphasis and in direction over short periods of time. However, in many ways a more difficult learning obstacle is the gaining of the experience managers need in order to do their jobs effectively since experience comes from being responsible for doing a job and not from observing how someone else does it.

Gaining experience takes time even if it is well planned and organized, but the learning process can be speeded up by managers being moved through a series of carefully chosen jobs which stretch them, and by being helped as required with their appropriate training and education. However the fact remains that manager training and development is a long-term business, and many decisions about the training and development of managers are comparable to those involving capital investment in plant and buildings. They must be taken well in advance of the time when the planned benefits will be needed as the lead times are often measured in years. This is one of the reasons why it is very difficult to evaluate management training and development, but *see* Whitelaw (1972).

AN APPROACH TO MANAGEMENT TRAINING AND DEVELOPMENT
A framework for successful management training and development commonly used by companies and which was originally recommended by the former Central Training Council (1967b, 1969) and by numerous ITBs, *see* for example, Chemical and Allied Products ITB (1969c), Food, Drink and Tobacco ITB (1971), has the following features:

Assignment of responsibility
The head of the organization, or one of his senior colleagues, must be directly and actively responsible for the training and development of managers. Experience has proved that unless this responsibility is accepted by a senior manager in the company and adequately discharged by him, management training and development will tend to be inappropriate to the organization's requirements and restricted to junior levels in the hierarchy. The example set by the senior executive largely determines

219

the training climate of the firm, and if he does not give a positive lead, the chances of his subordinate managers doing so in their own departments are reduced.

Deciding needs, policies and plans

If it is to be successful the training and development of managers must be intimately related to the organization's current and planned requirements for managerial talent. As we saw in chapter 4, senior management must decide short and long-term business objectives before effective training policies can be defined. Corporate objectives plus predicted vacancies (caused by promotion, retirement, ill-health, reorganization), provide the basic information needed to assess an organization's future requirements for managerial manpower. A management succession plan (*see* page 221) is prepared, showing which of the existing managers may be suitable for future vacancies, and the training and development they will need to prepare them for these jobs. The company then sets its management training and development objectives and evolves appropriate policies to cover existing staff and the recruitment of those needed to fill remaining vacancies.

Job training analysis

Before training can take place, a manager's training needs must be established. This may require a key task approach necessitating clarification of overall work objectives and targets and the skills and knowledge needed to achieve them *see* Forrest (1972), alternatively a problem centred approach may suffice, *see* chapter 5.

Performance appraisal

Personal training needs are mainly identified from appraisals of managers' work performance. An initial appraisal carried out when managers are appointed or when their jobs are radically changed, means that their ability to do the job can be assessed and any requirement which they may have for training can be identified and remedied. A tactical appraisal of managers' need for training emerges as a result of day to day assessment of their performance as they work towards their targets. This appraisal undertaken by the immediate superior is a valuable means of helping managers recognize their strengths and weaknesses and provides excellent opportunities for on the job coaching. A strategic appraisal takes place when managers' performance over a period of time, usually a year, is reviewed and their potential for further development assessed.

Information from these three kinds of appraisal enables a company to take stock of its managerial talent. Some of its managers will be found wanting in their jobs and corrective action will need to be taken, such as re-allocation of responsibilities or training. Other managers will have a successful record but will be assessed as having reached their promotion ceiling and unable to cope with a more senior job; for them updating training may be required. Still others will have shown by their performance that they have promotion potential. These managers are an important resource which no company can afford to lose, yet to retain and to develop their talent, particularly in a large organization, requires careful planning. Appraisers require special skills for which training is usually necessary and it is important to recognize that the training needs of others as well as those of the appraisee may become apparent during the interview. The performance of their peers, their subordinates, their superiors, may have prevented the managers from achieving their own targets, and the appraisers (particularly if they are also the immediate superior) must be prepared to recognise this. If it can be accepted as such, the whole appraisal procedure is a valuable learning experience for all concerned, *see* Randell *et al* (1974).

Succession planning and records
Although there are problems involved in developing and using a succession plan, it is essential for a company to have one if the continuity of the business is to be maintained with a minimum of disruption and if career staff are to be retained in the company. One of the main problems with succession plans is that they become rapidly out of date. Unpredictable events such as some managers leaving the company and others making unexpected progress or conversely falling short of what was expected of them, make succession planning a very fluid and at times a frustrating business. As part of its succession plans, a company needs to update personal records of its managers, including details of the training they have received, or will be receiving, and their progress in the company.

Career development
In considering management development and succession plan-

ning from the organisation standpoint, it is often forgotten that individuals have careers to which they are committed and which give them a personal identity which is extremely important to them, *see* Sofer (1970). As Glaser (1968) has put it, 'the organization career provides for people a stability in life plan, style and cycle, engendering their motivation to work'. People have expectations about their careers in which the timing of certain events forms an important part and several writers have suggested different stages of career growth, *see* Sofer (1970), Super and Jordaan (1973). As a result of a study by the Food, Drink and Tobacco ITB, Chadwick and Hogg (1978) suggest the following stages of growth as a general guide:

Exploration: 20-30 years of age
> Variety of career options, not tied by domestic circumstances, more frequent changes of employer, peak physical and intellectual ability, necessity for obtaining professional qualifications.

Establishment: 25-45 years of age
> Development of expertise, fewer career options, often a time for major career choice, maximum domestic constraints, possibility of disillusionment, mild decline in mental and physical ability (eg to work quickly and under stress), offset by knowledge and experience.

Maintenance: 40-60 years of age
> Less opportunity for change, adjustment to role, power and influence, greater freedom from domestic constraints, slight further loss of abilities.

Contraction: 55-65 years of age
> Preparing for a new role in life, reduction in physical and mental abilities, different anxieties, eg financial, health, concern for others, in particular immediate family.

The ITB examined the prime career development needs of managers during these stages of growth and suggested various development techniques available for meeting such needs. For instance, in the exploration stage, managers may need conceptual models, information and a chance to develop their self image. This implies professional counselling concentrating on such factors as identifying expectations and aspirations, revealing strengths and weaknesses in the individual's personality and abilities and help in setting attainable, self-determined and relevant goals in the short, medium and long-term. Suggested techniques include individual career planning, help in setting goals, and personality/ability profiles to assist in counselling. The ITB recommends the development of a five to 10 year education and training strategy for individual managers.

This kind of approach to career development has profound implications for appraisal sessions and might help to modify the judgemental aspect (with which they have traditionally been associated) towards an emphasis on counselling and constructive help. However, it relies heavily on the competence of managers and/or specialist staff in exercising the skills of counselling, although it is suggested that the techniques could be used in such a way as to throw much of the onus on to the individual manager.

The above features of management training and development are exemplified in medium and large organizations but should nonetheless be present, although in a less formalized way, in any organization attempting to train its managers. For example, a sophisticated system of appraisal is not required in a very small business where the owner knows his staff well and uses on the job training as a normal part of the day to day running of the business.

A different approach to management development (Delf and Smith (1978)) is based on the recognition that many successful managers have not relied for their growth on their companies but have deliberately taken charge of their own learning. Delf and Smith argue that the achievements of self-organized learners exemplify a successful manager self-development model, which companies should adopt alongside their existing management development schemes. Self-development is defined as:

the process by which individuals: identify their personal development goals; consciously take responsibility for planning and taking appropriate action to reach these goals; develop and use methods of monitoring progress and assess outcome; and re-assess goals in the light of new experiences.

The promotion by a company of a self-development approach which is not an *ad hoc,* random series of events but is integrated with other management development approaches, poses operational difficulties. This interesting self-help concept has also been analysed by Pedler *et al* (1978) who have developed a structured format for the manager interested in self-development.

223

TRAINING AND DEVELOPING THE MANAGER
Initial considerations
The following factors need to be borne in mind when operating manager training and development programmes:

> Training objectives must be based on an analysis of needs, which are agreed with the managers concerned before training is initiated. A considerable amount of time is usually required to clarify and define the purpose of the proposed training and to gain the agreement and, if possible, the enthusiasm of the managers for it. This is time well spent, for if they accept the need for the training and are committed to achieve the training objectives which they have helped to establish, the chances of success are greatly increased.

For the reasons given above, most manager training can only be carried out on the job by the manager's superior. As Farnsworth (1970) puts it:

> Managers are the best developers of their subordinates. They have immediate contact with them at all times and are in the best position to coach and to counsel them. This does not mean that a manager must undertake personally all the activities that may be necessary to develop his subordinate. It *does* mean that he is accountable for ensuring that they are provided with the opportunities, both on and off the job, which are necessary for their development.

Coaching subordinates means helping them to assess their own performance, to think through their own problems and to find appropriate solutions. Sometimes an external consultant may be required. For further discussion of coaching, *see* Hague (1973), Singer (1979), Megginson and Boydell (1979).

While courses can play a useful part in manager training, it is important that the precise contribution which they can make to skill and knowledge development is appreciated and their limitations understood. A company gains from a manager's attendance on a course only if he requires the particular training offered by the course, accepts the need for the training, and is encouraged to apply it at work.

We would stress that those responsible for the training and developing of managers must see that the organization in which the manager works is prepared for a successful outcome of the training. If this is not done, the benefits of the training can be

224

dissipated in friction and frustration. One common reason for the failure of manager training is that the manager returns to his company, having attended a successful course, to find little support for his ideas. Re-entry problems can be minimized only if they are foreseen and if appropriate action is taken in good time. Appendix 3 contains a simple control system which, with a minimum of paperwork, helps to ensure that attendance at a course is appropriate to a manager's needs and that the advantages gained from the training are not lost.

The Training Services Agency (1977b) suggests a useful framework which divides management knowledge and skills into three groups:

the main knowledge that managers need eg financial control, method study, production planning, legal and technical knowledge

skills such as analytical problem solving, decision making and social skills eg leading, negotiating, communicating

the ability to go on learning and improving, being able to move from abstract to practical thinking, and enable the manager to apply lessons learned in one situation to another, the ability to learn in different ways.

The major part of present management development activity helps with the first group and there are now signs that attention is being paid to the second group. The last group, however, receives very little attention, since although most managers would say that they learn by experience, what is not so commonly realized is that unless learning is carefully planned, it may not take place or it may not transfer (*see* page 94). 'Learning to learn' is becoming recognized as an important skill, particularly now that technology and economic considerations bring about rapid and radical changes in jobs.

Morris and Burgoyne (1976) stress that managerial work calls for 'varied qualities of resourcefulness' to cope with unprogrammed activities. They argue that 'management development must never lose contact with those forms of work in which the manager can experiment and become visible to himself and others', suggesting that the delicate job of management development is to help each manager discover the most important aspects of management development at first hand. Discovery learning and experiential learning are discussed in chapter 6.

Training programmes

The objectives and contents of training programmes for managers depend on such factors as: the size of the business and its training resources, the training requirements of managers, and particularly on the degree of sophistication of the company's approach to training at this level. *See,* for example, the case histories of management training and development systems and programmes in a variety of major companies described by Markwell and Roberts (1969).

Typically four stages can be identified in the evolution of company management training and development programmes:

Stage 1: the common skills approach: this is based on the assumption that the training requirements of most managers in a given category are similar and can be met by a common programme. It is the least sophisticated approach since the training is not derived from analysis and is usually limited to attendance on a course.

Stage 2: the manager as an individual: when a company introduces job training analysis, it usually concentrates initially on the more obvious of the manager's roles and functions, such as those which are readily apparent in relationship with superiors and subordinates. It is later realized that although a manager may gain some benefit from attending a general course, individual requirements for training cannot normally be met in this way and programmes have to be tailor made for each manager. Individual programmes result, with a strong emphasis on coaching by the manager's superior in the job situation, supported by off the job training.

Stage 3: the manager as a member of a management team: a further development in the degree of sophistication emerges with the recognition that by concentrating analysis and training on the vertical or superior/subordinate aspects of work, programmes are excessively department orientated. What is also needed is greater prominence to be given to helping managers fulfil horizontal roles in the company. Once it is accepted that managers' effectiveness also depends on their ability to work with other managers in the company, then in addition to the training referred to in the previous section, analysis is needed to identify their roles and functions in the overall management team, and the training, if any, they need. This broader and more complex approach calls for a higher order

226

of training expertise and a greater commitment on the part of senior management than is necessary for the two stages discussed previously. It has been adopted by few companies.

Stage 4: the manager and the organization: organization development (OD) is concerned with the preparation for and handling of change in an orderly but dynamic way. It follows that in this context, management training seeks to achieve inquiring attitudes of mind and the inter-personal skills necessary to secure cooperation and adaptability towards the actual process of change as it takes place. Above all, OD must ensure that managers accept responsibility not only for initiating change or developments but also for their own self-development. The change process within which they are working will of itself provide a potent learning opportunity. The concept of OD is new to the majority of firms and its practice is so far limited, see Bennis (1969) and Starbuck (1971).

An organization development approach to management training seeks to achieve a high degree of integration of the training requirements of managers with the firm's corporate objectives. It recognises that a company operates in a dynamic environment and that only if the firm is continuously being developed as an entity can it achieve its objectives. In this context, management training is a key tool in achieving organization development and at the same time in minimizing harmful effects that often result from change.

Although a company may possibly initiate its management training and development at any one of these four stages, the normal sequence is to begin at stage 1, and subsequently to adopt successively more sophisticated approaches.

It is interesting to compare the above stages with a framework given by Greiner (1972), who suggests five phases of organization growth, during which the management focus moves from the basic 'make and sell' through 'efficiency of operations', 'expansion of market', 'consolidation of organization' and finally to 'problem solving and innovation'. Each of these phases requires a different organization structure, which in turn has a typical style, ranging from individualistic and entrepreneurial in the first phase, to participative in the fifth phase. The validity of this framework is a matter of debate, but our purpose in mentioning it is to demonstrate that an organization can be regarded as having a career of its own and at each stage will probably require a different range of managerial skills. In rapid growth industries, these stages come in fairly quick succession, so that the span of a manager's working life in one organization can encompass a number of dynamic changes. As Stewart (1975) has pointed out, it is unlikely that sufficient thought is given to alterations in the behavioural demands of the job, although they can cause more stress and can ultimately be more costly to the organization than the well documented technical difficulties.

As the organization changes, it may also increase in sophistication and this, together with the management focus, will greatly influence the appropriate approach and techniques to be used in management development. To some extent this explains why there appear to be fashions in training techniques, one method having been given great acclaim for its success because it was absolutely right for a particular situation may fail elsewhere because it was inappropriate. Considerable diagnostic skill is therefore required not just in assessing the strengths and weaknesses of individuals, but in determining the stage of the organization's own development.

The process is of course reciprocal, and management development may itself be the catalyst for change 'just as education in general both reflects society and also helps to shape society, so management development is limited by the culture of the organization but can help to change that culture', Training Services Agency (1977b).

Managerial obsolescence

When radical change comes to an organization, some managers (often those with long service) seem rigid and inflexible in their approach. They become inefficient because they cannot adapt, possibly resisting change or preventing it, and in extreme cases are given a golden handshake. If we consider the points made at the end of chapter 1, and the proposition that employees are learning all the time from the organization, it can be argued that by rewarding them with promotion, praise etc, for certain types of behaviour, an organization can develop and fix attitudes and abilities, which are difficult and sometimes impossible to relinquish, if sudden change is required. Some attention has been paid to obsolescence of technical knowledge, but again very little to the behavioural aspects.

Bromley (1975) suggests that as people grow older they become more rigid, but the research on the effects of ageing is still sketchy. What evidence there is, suggests that 'learning to learn' transfers and that previous training facilitates new learning, even although not directly related to it. It would appear that training schemes which provide learning opportunities throughout working life are the best preparation for a flexible approach (and the ability) to learn new skills, see Nisbet (1957).

Categories of management training programmes

A training officer helps prepare and run programmes for four main categories of managers: young management trainees, older staff promoted to their first management job, existing managers to help make them more effective in their current jobs and existing managers being prepared for promotion.

Young management trainees

For the reasons discussed at the beginning of this chapter, companies look towards well-educated school and college leavers as an important source of potential managers. As explained in chapter 7, the programmes for 18 year olds with GCE A levels and those for graduates, differ in content and duration, but are based on a tour approach, a specific job training approach or, more commonly, a mixture of the two.

The tour aims to give trainees a comprehensive view of the company's organization and procedures before they are appointed to posts of responsibility and is achieved by the trainees spending one or more years working alongside staff in the major departments of the firm. The thinking behind this approach is that since, during their attachments, the trainees learn about the various aspects of the company's work and the inter-relationships of the different parts of the organization, both the company and the trainees are in a better position to decide the functional area of management for which they are best suited. When appointed to a manager's job, they should be able to apply their broad knowledge of the company to advantage, with a minimum of further training.

A different approach to training young potential managers is to appoint them directly to posts of appropriate responsibility and to give them the training they need for that particular job. When they have held the job for a year or more, and gained as much experience as they can, they are promoted, but only if they have merited it. This process is then repeated, with each of the moves taking place within a planned development programme.

Of these two approaches, the tour was more popular in the immediate post-war years but more recently companies have found that it is usually preferable to give a young man or woman a specific job soon after joining the firm. This is because extended tours have an unsettling effect which causes a high turnover of trainees. Moreover, a tour is knowledge rather than skill orientated, since the trainees acquire information about the company (much of which they do not need to know at their level), but gain little expertise at managing others.

In contrast, specific job training requires trainees to learn the necessary managerial skills and knowledge by actually doing a job rather than by watching others, and advancement depends on how well they perform under the pressures of responsibility. For the company this is a more satisfactory basis for promotion, and from the standpoint of other employees in the firm it is seen to be fair and merited. In practice, many companies have mixtures of the tour and job training approaches, thus combining the best of both. Berlew and Hall's (1966) study at the American Telephone and Telegraph Company is relevant here. They found that the first year in an organization is a critical period for learning, and that those who were exposed to high company expectations during the first year of employment attained far higher levels of performance in later years than those of apparent equal ability who were given less demanding jobs.

In parallel with in-company training, the potential manager follows, where possible, an appropriate course of business/management education. This may be a general course, for example, a Higher Certificate or Diploma in Business Studies for the A level trainee or a professional course in a functional area such as accounting (see page 118).

Older staff appointed to their first management post

According to Rose (1970), approximately 75,000 new managers are appointed every year in this country and it is probable that the majority of these are employees promoted within their own company. Promotion to manager is an important and often difficult step for most employees, since it involves adapting to significant changes in their work and in their relationships with other people in the organization. Ideally, they should be at least partly prepared for these changes in advance of their appointment, for example, by standing in for a manager when absent, or by being purposefully involved in different aspects of running the department. They also require specific training depending on their backgrounds and the jobs they will be doing.

The backgrounds of these new managers vary widely. Some have limited formal education, many are professionally qualified, some will be in charge of few and others of many staff, some will be in their twenties, others much older, and most of them will have had little previous experience of managing staff. For these reasons it is essential that training programmes for new managers are prepared on a tailor made basis with requirements being identified from an appropriate job training analysis and an appraisal of the new manager's abilities.

The recommendations of the Engineering ITB (1970) on the training of employees for their first managerial post are applicable to most situations and contain four main elements.

An off the job course: this can be held in the company or externally and it introduces new managers to the practice of management. It should also give them the opportunity to mix with others in a similar position and to reorientate themselves to their new responsibilities.

Coaching: a manager's superior is usually the best tutor. It is important that new managers receive feedback on their progress and have appropriate day to day guidance and direction.

Planned experience: new managers need to acquire a wider knowledge of the business than was previously necessary and they have to learn to recognize and take into account the many variables affecting their new job. Attachments to relevant departments in the company help achieve this broadening objective. During attachments they are introduced to the work of other parts of the company and meet the people they need to know in their new role. In this way they learn how their job fits into the organization and what others expect from their department. Attachments must be planned to meet specific objectives and not allowed to degenerate into a sitting next to Nelly exercise.

Self development: new managers need help to grow into their responsibilities and consolidate their position by being encouraged to develop themselves through their jobs. Self-development is also achieved by attending an appropriate

231

course, by directed reading, or by taking part in the activities of relevant management professional institutions.

Training managers to be more effective in their present jobs

Since, as we have seen, most managers have had no formal training, either on appointment or subsequently to keep them up to date, the majority of companies have a backlog of remedial management training to tackle. This neglected area deserves consideration because, although improvements in the work of individual managers as a result of training may not always be startling, collectively the impact can be very worthwhile, particularly since many of the managers concerned will probably remain with the company for the rest of their working lives. As Drucker (1968) puts it:

> The men who need manager development the most are not the 'balls of fire' who are the back-up men and promotable people. They are those managers who are not good enough to be promoted, but not poor enough to be fired. They constitute the great majority, and they do the bulk of the actual managing of the business. Most of them will, 10 years hence, still be in their present jobs.

Training for these managers has the following characteristics:

The content of programmes must be demonstrably relevant. Training should, where possible, be problem-centred, that is, aimed at resolving specific difficulties. These difficulties will be known to the manager's superior and probably to the manager himself and are defined as a result of appraisal. Detailed comprehensive job training analyses are unnecessary.

Training methods are chosen to achieve maximum involvement of the managers and training consists of planned on the job coaching, with occasional attendance on a course in which formal instruction is kept to a minimum. Case studies and other similar techniques are used to encourage the sharing of knowledge and experience, with trainers applying the dictum that 'men must be taught as if you taught them not, and things unknown proposed as things forgot!' *see* chapter 6.

The success of this training is measured by regular appraisal. This also highlights those managers whose talents have not previously been recognized by the company.

When training for in-post managers is introduced successfully into a company, it causes considerable changes; objectives are questioned, established policies and procedures are reappraised, individual managers' personal expectations are raised and work standards improved. These developments are healthy for the organization and need encouragement, but frustration and a lowering of morale result if the enthusiasm and energy released by the training are not followed by action on the part of senior management.

Developing managers for promotion

We have already stressed that the process of developing managers takes time and that to be effective it should be carried out systematically. This involves, at an appropriate level of sophistication, manpower analysis and succession planning, together with the monitoring of managers' progress through performance appraisals. With an efficient system of management development a company is aware and able to use the talents of its managers and at the same time is able to satisfy the organization's short and longer term requirements for managerial expertise. Ideally, although it is not always feasible, managers should be prepared as far as possible for promotion before taking up their appointment. Training for this purpose must be tailor made, and will depend on the requirements and potential of the individual manager and on the job in question. There are, however, basically two categories of programmes: those for managers with limited promotion ceilings, and those for managers who appear to have the ability to go to the top.

In the former case, candidates for development are often in the position of being a natural successor for a job and so can be groomed over a period of years to take over their superior's post when the latter retires or leaves. In this situation, on the job coaching is the mainstay of the training, with attendance on courses, if required. Much depends on the skill of the senior manager as a coach, and especially on the senior manager's willingness to delegate responsibility and authority at a pace which helps the subordinate manager to grow into the new job.

Development programmes for high flyers are more complex with the tendency to adjust the organization to make the best use of the talents of individual managers. Moreover, promotion paths are not restricted to within a single department and are

233

planned so that managers move through a series of different types of job to widen their experience and to equip them with the broader outlook needed by senior management. Their rate of progress through the different jobs is rapid and they normally attend a number of senior management development courses at various stages in their career.

MANAGEMENT EDUCATION

After many years in which very little management education was available in this country, the last two decades have seen an explosion in the provision of education courses for managers. During this period undergraduate, post-experience and post-graduate programmes were established and flourished in many colleges and universities.

Wheatcroft (1970) has discussed the aim of management education and concluded that, while the motives and priorities of the main parties concerned with education for managers (the government, industry, the individual manager, and the educationalists) may differ, 'the fundamental objective of developing the capacity and performance of the individual manager is common to them all'. This general aim is unlikely to be contentious, but how it can and should be achieved is another matter, and management education is not without its critics. For example, after studying the career records of nearly 1,000 graduates of the Harvard Business School, Marshall (1971) concluded that:

> academic success and business achievement have relatively little association with each other, and that too much attention is paid to problem solving (respondent behaviour), and not enough to problem finding or the exploitation of opportunities (operant behaviour).

Price (1978), however, quotes a number of major UK companies who are very satisfied with business graduates!

Many of the difficulties that faced management education in the UK stemmed from its recent growth. For example, its value is hard to assess since it has yet to stand the test of time. The quality of courses varies considerably, an inevitable consequence of the dramatic expansion which at times took place with insufficient resources, while the right mix of theoretical and applied material in courses is not easily determined and is unlikely to be resolved in the short term. As Stewart (1968) has
234

pointed out, the assumptions commonly made in management education can only be tentative until there has been much more research into managers' activities and the role of education more clearly defined.

The range of business and professional courses available for school leavers seeking a management career in industry and commerce is now extensive and includes BEC National and Higher National Diplomas and Certificates, honours and ordinary degrees (including sandwich degrees) and courses leading to membership of professional institutions. The provision of master's degrees in general management, an MBA, or in a specific area of management such as an MSc in Operational Research and, since 1970, of doctoral programmes, completes the educational range for people starting a management career in business.

In contrast, for the practising manager and the older employee about to become a manager, the choice of educational programme is limited. Given a professional background, it is possible for him to take a higher degree in management, but in practice this is rarely feasible. Despite TOPS support, the majority of managers are unable to take a year or more off work to follow a full time course and very few are given day release. The number of advanced courses which can be taken on an evenings only basis is limited, and the difficulties of studying after a day's work daunt all but the most persistent. Since 1961, the Diploma in Management Studies (DMS) course has fulfilled a major role in providing a broad general management programme for post-graduate and post-experience managers. It is shorter than many degree courses (seven or eight months if taken full time) and is offered in a variety of part time modes.

For the non-graduate trainee manager, the courses provided by the National Examinations Board for Supervisory Studies (NEBSS) provide a valuable and practical introduction to junior management. The older manager without graduate or professional status is not at present well catered for in the plethora of management education courses available.

Few would doubt the important contribution that management education can make in improving the standard of management performance of individuals and of companies, yet it remains true that:

. . .Managers learn by managing. Management performance

can in the last resort only be improved by the manager himself. He may be helped by the guidance of his superior to build up his strong points and make good his weaknesses, and to gain wider experience and enlarge his perspectives. He may be given the authority and the facilities to develop the skills he requires to do the job but. . . no system of training can be a substitute for what an individual can achieve for himself. An individual's efforts to develop himself and to define his objectives against which he can measure his performance are key factors and every management development programme must provide opportunities for this personal initiative, *see* Central Training Council (1969).

Chapter 15

National Training Policy

Legislation for training — the Industrial Training Act
1964 — the Employment and Training Act 1973 — the
impact of legislation — problems and trends

LEGISLATION FOR TRAINING

Prior to 1964, the *laissez-faire* approach to industrial training in
the UK had consistently failed to supply adequate numbers of
skilled workers and this was especially so in engineering, where
dissatisfaction was expressed at the inability of the centuries old
craft apprenticeship structure to meet the changing economic
conditions of the twentieth century. Although some organizations had excellent training schemes, attempts to improve the
general situation by persuasive methods such as those recommended in the Carr Report (1958) on craft training, had only a
minimal effect. In addition to the craft problem there were
shortages of technologists and technicians while, as the Robbins
Committee (1963) reported, the provision for management
education was inadequate. The overall position was regarded as
particularly serious because as a nation we depend on our skills
rather than natural resources and, it was claimed, that the lower
productivity of certain UK industries compared with the USA
was due to our less efficient management.

Moreover in the early sixties, there was growing interest in
the UK joining the European Economic Community, and it
became clear that much of our industrial training compared
unfavourably with that in countries such as Germany and
France. Section 3 of the Treaty of Rome, which deals with the
free movement of persons, services and capital, posed problems
for the UK, as did the EEC directives for the national recognition of diplomas and other qualifications.

THE INDUSTRIAL TRAINING ACT 1964

Although industrial training was a politically neutral issue, successive post-war governments had been wary of introducing legal compulsion in this field. A dramatic change in government thinking was contained in the *Government Proposals Industrial Training* (1962), which marked the beginning of a new era for industrial training by officially recognizing that exhortation had failed and that legislation was necessary to meet the UK's training needs. The (Conservative) Government argued that the shortage of skilled manpower was retarding the rate of industrial expansion, that the quality of much of the country's training was inadequate, and that the cost of training should be equitably distributed. These points formed the cornerstone of the Industrial Training Act, which became law in 1964. For detailed accounts of the developments leading to the Industrial Training Act, *see* Page (1967) and Hansen (1967).

The Industrial Training Act is a short document of only 15 pages and its three main objectives are described in an official guide to the Act (1964) as follows:

to ensure an adequate supply of properly trained men and women at all levels of industry

to secure an improvement in the quality and efficiency of industrial training

to share the cost of training more evenly between firms.

The Act laid down that these objectives would be achieved through the establishment of Training Boards on an industry basis. Each Industrial Training Board (ITB) would be responsible for the development of training recommendations, the approval of training standards and facilities, and the encouragement of research into training problems. Under the Act an ITB had a duty to levy employers in its industry and, with the money collected from this levy, to provide companies with financial incentives to carry out training. The levy income was also used to finance the Boards' administrative costs. ITBs were given the authority to pay training grants, assess industries' training needs and require companies coming within scope to supply information about the numbers, categories and training of their employees.

Despite these provisions, the Act was basically enabling or permissive, in that although an ITB had to levy companies in scope, employers had no legal obligation to train their person-
238

nel. They could, if they wished regard the levy as a training tax and decline to carry out any training. The Act was therefore a compromise between the two extremes of a *laissez-faire* approach to training and compulsion to train.

The Central Training Council (CTC) was established under the 1964 Act to advise the Secretary of State for Employment on the exercise of his functions under the Act and on any other training matters about which either he or the ITBs required advice. The Council had some severe critics and it was discontinued with the advent of the Employment and Training Act (1973). The criticisms of the CTC mainly focused on its lack of executive authority, but it must be said that the Council published basic recommendations for training in various functional areas which have stood the test of time, ITBs having adapted them to suit their own industries.

The structure of training boards

Prior to setting up an ITB, the Secretary of State at the Department of Employment (DE) consulted employer and trade union or other staff representatives in the industry to sound out their views on the scope of the proposed board. When this was agreed, a statutory instrument was drafted in the form of an Industrial Training Order and laid before Parliament for approval. The Training Order was concerned with the definition of the industry to be covered by the new ITB and also laid down its membership and the procedure to be adopted at its meetings. Members are appointed to hold office for a three year period, after which the board is normally reconstituted.

Each ITB has an independent chairman, an equal number of employer and employee members, and some educationists. Members are appointed on a part time, unpaid basis and sit on the board in their personal capacities and not as delegates of their organizations. Employer and employee organizations usually have about six members each, although this number is higher where several trades exist within one ITB. The purpose of the educational membership is to foster a close link between the ITB and the educational system. The importance of this link is underlined in the Act and in many ITB publications, which stress the need for integrated education and training programmes. Board membership also includes government assessors from relevant departments, whose main functions are to advise the board and to assist in communications between the ITB and government.

239

The development and work of the training boards

During the six years following 1964, 29 boards were established (this number has since been reduced to 23), and efforts were made by the ITBs to meet the objectives imposed upon them by the 1964 Act. This they did in a number of ways:

The ITB's advisers offered firms a training consultancy service.

They published training recommendations, especially prepared for the industry which could be adapted, with minimum alteration, to suit a company's training requirement. The adoption of an ITB's recommended training programme reduced the need for job training analyses and for designing training programmes.

Some ITBs established centres in which they offered training facilities, normally restricted to trainees from in-scope companies. Examples include the Construction ITB's training centre at Bircham Newton in Norfolk for construction operatives and others, and the Road Transport ITB's Multi Occupational Training and Educational Centres (MOTECs), established to provide a wide range of training for road transport employees.

They developed special training programmes in collaboration with colleges of further education and other course-running organizations.

They paid grants to those companies whose training satisfied the ITB's requirements.

Levy grant schemes 1964–1972

During this period, an ITB's levy grant scheme generally required all companies within its scope to pay a levy, but only those firms which carried out training approved by the ITB received grants. In this way, an attempt was made to distribute the training costs more fairly within the industry, since those companies that did no training received no ITB grant and so paid their levy (in effect) to those firms which trained systematically. This meant that a company undertaking an above average amount of approved training received from its ITB more money in training grant than it paid in levy. There was, however, an upper limit to the amount of grant which a company could claim in any one year, usually expressed as a percentage of the amount paid in levy.

Problems associated with the Industrial Training Act 1964

Some of the measures arising from this Act gave rise to considerable criticism, *see*, for example, *Training for the Future*, the Department of Employment (1972) discussion document which heralded the 1973 Act including the following:

A substantial number of people worked in occupations which were not covered by training boards.

The ITBs did nothing for the unemployed, and little for the declining industries.

Determining equitable criteria by which to judge the standard and quantity of training caused many problems. For instance, firms with a high labour turnover could claim to be undertaking a great deal of training, although there was no guarantee that those who had left would be re-employed within the industry.

It was an almost impossible task to ensure that the statistical returns made by firms were 100 per cent accurate. Extensive inspections would have required large numbers of ITB staff, which in turn would have raised administrative expenses, so reducing the money available to be repaid to industry in grant. Moreover it was difficult for ITB staff to adopt the dual role of inspector and adviser.

The payment of levy at the beginning of the year (especially a high levy such as the Engineering ITB's two and a half per cent of payroll), caused cash flow difficulties to many firms, since training grants were not paid by ITBs to eligible companies until months later.

It was felt that the training activities of ITBs should be co-ordinated and manpower planning implemented.

On the credit side, the 1964 Act had many beneficial effects which will be discussed later. However, it is probably best viewed as the means by which companies were induced to give systematic training a trial, and in this respect the first ITBs carried a greater responsibility than they may have realised. The ITBs had few excuses for failure; they had access to top management and, whatever time span had been allowed for the trial, if the training boards could not convince companies that training was a sound business proposition, then it could not be bolstered up forever as an activity to which lip service had to be paid in order to retrieve a punitive levy. It is a matter of debate as

241

to whether the ITBs were given enough time to implement successfully the 1964 Act, but in the event the deficiencies in the Act led to a major review of training legislation, and to the passing of the Employment and Training Act 1973.

THE EMPLOYMENT AND TRAINING ACT 1973
The 1973 Act had four main functions:

> it set up three bodies, the Manpower Services Commission, the Employment Service Agency (ESA) and the Training Services Agency (TSA)
>
> it conferred upon the Secretary of State of Employment the power to provide temporary employment for 'persons in Great Britain who are without employment'
>
> it laid upon each local authority the duty to provide career services
>
> it amended the Industrial Training Act 1964, notably in the revision of arrangements for collection of levy by ITBs, and in the provision of certificates of exemption from levy to companies whose training is 'in accordance with proposals published by the board'.

The Manpower Services Commission
The Commission has 10 members: a chairman, three members appointed after consultation with the TUC, three after consultation with the CBI, two after consultation with local authority associations, and one with professional education interests. It is responsible to the Secretary of State for Employment, and the Secretaries of State for Scotland and for Wales. In the words of the Act, it is the duty of the Commission to 'make such arrangements as it considers appropriate for the purpose of assisting persons to select, train for, obtain and retain employment suitable for their ages and capacities and to obtain suitable employees. . . .' In contrast to the 1964 Act, it acknowledges a social responsibility for the individual, as well as providing for the needs of the company.

By working through its two arms, the TSA and the ESA, it was hoped that the Commission would be able to link the problems of manpower planning and supply with an integrated national training provision. Following a review of the organization in 1978, the whole of the Commission's operations was integrated into a single manpower services organization, and both the ESA and TSA became operational divisions (ESD

242

and TSD) of the Commission. Greater emphasis was placed on the oversight of all manpower services at regional level. A third division was also formed to be in charge of Special Programmes, including those for young people (such as Youth Opportunities), and programmes providing temporary employment for adults, *see* chapter 7.

Through its Training Services Division, the Manpower Services Commission (MSC) oversees the 23 ITBs, has responsibility for the non-ITB sector and for the Training Opportunities Scheme (TOPS), under which over 100,000 people were trained in 1977. The TSD also has direct training services of its own, including the Training Within Industry unit (TWI), the Skill Centres, and a mobile instructor service. The Division has three main aims (MSC (1978a)):

meeting the training needs of industry
meeting the training needs of individuals
improving the effectiveness and efficiency of training.

Meeting the training needs of industry
This is achieved largely through the work of the ITBs which cover firms employing about two thirds of the working population, MSC (1977b). Since the 1973 Act, the ITBs discuss their arrangements for training levies and exemptions with the Training Services Division, within the constraint that the maximum levy must not exceed 1 per cent of payroll. TSD subsidies are also available to ITBs to encourage key training activities in their industries.

It is claimed that under this organization, the ITBs are able to play a major part in training programmes which are of national importance by relating wider national requirements to the needs and situations of particular industries. Whilst each industry has its specific requirements and the MSC helps each ITB with its own priorities, there is, nevertheless, considerable overlap in areas such as management development and clerical training. Co-ordination in these areas and collaboration between boards on common projects are facilitated by the TSD-ITB structure.

The non-ITB sector contains about 37 per cent of the working population and the TSD has undertaken to establish relationships with the organizations concerned, and to make a study of training needs in a number of priority areas such as banking, insurance, finance and the National Health Service. In addition, the TSD has produced a set of multi-industry training needs of national importance such as those for young entrants, women, management development and safety and health at work.

Meeting the training needs of individuals
These will be met by improving training provisions generally, but also through the expansion of the Training Opportunities Scheme (TOPS) introduced in 1972 for adults who need training to take up new employment. TOPS training courses are available in the Skill centres or at colleges or employers' establishments and a wide range of courses is offered. Three main occupational areas have been given priority: technicians, clerical and commercial occupations, and jobs in hotel and catering. Again particular attention is paid to special groups of people such as the disabled, the long term unemployed, immigrants and young people.

Improving the effectiveness and efficiency of training
Activities to this end include: co-ordinating the research and information work of the ITBs, sponsoring external research and development and providing advice and information, including publications. For reviews of the 1973 Act, *see* British Association for Commercial and Industrial Education (1978), Cooper (1978).

THE IMPACT OF LEGISLATION
Initially, the ITBs made slow progress in repairing deficiencies in the country's training but this was not surprising, since they had first to organize themselves before they could start influencing training in their industries. Moreover, the requirement that newly-established ITBs had to be self-financing within 12 months of their formation, aggravated rather than helped the initial difficulties which most new ITBs encountered when assessing the volume and quality of training taking place in their industry, determining training priorities, deciding levy grant schemes and compiling registers of names and addresses of all companies within their scope. For example the Chairman of the Distributive ITB Spencer (1971) reported, nearly three years after his board had been established, that there were still probably 250,000 small firms within its scope which had not been registered.

244

Nonetheless, the first six years after the 1964 Industrial Training Act became law saw the evolution of a network of ITBs covering, with a few important exceptions, most industries of any size in the country. This was itself a major development in the British industrial scene and was achieved, in spite of its radical nature, with the continued support of the Confederation of British Industries, the Trades Union Congress and the further education system.

Earlier we quoted the aims of the 1964 Act as being to increase the quantity of training, the quality of training at all levels in industry and to share the cost more equitably. To what extent have these aims been met?

The increase in the quantity of training

It would be wrong to attribute the substantial increase in training that took place in the years after the Act exclusively to the work of the ITBs, but there can be little doubt that their advice and incentives played a major part in this expansion. Government and ITBs' statistics, and research projects, Giles (1969), Mukherjee (1970), provide evidence of the rapid growth in the quantity of training, particularly in those industries covered by ITBs. Between 1964 and 1968, for example, there was an increase of 15 per cent in the number of employees under training in the manufacturing industries alone. Much of this growth was in operative and craft training, which were then high on the list of the nation's training priorities. It is also interesting to note that the number of group training schemes rose from 60 in 1965 to 700 in 1975, an indication that small firms, by pooling their resources and forming groups, were also involved in the expansion. The ITBs also encouraged off the job training and there was a slow but steady increase in the proportion of young people under 18 on day release courses: from 19 per cent in 1964 to 22.6 per cent in 1973.

The increase in the number of people being trained under TOPS has already been noted. Approximately 33 per cent of TOPS trainees are in the main traditional craft skills, 36 per cent in clerical and commercial training and 31 per cent in a miscellaneous group, among which increasing attention is given to managers and technicians, for whom training provisions are still inadequate. The concentration of all manpower services under a single Commission has helped to focus attention and resources on national priority areas and to place training, quite

245

properly, as one consideration in a scheme of interrelated manpower policies.

However, despite all the progress there are some disturbing features. For example, the operation of the TOPS scheme, which cost £226 million in 1977, has been criticised by the Controller and Auditor-General, *see* Perry (1978): the trainee drop-out rate of 27 per cent is considered very high, and the proportion of TOPS training in commercial and clerical skills has been criticized as being unlikely to give the necessary boost to the manufacturing industries. As far back as 1947 there was trade union opposition to 'dilutees' trained at (the then) Government Training Centres over a shorter period than the traditionally agreed time, and this problem has still not been resolved. The Boilermakers' Union, for example, will not admit as members men retrained in this way, while in 1976 the Civil Service Department refused to consider TOPS trained computer operators for appointments in government departments.

Far more serious, however, is the indication contained in the CBI Industrial Trends Surveys from 1960 to 1978, that even in times of severe unemployment, almost a quarter of Britain's manufacturers faced a shortage of skilled labour, which limited their output. In the capital goods industries just over a third of firms faced this constraint, in machine tools the figure was 50 per cent, while in spinning and weaving it was 58 per cent. These surveys show a consistent gap each year since 1960, between the percentage of companies which stated they were working at full capacity (used as a barometer of the state of economic demand), and the pecentage of those which reported that the shortage of skilled labour limited output. In 1978, whilst almost 40 per cent of employers claimed to be at full capacity, between 20 and 25 per cent claimed they had a shortage of skilled labour.

It is, of course, possible to contest these figures (a lack of skilled people is a convenient explanation for not achieving production targets), but they appear to be backed by a substantial amount of other evidence, ranging from that of the Engineering Construction Economic Development Council's estimate of a shortage of 500 draughtsmen, to the NEDC working party report of 'a chronic shortage of high calibre design engineers and draughtsmen, to the cancellation by ICI of a major investment at Wilton, because of the lack of sufficient skilled instrument artificers', Carvel (1978).

246

The MSC (1976b) reaches a similar conclusion:

There is good reason to believe that taking all employers together, industry has never provided as much training in vital skills as the economy requires. Since recruitment is cut back heavily in periods of recession, and training in transferable skills takes some years to complete, the effects of the cutback tend to become apparent just as demand is increasing with economic upturn. By definition, the gap between supply and demand cannot be plugged rapidly by long-term training.

However, these problems are partly a reflection not only of recruitment and training, but also of labour wastage, caused for example by lack of promotion prospects, drastic erosion of skill differentials and, in some cases, of redundancy. But the major problem seems to stem from the cyclical nature of the economy, when too little training during a depression results in shortage of skilled labour during the ensuing boom. For instance, the total number of trainees fell by 400,000 from 1.6 million in 1970 to 1.2 million in 1971.

It is easy to take a macro view and point to national shortages, but from a company's standpoint the answer is not simple. Constant rising wage rates, as well as increases in the cost of training, have made it expensive for a company to maintain surplus labour either of trainees or its own longer serving personnel, in anticipation of a possible upturn in the economy.

Some measures which improve training may also prove to be a deterrent to firms. For instance, the Engineering ITB's (1978b) proposals for craft training may help employers to balance the supply and demand situation more quickly, because training time would be reduced, but it may also inhibit them from recruiting apprentices they do not need at that time if they have to pay a full craftsman's wage at age 18, a much more expensive form of investment than the traditional apprentice, who would fetch and carry on the factory floor for five or more years at a low rate of pay. This is not a plea for a return to old training methods, nor a criticism of systematic training, but a reminder that changes in training strategy, however desirable, can have undesirable side effects. Furthermore, motivation and morale play a vital part in training, and the brightest recruits are unlikely to be attracted to an industry which is in recession. If learning is to be really effective, skills require consolidation,

247

practice and experience immediately after acquisition. But this would take production work from the existing labour force and so be unacceptable to employees worried about job security. These difficulties appear to make a strong case for more state responsibility for training, so that in a recession expenditure can actually be increased (counter cyclical training), but it is not easy to predict exactly what skills will be required in a boom, particularly in view of regional variations, and there would still be motivational problems for many trainees.

What constitutes an adequate supply of skilled labour is a complex question. Workers are not a disposable commodity and, if there is an ample supply of skilled people to cope with any upsurge of the economy, they must either be made redundant or retained at a loss during a slump and both alternatives are costly to a company. It is understandable why for reasons of caution, or even for sheer survival, organizations deliberately take a middle of the road approach, and never recruit or train right up to the peak of their requirement.

The MSC (1976b) has suggested two possible approaches to remedying the shortfall problem. One involves a public subsidy for amounts of training in transferable skills above a norm, and the other involves collective funding to encourage relevant employers to increase their recruitment for training, by repaying them the whole or part of the cost of the initial stages of this training. The funding for the latter approach would be geared to regular decisions about the level of intakes into training for the occupations selected. But, as we have seen, companies are not only concerned with the cost of training they may decide to limit production rather than risk enlarging their labour force beyond their permanent need. Thus, it is clear that a range of national policies affect company decisions about the training of skilled manpower, and the aim of the 1964 Act, 'to ensure an adequate supply of properly trained men and women' could never be achieved by training alone.

Improvement in the quality of training
One of the three main aims of the 1964 Act was to raise the quality of training in this country. To what extent has this happened? This is not an easy question to answer because the ITBs have had a difficult role in creating better quality training, since companies decide for themselves what training their employees need and how best to provide it. An ITB's influence over
248

training standards has, therefore, been indirect. Managements have become more conscious of the costs involved in learning and as a result are more critical of inefficient training but the process of raising the general standards of training is a lengthy one.

The ITBs encouraged the use of systematic methods, which in turn brought about a new approach to training. A major factor here has been the application of job analysis, which in some extreme instances resulted in massive paper work exercises and very little training, but has in general undoubtedly counteracted loose thinking in deciding objectives and relevant content for company training programmes. The advice given by ITBs on the criteria to use in selecting external courses has certainly stimulated colleges and commercial organizations to set more precise training objectives and to meet these with appropriate course designs.

A vast amount of analytical work has been completed by the ITBs so that training officers can now find in their own ITB's publications a basic job or task analysis, which they can adapt for most jobs within their organizations, whereas in the past they had to carry out all their own analytical work. The ITBs have also made good progress in streamlining the country's training systems, for example, the development by the Engineering ITB of training modules for craft apprentices (*see* chapter 11), while other boards have taken the initiative in working through Joint Examination Committees, examination councils, BEC and TEC, to improve the integration of in-company and college elements of training programmes.

The orientation of analysis has changed through the years. In the 1950s, the emphasis was on the analysis of what were basically motor and perceptual skills, Seymour (1966). Gradually, as these types of job were analyzed or replaced by automation, the emphasis changed towards the analysis of problem solving and decision making skills, which in turn stimulated the study of intellectual and social skills, *see* Youngman *et al* (1978). Researchers such as Argyle (1970) were working on methods of analysing interpersonal skills, and while this research proceeded independently of the ITBs, it would be true to say that they were able to encourage its practical application. Much of the early work of the ITBs was understandably concerned with relatively mechanistic aspects of analysing jobs, but more recently there are signs that they are drawing upon the wider findings of behavioural science. A good example of this is the study of Career Development by the Food, Drink and Tobacco ITB, *see* chapter 14. Contributions which helped improve the quality of training came from research projects financed originally by the former Central Training Council and currently by the Training Services Division, which maintains a research register, the current edition of which contains several hundred items relating to a wide range of activities connected with training. The Industrial Training Research Unit was set up at Cambridge to supply information and advice in this rapidly changing field.

Another noticeable development has been the increase in the quality of people who are now being appointed to training officer positions. There were few high calibre training specialists before 1964, and this shortage of people with the appropriate knowledge and skills to staff the training boards was a major problem for all the ITBs. Many of the company training officer appointments made in response to the 1964 Act, reflected the very low status in which the training function was then held. People were not selected on relevant job criteria but rather the training officer post was sometimes used to accommodate an 'unwanted' person from elsewhere in the organization, or a former, often highly successful, craft instructor. The latter was understandably often quite out of his depth in coping with organizational problems and levy grant matters and was severely handicapped by his lowly position in the company hierarchy. Today, the general calibre of company training staff has greatly improved although the MSC (1978b) has expressed concern that 'the level of status and influence of many training staff was (still) relatively low'. Increased professionalism in training has also been reflected in the rising membership of the Institute of Personnel Management and the Institution of Training Officers. These organizations have done a great deal to raise the standards of the training profession by their examination schemes and educational activities, which now attract many graduates. All of these developments stimulated a rapid growth in training literature — from documents published by official bodies such as the Department of Employment, the CTC and later the MSC, to training journals and literature of many kinds.

Thus it is clear that the quality of training in the UK has greatly improved in recent years and, bearing in mind the pre-1964 situation, credit for the lion's share of the improvements must be attributed to the 1964 and 1973 Acts.

Sharing the cost of training more equitably
This aim was included in the 1964 Act primarily to compensate those companies who trained staff and then had them poached by other employers, often, it was said, by smaller firms who did not or could not train their own employees. Whether this was as common a problem as had been suggested is now open to doubt, as many small firms are known to have a negligible labour turnover and so have little need to poach.

Nonetheless, it remained true that some companies trained and others did not, and ITBs designed levy grant schemes in an attempt to correct the situation. Boards were in a dilemma in trying to keep their schemes as simple as possible and yet making them flexible enough to accommodate the variety of conditions within their industries. For example, it was argued that although smaller companies were helped by the expansion of ITB sponsored group training schemes, there was a tendency for grant proposals to benefit the medium or large company, *see* the Confederation of British Industries CBI (1971).

It has also to be remembered that a levy grant scheme was designed to meet the industry's training needs, which were unlikely to be similar to those of the individual company. A firm could therefore be in the position of having to choose between training to the national guidelines as laid down by the ITB and maximizing grant, or training to meet its own needs and, as a result, possibly being eligible for a smaller grant.

Companies reacted differently to levy grant. Some paid the levy, trained to meet their own needs and tended to look on grant payments as of secondary importance. Others saw the levy as a tax, paid it and did no training. Still other companies were motivated to train for the wrong reasons. They believed that by receiving grant they retrieved their levy, but as Forrester (1968) pointed out, this ignored the fact that levy and grant were not the only elements in the training cost equation. This equation can be expressed as: cost of training plus levy minus grant minus benefits of training equals net cost. Significant though the amounts of levy and grant may have been, what really mattered was the net cost which a company had to pay for its training. Obtaining a high percentage return of levy was to the net advantage of a company only if the costs of training involved were not excessive. Looking at levy and grant in

251

isolation from other costs and benefits did not and could not give a true picture of the training costs, yet many companies were slow to realize this.

Another problem (*see* page 241) was that many ITBs operated their finances on the basis of invoicing companies for levies at the beginning of a levy year, and then at a later date paid grant to those firms which had earned it. This procedure suffered from two major disadvantages. First, companies had to forego the use of their levy payments while the ITBs held the money and, apart from their administrative expenses (which on average amounted to approximately two to three per cent of the levy income), subsequently paid most of the levy back to industry in grants. Secondly, there were also, as mentioned above, unnecessary and costly transfers of money between companies and the ITB. Boards, therefore, eventually adopted a system of netting payments ie at the end of the grant year, a company's levy and grant were assessed and only the difference between them, if any, was settled by the ITB paying grant or invoicing for the balance of the levy due. This netting system allowed all but the balance of levy paid to remain in the industry, so helping company liquidity.

Certain ITBs also had difficulties because of their open-ended levy grant schemes and the considerable financial problems which arose in predicting the extent to which the firms within an industry would claim grant. The Construction ITB, for example, raised levies in 1967/68 which it considered adequate to meet anticipated claims for grants, but was left with a substantial surplus as many companies did not claim the grants to which they were entitled. Later, this ITB had the opposite problem of grant claims exceeding levy income, with the result that in the levy year ending March 1970, it had a deficit of 4.5 million pounds.

The objective of cost-sharing through the medium of a levy grant system therefore proved very difficult to achieve. Indeed, in the light of experience, the validity of the argument that training costs should and could be more equitably distributed was seriously doubted. For example, the CBI (1971) regarded the sharing of the cost of training more evenly between firms as impracticable as well as an undesirable objective. The CBI argued:

that no employer should be expected to bear more than his
252

fair share of training costs in his industry, but the conception that one employer should be subsidized by others when he does more than his fair share should be approached with great care. Experience indicates that the use of levy and grant schemes to this end may create as much inequity as it resolves.

The Department of Employment (1972) also concluded that:

In practice the idea of full cost redistribution has been largely abandoned by Boards. . . . in general the employer who trains beyond the needs of his own business receives little compensation for his extra costs from the levy grant system, and equally firms who rely on recruiting workers trained by others do not contribute substantially to the cost of their training.

Thus, the evidence shows that the aim of the 1964 Act to share the costs of training more equitably, was not achieved by the ITBs. For a detailed analysis of the development of training legislation in the UK the reader is referred to Perry (1976), whose major survey includes explanations of the main factors determining the training policies of successive governments and of the ITBs.

PROBLEMS AND TRENDS
Individual versus organizational needs
As well as being concerned with the needs of companies, the 1973 Act made provision for the training of the individual. These two aspects are contained in the principles of the Council of the Ministers of the EEC Common Vocational Policy (1963):

to relate closely the different forms of vocational training to the sectors of the economy so that vocational training best meets both the needs of the economy and the interests of the trainees.

The potential conflict here, however, cannot be brushed aside: should the individual be subsidized to train according to his own vocational inclinations, or be persuaded into occupations or professions of national need, eg away from declining industries into those which appear likely to expand?

The idealistic objective of the Council of Ministers of the European Economic Community (1963) 'To offer everyone in accordance with his aspirations, skills, knowledge and working experience and by permanent means for vocational improvement, eligibility for a higher occupational level or instruction for a different activity at a higher level', is highly commendable, but can it be achieved in practice? Will the employment opportunities afforded by the nation ever equal the sum of the aspirations and capabilities of its workforce? (For an interesting development of this idea, *see* Wellens (1963)). To some extent it may be feasible because, for example, it can be argued that increased knowledge begets further research which, in turn, may lead to further jobs and/or changes in the pattern of employment. However, the debate on this subject has hardly begun and certainly further consideration must be given to the question of how far it is possible to make accurate predictions about future national manpower needs. There are so many relevant variables such as technical change, capital, stocks, output, prices etc, that the commonly held view is that:

.... the task of forecasting how much change there will be in demand at any date in the future and to what extent there may be a shortfall or excess of supply is so formidable as to verge on the impossible, *see* Mukherjee (1974).

The training requirements for the development of the individual will, at times, be in conflict with those of his organization. For instance, the former Central Training Council (1966c) pointed out the danger in encouraging firms to construct commercial and clerical training syllabuses for their own, perhaps quite limited, requirements which may not enable the trainee subsequently to work in a different firm or move to a more demanding or responsible job. Upward and lateral mobility must be encouraged by the training given. The Engineering ITB's module system incorporates this principle by requiring companies to provide a complete programme for their craft trainees, even although in some cases the specified content may include skills which the company will never require.

Furthermore, the aims and training needs of individual organizations can conflict with the overall requirements of the industry, which again may not coincide with national requirements. Now that the ITBs are grouped together under the Training Services Division and their funding has been switched to the Exchequer, there are fears that industries' influence over their ITBs will be lessened and the boards' main efforts will be directed towards national and political problems such as unemployment, rather than to the specific training problems of their own industries. It would be naïve to imagine that all of these competing interests can be satisfied at the same time, particularly in the face of serious difficulties such as high unemployment, and so criticism from one quarter or another is inevitable. The MSC training policy appears so all embracing that there does not seem to be anyone who is not supposed to benefit from it, and so the only way of making progress appears to be that of the 'best fit' in the circumstances. This being so, some explanation must surely be given as to the priority which policy makers attach to each of the objectives. Whilst the legislation cannot serve all masters at once, it certainly contains provisions to give help where and when it is most urgently needed. The danger is that approaches which attempt to please all parties are in danger of satisfying none.

National training policy is also affected by other government measures, and although a full discussion of this relationship is not possible here, an example illustrates the point. Industrial subsidy policy:

> creates a conflict between the skill implications of job preservation and the skill requirements of the expanding sectors some of which might involve new techniques. Either way, governments cannot avoid a decision on society's attitude to change. They have to choose between preventing change or accepting it and being more concerned with the adjustment period and the adequacy of arrangements for re-allocating resources (eg retraining), *see* Hartley (1976)

These considerations as to the nature of training lead to the fundamental question of how far legislation is an appropriate means of bringing about more and better training in organisations. Clearly, the day to day commitment so necessary for successful training cannot be enforced by Act of Parliament. The role of legislation is better viewed as providing a supportive environment and acting as an external agent in trying to break the vicious circle where, until successful training has been carried out in an organization, managers, particularly if they themselves have not been trained, are likely to undervalue its contribution. This role is not an easy one, particularly in the light of problems of training evaluation, but the legislation appears to be moving in the right direction by creating conditions where

255

ITB staff are advisers rather than inspectors. At the end of the day, however, in training as in culinary matters, the 'proof of the pudding is in the eating!'

Potential conflict also exists in training the unemployed for job vacancies, which it is hoped will occur in the future. The case for doing this is strong and it can be argued, for example, that the cost of training can be set against the cost of paying unemployment benefit. However, the prospect of the money being used in a very different way, eg to encourage capital investment, which might result in more opportunities for permanent employment, cannot be ignored. It is also argued that even if the precise jobs do not materialize, 'learning to learn' transfers, and so the experience should help future learning. Thus school leavers should be given the opportunity to acquire a firm vocational basis, whilst they are near the height of their intellectual ability and learning is easiest. On the other hand, there are motivational problems, and the need to consolidate learning by related experience which may not be available. On this side of the argument also is the possibility that frustration in one learning situation may transfer to another.

Our cyclical economy and the speed of technical change suggest that 'learning to learn' is the central training problem of our time. This view is featured in the EEC Guidelines, *see* Perry 1972, where at one point mention is made of it as 'the permanent ability to adapt to the technical pattern of work'. There is a need for further research in this area, both into the conditions necessary for learning transfer to take place (what are 'transferable skills'?), and into what 'families of skills' can be taught at school which are likely to have applicability in later life. In this context, it is encouraging and interesting to note that the Industrial Training Research Unit has started a project which aims to improve the learning skills of young people aged 16 and above. It is intended to explore individual differences in learning style and to determine what aspects of learning give difficulty, and then to develop 'learning to learn' courses suitable for school leavers, immediately before they enter industry or further education. Raising the school leaving age may be a help but only if greater integration between the education system and vocational training really takes place. Versatility is not, however, just a matter for school leavers, it is likely that in consideration of future national needs, versatility of the labour force will be rated as of equal, if not of greater importance, than the some-
256

what mechanistic assessments of quantity and quality of training provided for specific jobs. Retraining for new occupations and adaptation within the same job will be permanent features of the employment scene.

We have already demonstrated that there has been a gradual harmonization of UK training provisions with those suggested in the EEC guidelines. Partly under this influence and partly because of pressing problems of growing unemployment, the State has gradually assumed more responsibility for vocational training. Although this has inherent dangers, such as costly bureaucracy, it has obvious advantages both in breadth of provision and in the possibility of isolating and remedying problem areas. However, just as an organization requires a total policy (of which training should be an integral element), derived from its basic objectives, so a nation needs to work out a coherent plan around basic principles and priorities. The piecemeal pattern outlined above suggests that this is far from being achieved.

The training needs of an individual, an organization or a nation will vary from time to time according to background and circumstance. Training will never be an exact science but since perhaps the first skill of the training specialist is the ability to ask the right questions, it is fitting that we have concluded by raising a series of questions! The reader may well have been looking for prescribed answers — we hope that at least we have given some guidance and ideas and in addition, a deeper and more sensitive understanding of training and development.

List of Abbreviations

ABCC	Association of British Chambers of Commerce
BACIE	British Association for Commercial and Industrial Education
BEC	Business Education Council
BIM	British Institute of Management
CBA	Cost Benefit Analysis
CBI	Confederation of British Industry
CGLI	City and Guilds of London Institute
CIR	Commission on Industrial Relations
CNAA	Council for National Academic Awards
CTC	Central Training Council
DE	Department of Employment
DES	Department of Education and Science
DMS	Diploma in Management Studies
EEC	European Economic Community
ESA	Employment Services Agency
ESD	Employment Services Division
EWS	Experienced Worker Standard
ICI	Imperial Chemical Industries
IPM	Institute of Personnel Management
ITB	Industrial Training Board
MBA	Master of Business Administration
MBO	Management by Objectives
MOTECs	Multi-Occupational Training and Educational Centres
MSA	Manual Skills Analysis
MSC	Manpower Services Commission
NCTA	National Council for Technical Awards
NEBSS	National Examinations Board for Supervisory Studies
NEDCO	National Economic Development Council Office
OD	Organization development
O and M	Organization and Method
SCOTBEC	Scottish Business Education Council
SRC	Science Research Council
TA	Transactional Analysis
TEC	Technician Education Council
TOPS	Training Opportunities Scheme
TSA	Training Services Agency
TSD	Training Services Division
TUC	Trades Union Congress
TWI	Training Within Industry

APPENDIX 1

LIST OF TRAINING ACTIVITIES — Reproduced
with the permission of The Local Government Training
Board, from Training Recommendation 17, Training
and Development of Training Officers (1976)

The following list of activities is not intended to be exhaustive.
However, this list has been compiled from the results of various
questionnaires, surveys and interviews, and from the discussions at the 1972 National Conference of Central Training
Officers. It covers the main areas of present commitment as
well as those areas in which most training officers see themselves being involved in the near future. It also corresponds
with the Board's views of which activities should be carried out
within the training function in local government.

1   Training policy:
  (i)   Make recommendations on the authority's training policy and assist in its formulation.

2   Identify training needs and priorities:
  (i)   Participate in the identification of future manpower needs and in decisions on ways of meeting these
  (ii) Liaise with other training staff in the authority and with management
  (iii) Identify the long and short-term training needs of the authority, departments and sections, job categories and individual employees
  (iv) Define overall training objectives to meet the training needs within the confines of the authority's training policy
  (v)   Estimate the resources required to meet the objectives

(vi)   Recommend areas of training priority, taking into account the authority's training policy and limited resources available

(vii) Advise individuals on training problems.

3   **Plan training:**

(i)   Formulate a training plan taking account of the overall manpower plans for the authority

(ii)   Liaise with other staff in the authority with a responsibility for training

(iii)   Liaise with colleges and other outside organisations concerned with training (eg training boards and provincial councils)

(iv)   Evaluate various ways of meeting training needs

(v)   Set objectives for training programmes

(vi)   Prepare training programmes to meet the long and short-term training needs of the authority, departments and sections, job categories and individual employees

(vii) Prepare training estimates and budgets

(viii) Prepare any necessary training controls, records, and validation procedures.

4   **Implement training:**

(i)   Advise on the preparation of man specifications for recruitment and selection purposes and assist in selection of staff, if required

(ii)   Organize and supervise internal courses to meet the planned objectives

(iii)   Make and supervise practical training arrangements

(iv)   Select, train and brief instuctors

(v)   Prepare training material for internal courses, and operate and maintain training equipment

(vi)   Participate in internal courses

(vii) Select external courses; advise management on the suitability of external courses to meet planned objectives; supervise the operation of externally conducted training programmes and the associated on the job training

(viii) Maintain records of training

(ix)   Carry out evaluation and validation procedures, amending training plans accordingly.

5   Management of training:
  (i)   Set objectives of training section to meet the authority's training policy
  (ii)   Plan work load and priorities of the training section; organise the staff to meet the objectives
  (iii)   Ensure an effective utilization of the authority's training resources (staff, premises, equipment, etc); operate within the approved budget
  (iv)   Keep management informed of the progress of training
  (v)   Organise and carry out the training and development of all the authority's training staff
  (vi)   Liaise with senior managers on the future objectives of the authority and the need for development of particular categories of staff
  (vii)   Help to establish the best conditions for learning in the authority.

A BRIEF GUIDE TO TRAINING TECHNIQUES

The following is intended only as a general guide to the more common methods of instruction

Method	What it is	What it will achieve	Points to watch
Lecture	A talk given without much, if any, participation in the form of questions or discussion on the part of the trainees.	Suitable for large audiences where participation of the trainees is not possible because of numbers. The information to be put over can be exactly worked out beforehand – even to the precise word. The timing can be accurately worked out.	The lack of participation on the part of the audience means that unless the whole of it, from beginning to end, is fully understood and assimilated the sense will be lost.
Talk	A talk incorporating a variety of techniques, and allowing for participation by the trainees. The participation may be in the form of questions asked of trainees, their questions to the speaker, or brief periods of discussion during the currency of the session.	Suitable for putting across information to groups of not more than twenty trainees. Participation by the trainees keeps their interest and helps them to learn.	The trainees have the opportunity to participate but may not wish to do so. The communication will then be all one way and the session will be little different from a lecture.
Job (skill) instruction	A session during which a job or part of a job is learned to the following formula: (a) The trainee is told how to do the job. (b) The trainee is shown how to do the job. (c) The trainee does the job under supervision. Each of these parts may be a complete session in itself. (a) talk (b) demonstration (c) practice	Suitable for putting across skills. The job is broken down into small stages which are practised. The whole skill is thus built up in easily understood stages. This gives the trainees confidence and helps them to learn. More suitable when the skill to be learned is one which depends on a lot of knowledge first being learned. Many clerical skills are of this sort.	The skill to be acquired may best be learned as a 'whole' rather than as parts. It is difficult for trainees to absorb large chunks of information and then to be shown what to do at some length before they get the opportunity to put the learning into practice.

Method	What it is	What it will achieve	Points to watch
Discussion	Knowledge, ideas and opinions on a particular subject are freely exchanged among the trainees and the instructor.	Suitable where the application of information is a matter of opinion. Also when attitudes need to be induced or changed. Trainees are more likely to change attitudes after discussion than they would if they were told during a talk that their attitude should be changed. Also suitable as a means of obtaining feedback to the instructor about the way in which trainees may apply the knowledge learned.	The trainees may stray from the subject matter or fail to discuss it usefully. The whole session may be blurred and woolly. Trainees may become entrenched about their attitudes rather than be prepared to change them.
Role-play	Trainees are asked to enact, in the training situation, the role they will be called upon to play in their job of work. Used mainly for the practice of dealing with face-to-face situations (ie where people come together in the work situation).	Suitable where the subject is one where a near-to-life practice in the training situation is helpful to the trainees. The trainees can practise and receive expert advice or criticism and opinions of their colleagues in a 'protected' training situation. This gives confidence as well as offering guidelines. The trainees get the feel of the pressures of the real life situation.	Trainees may be embarrassed and their confidence sapped rather than built up. It can also be regarded a 'a bit of a lark' and not taken seriously.
Case-study	A history of some event or set of circumstances, with the relevant details, is examined by the trainees. Case-studies fall into two broad categories: (a) Those in which the trainees diagnose the causes of a particular problem. (b) Those in which the trainees set out to solve a particular problem.	Suitable where a cool look at the problem or set of circumstances, free from the pressures of the actual event, is beneficial. It provides opportunities for exchange of ideas and consideration of possible solutions to problems the trainees will face in the work situation.	Trainees may get the wrong impression of the real work situation. They may fail to realize that decisions taken in the training situation are different from those which have to be made on the spot in a live situation.

263

Method	What it is	What it will achieve	Points to watch
Exercise	Trainees are asked to undertake a particular task, leading to a required result, following lines laid down by the trainers. It is usually a practice or a test of knowledge put over prior to the exercise. Exercises may be used to discover trainees' existing knowledge or ideas before further information or new ideas are introduced. Exercises may be posed for individuals or for groups.	Suitable for any situation where the trainees need to practise following a particular pattern or formula to reach a required objective. The trainees are to some extent 'on their own'. This is a highly active form of learning. Exercises are frequently used instead of formal tests to find out how much the trainee has assimilated. There is a lot of scope in this method for the imaginative trainer.	The exercise must be realistic and the expected result reasonably attainable by all trainees or the trainees will lose confidence and experience frustration.
Project	Similar to an exercise but giving the trainee much greater opportunity for the display of initiative and creative ideas. The particular task is laid down by the trainer but the lines to be followed to achieve the objectives are left to the trainee to decide. Like exercises, projects may be set for either individuals or groups.	Suitable where initiative and creativity need stimulating or testing. Projects provide feedback on a range of personal qualities of trainees as well as their range of knowledge and attitude to the job. Like exercises, projects may be used instead of formal tests. Again there is a lot of scope for the imaginative trainer.	It is essential that the project is undertaken with the trainee's full interest and co-operation. It must also be seen by the trainee to be directly relevant to his needs. If the trainee fails, or feels he has failed, in the project there will be severe loss of confidence on his part and possible antagonism towards the trainer. Trainees are often hypersensitive to criticism of project work.
In-tray	Trainees are given a series of files, papers and letters similar to those they will be required to deal with at the place of work (ie the typical content of a desk-worker's in-tray). Trainees take action on each piece of work. The results are marked or compared one with another.	Suitable for giving trainee desk-workers a clear understanding of the real-life problems and their solutions. The simulation of the real situation aids the transfer of learning from the training to the work situation. A valuable way of obtaining feedback on the trainees' progress. Also useful for developing attitudes towards the work, eg priorities, customers' complaints, superiors, etc.	It is important that the contents of the in-tray are realistic. The aim should be to provide trainees with a typical in-tray. The marking or comparison of results must be done in a way which will not sap the confidence of the weaker trainee.

Method	What it is	What it will achieve	Points to watch
Business and management games	Trainees are presented with information about a company — financial position, products, market, etc. They are given different management roles to perform. One group may be concerned with sales, another with production and so on. These groups then 'run' the company. Decisions are made and actions are taken. The probable result of these decisions in terms of profitability is then calculated.	Suitable for giving trainee managers practice in dealing with management problems. The simulation of the real-life situation not only aids the transfer of learning but is necessary because a trainee manager applying only broad theoretical knowledge to the work situation could cause major problems. Also a valuable way of assessing the potential and performance of trainees. It helps considerably in developing many aspects of a manager's role.	The main difficulty is in assessing the probable results of the decisions made. Sometimes a computer is used for this purpose. The trainees may reject the whole of the learning if they feel the assessment of the probable outcome of their decisions is unrealistic. There is also a risk that the trainees may not take the training situation seriously.
Group dynamics	Trainees are put into situations in which: (a) the behaviour of each individual in the group is subject to examination and comment by the other trainees, (b) the behaviour of the group (or groups) as a whole is examined. (The trainer is a psychologist, sociologist or a person who has himself received special training).	A vivid way for the trainee to learn of the effect of his behaviour on other people and the effect of their behaviour upon him. It increases knowledge of how and why people at work behave as they do. It increases skill at working with other people and of getting work done through other people. A valuable way of learning the skill of communication.	Difficulties can arise if what the trainee learns about himself is distasteful to him. Trainees may 'opt-out' if they feel put off by the searching examination of motives. It is important that problems arising within the group are resolved before the group breaks up.

Reproduced with permission from the Ceramics, Glass and Mineral Products ITB. Paper Number 5

APPENDIX 3

MANAGEMENT TRAINING AND DEVELOPMENT
CONFIDENTIAL

PART A

This part of the form should be a) completed by the nominating Manager; b) its contents notified to the Nominee (as appropriate) before he goes on the course; c) returned to the Training Manager.

Name of Course Member: .... Title:..............................
Subject:.. Department: ....
Run by:... Location: ....
Date(s): ....

---

1. *Training Objective(s)*
   The reason for nominating the above for this course is to:
   — improve the skills which he needs for his present job   . . . . yes/no
   — give him a broader understanding of his present job
      and its relationships with those in other parts of the
      Company   . . . . yes/no
   — prepare him for promotion   . . . . yes/no
   Additional comments:

2. *Has the Nominee been informed of:*
   — the objectives of the course   . . . . yes/no
   — its outline content   . . . . yes/no
   — why he has been selected to go on this course   . . . . yes/no

3. *Was his reaction*
   enthusiastic?   . . . . yes/no
   agreeable?   . . . . yes/no
   other? (please comment)   . . . . yes/no

4. *Has the Nominee had any previous instruction or training
   in the subject matter covered by the course?*   . . . . yes/no
   Please specify, as this information is needed to ensure
   that the proposed training is at an appropriate level:

5. *What plans have you made to ensure that after the course the
   Nominee will use the skills and/or knowledge he has learnt?*

   Signed...

   Date...

NB This form has been reduced for printing purposes

266

APPENDIX 3 (contd)

MANAGEMENT TRAINING AND DEVELOPMENT
CONFIDENTIAL

PART B

This part of the form should be completed by the nominating Manager approximately three months after his Nominee has finished his course, and then returned to the Training Manager.

Name of Course Member: .... Title:...............................
Subject:................................... Department: ....
Run by:................................... Location: ....
Date(s): ....

---

6. *Has the training objective as stated in Question 1 been achieved*
      fully? .... yes/no
      largely? .... yes/no
      not at all? .... yes/no
  Please give details:

7. *Have your plans outlined in Question 5 been implemented*
    completely successfully? .... yes/no
    satisfactorily? .... yes/no
    to a limited extent only? .... yes/no
  Please give details:

8. *If you were to nominate another manager to this course what, if any, additional information would you require about it?*

9. *In the light of your experience of this course, would you recommend any alterations to its content? (Tailor made courses only).*

          Signed...
          Date...

References and Bibliography

ANNETTE J and DUNCAN K D, 1968, in *New media and methods in industrial training*, editors, Robinson J and Barnes N, British Broadcasting Corporation

ANNETTE J, DUNCAN K D, STAMMERS R B and GRAY M J, 1971, *Task analysis*, Training Information Paper No 6 HMSO

ARGYLE M, 1970, *Psychology of interpersonal behaviour*, Penguin

ASSOCIATION OF TEACHERS IN TECHNICAL INSTITUTIONS, 1970, *The Technical Journal*, February

BASS B M and VAUGHAN J A, 1966, *Training in industry — the management of learning*, Tavistock Publications

BELBIN E, 1964, *Training and the adult worker*, Problems of Progress in Industry, No15, HMSO

BELBIN E and BELBIN R M, 1972, *Problems in adult retraining*, Heinemann

BELBIN R M, 1965, *Employment of older workers*, No 2, training methods, OECD, Paris

BELBIN R M, 1969, The discovery method in training, *Training Information Paper* No 5, HMSO

BENNIS W G, 1969, *Organization development — its nature, origins and prospects*, Addison-Wesley

BERLEW D E and HALL D T, 1966, The socialization of managers, effects of expectations on performance, *Administrative Science Quarterly*, Vol 11, No 2

BEVERSTOCK A G, 1968, *Industrial training practices*, Classic Publications

BIENVENU B J, 1969, *New priorities in training, a guide for industry*, American Management Association

BINGHAM V N, 1968, The training officer's guide to commercial apprenticeship, *Training manual* No 3, British Association for Commercial and Industrial Education

BLAKE R P and MOUTON J S, 1964, *The managerial grid*, Gulf Publishing, Houston

268

BLOODWORTH M E, 1969, *Retail training and education,* Pitman

BOSWORTH REPORT, 1966, *Education and training requirements for the electrical and mechanical manufacturing industries,* HMSO

BOSWORTH REPORT, 1970, *Graduate training in manufacturing technology,* HMSO

BOYDELL T H, 1976, *A guide to the identification of training needs,* British Association for Commercial and Industrial Education

BOYDELL T H, 1977, *A guide to job analysis,* British Association for Commercial and Industrial Education

BRAMHAM J 1978, *Practical manpower planning,* Institute of Personnel Management

BRITISH ASSOCIATION FOR COMMERCIAL AND INDUS- TRIAL EDUCATION, 1976, *A training officer's guide to the education system of Great Britain,* BACIE

BRITISH ASSOCIATION FOR COMMERCIAL AND INDUS- TRIAL EDUCATION, 1977, *Report writing,* BACIE

BRITISH ASSOCIATION FOR COMMERCIAL AND INDUS- TRIAL EDUCATION, 1978, Review of the 1973 Employment and Training Act, *BACIE Journal,* February, Vol 32, No 2

BRITISH ASSOCIATION FOR COMMERCIAL AND INDUS- TRIAL EDUCATION, 1979,Training for skills, *BACIE Journal,* February, Vol 33, No 2

BRITISH INSTITUTE OF MANAGEMENT, 1975, Managing the export function, *Management Survey Report* No 26, British Institute of Management

BROMLEY D B, 1975, *The psychology of human ageing,* Penguin

BURNS T and STALKER G N, 1966, *The management of innovation,* Tavistock Publications

BUSINESS EDUCATION COUNCIL, 1976, *First policy statement,* Business Education Council

CARBY K and THAKUR M, 1976, *Transactional analysis at work,* Information report No 23, Institute of Personnel Management

CARBY K and THAKUR M, 1977, *No problems here?* Institute of Personnel Management

CARPET INDUSTRY TRAINING BOARD, 1967, *Guide to recruitment and selection for manual jobs,* carpet ITB

CARR COMMITTEE REPORT *Training for skill, recruitment and training of young workers in industry,* 1958, National Joint Advisory Council, HMSO

CARVEL J, 1978, Where have all the skilled men gone? *Financial Guardian,* 15 August

CENTRAL TRAINING COUNCIL, 1966(a), *Industrial training and further education,* HMSO

CENTRAL TRAINING COUNCIL, 1966(b), *Training of training officers – introductory courses,* HMSO

CENTRAL TRAINING COUNCIL, 1966(c), *Training for commerce and the office,* HMSO

CENTRAL TRAINING COUNCIL, 1967(a), *Training of training officers – the pattern for the future,* HMSO

CENTRAL TRAINING COUNCIL, 1967(b), *An approach to the training and development of managers,* HMSO

CENTRAL TRAINING COUNCIL, 1968(a), *Training for office supervision,* HMSO

CENTRAL TRAINING COUNCIL, 1968(b), *The training of export staff,* HMSO

CENTRAL TRAINING COUNCIL, 1969, *Training and developing of managers – further proposals,* HMSO

CERAMICS, GLASS AND MINERAL PRODUCTS INDUSTRY TRAINING BOARD, 1968(a), *How to assess your training needs,* Ceramics, Glass and Mineral Products ITB

CERAMICS, GLASS AND MINERAL PRODUCTS INDUSTRY TRAINING BOARD, 1968(b), *A guide to job analysis for the preparation of job training programmes,* Information paper No 3, Ceramics, Glass and Mineral Products ITB

CERAMICS, GLASS AND MINERAL PRODUCTS INDUSTRY TRAINING BOARD, 1968(c), *Designing programmes,* Information paper No 5, Ceramics, Glass and Mineral Products ITB

CERAMICS, GLASS AND MINERAL PRODUCTS INDUSTRY TRAINING BOARD, 1969, *Selection of external training courses,* Information paper No 1, Ceramics, Glass and Mineral Products ITB

CERAMICS, GLASS AND MINERAL PRODUCTS INDUSTRY TRAINING BOARD, 1971, *Training guideline, young operatives in the glass industry,* Ceramics, Glass and Mineral Products ITB

CHADWICK D and HOGG Y, 1978, *Career planning and development for managers,* Food, Drink and Tobacco ITB

CHEMICAL AND ALLIED PRODUCTS INDUSTRY TRAINING BOARD, 1969(a), *Recommendations for the immediate postgraduate training of engineers, scientists and technologists,* Training recommendation No 2, Chemical and Allied Products ITB

CHEMICAL AND ALLIED PRODUCTS INDUSTRY TRAINING BOARD, 1969(b), *Recommendations for sales training,* Recommendation No 5, Chemical and Allied Products ITB

CHEMICAL AND ALLIED PRODUCTS INDUSTRY TRAINING BOARD, 1969(c), *Recommendations for management and supervisory training and development,* Training recommendation No 1, Chemical and Allied Products ITB

CHEMICAL AND ALLIED PRODUCTS INDUSTRY TRAINING BOARD, 1970(a), *Analysis of training needs — how to go about it, a guide for smaller companies,* Chemical and Allied Products ITB
270

CHEMICAL AND ALLIED PRODUCTS INDUSTRY TRAIN-
ING BOARD, 1970(b), *Information paper on productivity agreements,*
Chemical and Allied Products ITB
CHEMICAL AND ALLIED PRODUCTS INDUSTRY TRAIN-
ING BOARD, 1970(c), *Recommendations for the training of punch
operators or verifiers (electronic data processing),* Recommendation No
7, Chemical and Allied Products ITB
CHEMICAL AND ALLIED PRODUCTS INDUSTRY TRAIN-
ING BOARD, 1971, *Industrial training associated with sandwich courses
(science and engineering),* Training recommendation No 11, Chemi-
cal and Allied Products ITB
CHERRINGTON P, 1970, *Wider business objectives in management
education,* Occasional paper No 8, Industrial Education and
Research Foundation, London
CLOTHING AND ALLIED PRODUCTS INDUSTRY TRAIN-
ING BOARD, 1977, *Levy exemption and key training grants,* Clo-
thing and Allied Products ITB
COMMISSION ON INDUSTRIAL RELATIONS, 1972(a), *Indus-
trial relations training,* Report No 33, HMSO
COMMISSION ON INDUSTRIAL RELATIONS, 1972(b), *A prac-
tical guide for unions and employers,* HMSO
COMMISSION OF THE EUROPEAN COMMUNITIES, 1976,
From education to working life in *Bulletin of the European Com-
munities Supplement 12/76*
COMMITTEE ON MANPOWER RESOURCES FOR SCIENCE
AND TECHNOLOGY, 1965, 1968, *Triennial scientific manpower
survey,* HMSO
CONFEDERATION OF BRITISH INDUSTRY, 1971, Operation
of the Industrial Training Act, statement by the CBI, *Supplement to
the Education and Training Bulletin,* February, CBI
CONFEDERATION OF BRITISH INDUSTRY, 1978, *Evidence to
the Finniston Committee of Inquiry into the Engineering Profession,* CBI
COOPER K, 1978, Review of the Employment and Training Act,
BACIE Journal, March, Vol 32, No 3
CORLETT E N and MORCOMBE V J, 1970, Straightening out
learning curves, *Personnel Management,* June, Vol 2, No 6
COTTON AND ALLIED TEXTILES INDUSTRY TRAINING
BOARD, 1970(a), *Guide to induction training,* Cotton and Allied
Textiles ITB
COTTON AND ALLIED TEXTILES INDUSTRY TRAINING
BOARD, 1970(b), *Recommendations for marketing and sales training,*
Cotton and Allied Textiles ITB
COUNCIL OF THE MINISTERS OF THE EUROPEAN
ECONOMIC COMMUNITY, 1963, *General principles for imple-
menting a common vocational training policy,* 63/266 OJ No 63, April
CRISP J, 1978, Tapping hidden talents, *Financial Times,* 26 April

CROSSMAN E R F W, 1960, Automation and skill. *Problems of Progress in Industry,* No 9, HMSO

DAINTON REPORT, *Enquiry into the flow of candidates in science and technology in higher education,* 1968, HMSO

DANIEL W W and PUGH H, 1975, *Sandwich courses in higher education,* Report on CNAA degrees in business studies, Political and Economic Planning

DAVIES I K, 1971 *The management of learning,* McGraw-Hill

DELF G and SMITH B, 1978 Strategies for promoting self development, *Industrial and Commercial Training,* December, Vol 10, No 12

DENERLEY R A and PLUMBLEY P R, 1969, *Recruitment and selection in a full employment economy,* Institute of Personnel Management

DENNY E, 1970, *The merchant apprentices,* Collins

DEPARTMENT OF EMPLOYMENT AND PRODUCTIVITY, 1968, *Company manpower planning,* Manpower Paper No 1, HMSO

DEPARTMENT OF EMPLOYMENT AND PRODUCTIVITY, 1970, Training adults for office work, *Employment and Productivity Gazette,* February

DEPARTMENT OF EMPLOYMENT, 1971, *Glossary of training terms,* HMSO

DEPARTMENT OF EMPLOYMENT, 1972, *Training for the future — a plan for discussion,* HMSO

DEPARTMENT OF EMPLOYMENT, 1974, Employment prospects for the highly qualified, *Manpower paper* No 8, Department of Employment

DEPARTMENT OF EMPLOYMENT, 1975, Young persons entering employment, *Employment and Productivity Gazette,* December

DEPARTMENT OF EMPLOYMENT, 1978, *The work of the careers service,* HMSO

DONNELLY E L and KENNEY J P J, 1970, Training analysis of 'semi-skilled' work — the importance of pre-analysis groundwork *Industrial and Commercial Training,* Vol 2, No 6, June

DONOVAN REPORT, *Royal Commission on trade unions and employers' associations,* 1968, HMSO

DOWNS S, 1977, Trainability testing, *Training information paper* No 11, HMSO

DRUCKER P F, 1968, *The practice of management,* Pan Books

ELECTRICITY SUPPLY INDUSTRY TRAINING BOARD, 1968(a), *Recommendations on the training of salesmen, saleswomen and demonstrators,* Electricity Supply ITB

ELECTRICITY SUPPLY INDUSTRY TRAINING BOARD, 1968(b), *The training of student engineering apprentices,* Electricity Supply ITB

EMPLOYMENT AND TRAINING ACT, 1973, HMSO

ENGINEERING INDUSTRY TRAINING BOARD, 1967, *The training of adult operators,* Booklet No 3, Engineering ITB
272

ENGINEERING INDUSTRY TRAINING BOARD, 1968(a), *Training for engineering craftsmen — the module system,* Engineering ITB

ENGINEERING INDUSTRY TRAINING BOARD, 1968(b), *Training of professional engineers,* Booklet No 5, Engineering ITB

ENGINEERING INDUSTRY TRAINING BOARD, 1969(a), Training of clerks, *Training recommendation* No 5, Engineering ITB

ENGINEERING INDUSTRY TRAINING BOARD, 1969(b), *The training of technician engineers,* Booklet No 9, Engineering ITB

ENGINEERING INDUSTRY TRAINING BOARD, 1970, *The selection and preparation of supervisors for first appointment,* Booklet No 12, Engineering ITB

ENGINEERING INDUSTRY TRAINING BOARD, 1971(a), *The training of technicians,* Booklet No 14, Engineering ITB

ENGINEERING INDUSTRY TRAINING BOARD, 1971(b), *The analysis of certain engineering craft occupations,* Research report No 2, Engineering ITB

ENGINEERING INDUSTRY TRAINING BOARD, 1977, *The relevance of school leaving experience to performance in industry,* Engineering ITB

ENGINEERING INDUSTRY TRAINING BOARD, 1978(a), *The Finniston Inquiry: the Board's submission to the Committee of Inquiry into the engineering profession,* Supplement to Blueprint, April, Engineering ITB

ENGINEERING INDUSTRY TRAINING BOARD, 1978(b), *Review of craft apprenticeship in engineering,* Information paper No 49, Engineering ITB

ENGINEERING INDUSTRY TRAINING BOARD AND SHELL CENTRE FOR MATHEMATICAL EDUCATION, 1978, *Basic skills in mathematics for engineering,* Nottingham University

EUROPEAN ECONOMIC COMMISSION, 1971, *Preliminary guidelines for a community social policy programme,* Sec (71), 600 Final, 17 March

FARNSWORTH T 1970, Management development — establishing a policy, *Industrial and Commercial Training,* November, Vol 2, No 11

FOOD, DRINK AND TOBACCO INDUSTRY TRAINING BOARD, 1971, The training of retail shop managers, *Training recommendation* No 1, Food, Drink and Tobacco ITB

FOOD, DRINK AND TOBACCO INDUSTRY TRAINING BOARD, 1972, How to use job analysis for profitable training, *Systematic training guide* No 2, Food, Drink and Tobacco ITB

FOOD, DRINK AND TOBACCO INDUSTRY TRAINING BOARD, 1977, *Industrial relations training step by step,* Food, Drink and Tobacco ITB

FORREST A, 1972, The manager's guide to setting targets, *Industrial Society*

FORRESTER D, 1968, quoted by HARLEY J in How to assess your training costs, *British Industry Week*, 22 November

FOUNDRY INDUSTRY TRAINING COMMITTEE, 1966, *Recommendations on the training of technologists*, Foundry Industry Training Committee

FOUNDRY INDUSTRY TRAINING COMMITTEE, 1969, *Recommendations on technician training*, Foundry Industry Training Committee

FRASER J M, 1966, *Employment interviewing*, McDonald and Evans

FRENCH H W, 1970, National certificates — the past, the present — and the future, *The Technical Journal*, October, Association of Teachers in Technical Institutions

GAGNE R M, 1967, *Learning and individual differences*, Merrill Publishing

GARBUTT D, 1969, *Training costs with reference to the Industrial Training Act*, Gee and Company, Ltd

GILES W J, 1969, Training after the Act, *Personnel Management*, June, Vol 1, No 2

GILL D, 1978, *Appraising performance, present trends and the next decade*, Information report No 25, Institute of Personnel Management

GLASER B G (Editor), 1968, *Organizational careers*, Aldine

GLASER R, 1965, *Training research and education*, Wiley and Sons, New York

GOVERNMENT PROPOSALS, *Industrial training*, 1962, HMSO

GREINER L E, 1972, Evolution and revolution as organizations grow, *Harvard Business Review*, July–August

GRONLUND, N E, 1970, *Stating behavioural objectives for classroom instruction*, MacMillan

HAGUE H, 1973, *Management training for real*, Institute of Personnel Management

HALL K and MILLER I, 1970, Supplying skills the government way, *Personnel Management*, April, Vol 2, No 4

HALL N, 1976, Cost benefit analysis in industrial training, *Manchester Monographs* No 6, University of Manchester, Department of Adult and Higher Education

HAMBLIN A C, 1974, *Evaluation and control of training*, McGraw-Hill

HANSON G B, 1967, *Britain's Industrial Training Act, its history, devolopment and implications for America*, National Manpower Policy Taskforce, Washington D C

HARTLEY K, 1976, *Training and retraining for industry*, Conference on fiscal implications of manpower planning, Stirling University

HASLEGRAVE REPORT, *Report of the committee on technician courses and examinations*, 1969, HMSO
274

HERZBERG E, 1964, *Some principles of training applied to the retail trade*, Institute of Personnel Management

HERZBERG F, 1975, *Work and the nature of man*, Lockwood

HESSELING P, 1966, *Strategy of evaluation research*, Van Gorcum

HOBSON B and HAYES J, 1968, *The theory and practice of vocational guidance*, Pergamon

HOLDING D H, 1965, *Principles of training*, Pergamon

HONEY P, 1976, *Face to face: a practical guide to interactive skills*, Institute of Personnel Management

HOTEL AND CATERING INDUSTRY TRAINING BOARD, 1971, *Technical training recommendations*, Hotel and Catering ITB

HOWELLS R and BARRETT B, 1975, *The Health and Safety at Work Act*, A guide for managers, Institute of Personnel Management

HUGHES J J, 1970, *Cost benefit aspects of manpower retraining*, Manpower paper No 2, HMSO

HUMBLE J W, 1973, *Management by objectives*, British Institute of Management

HUNT A, 1968, *A survey of women's employment*, Vol 1, HMSO

HURLEY F G, 1971, *Training retail managers – a symposium*, Institute of Personnel Management

INDUSTRIAL TRAINING ACT, 1964, *General guide, scope and objectives*, HMSO

INSTITUTION OF PRODUCTION ENGINEERS, 1978, *Evidence to the Finniston inquiry into the engineering profession*, Institution of Production Engineers

IRON AND STEEL INDUSTRY TRAINING BOARD, 1966, *Recommendations for the training of operatives*, Iron and Steel ITB

IRON AND STEEL INDUSTRY TRAINING BOARD, 1970, *Retraining of older workers*, Iron and Steel ITB

IRON AND STEEL INDUSTRY TRAINING BOARD, 1976, *The management of health and safety*, Iron and Steel ITB

JACKSON W, 1969, Manpower for engineering and technology, *British Association for Commercial and Industrial Education Journal*, December, Vol 23, No 4

JACQUES E, 1967, *Equitable payment, a general theory of work, differential payment and individual progress*, Heinemann

JAHODA M, 1963, *The education of technologists*, Tavistock Publications

JEFFRIES A A and DUXFIELD T S, 1969, *Management and training of technical salesmen*, Gower Press

JOINT COMMITTEE FOR TRAINING IN THE FOUNDRY INDUSTRY, 1966, *Recommendations on craft apprentice training – patternmakers*, Joint Committee for Training in the Foundry Industry

JONES REPORT, *The brain drain, report of the working group on emigration*, 1967, HMSO

JONES J A G and MOXHAM J, 1969, Costing the benefits of training, *Personnel Management,* August, Vol 1, No 4

JONES J A G, 1970, *The evaluation and cost effectiveness of training,* Seminar August, Industrial Training Service

JONES S, 1968, *Design of instruction,* Training Information Paper, No 1, HMSO

KENNEY J P J and DONNELLY E L, 1969, Diploma course in industrial training, *Industrial Training International,* July, Vol 4, No 7

KENNEY J P J and MARSH P J, 1969, Management schools and industrial training, *Industrial and Commercial Training,* December, Vol 1, No 2

KING D, 1964, *Training within the organization,* Tavistock Publications

KNITTING, LACE AND NET INDUSTRY TRAINING BOARD, 1970(a), Operatives, *Training recommendation,* No 3, Knitting, Lace and Net ITB

KNITTING, LACE AND NET INDUSTRY TRAINING BOARD, 1970(b), Professional and administrative staff, *Training recommendation,* No 5, Knitting, Lace and Net ITB

KNITTING, LACE AND NET INDUSTRY TRAINING BOARD, 1971, Technicians and technologists, *Training recommendation,* No 6, Knitting, Lace and Net ITB

KOLB D A, RUBIN I M and McINTYRE J M, 1974, *Organizational psychology, an experimental approach,* Prentice Hall

LAWRENCE S, 1970, Much ado about modules, *Personnel Management,* March, Vol 2, No 3

LEPPARD J W and KAUFMAN M, 1972, English for Asian workers, *Industrial and Commercial Training,* September, Vol 4, No 9

LESTER T, 1970, The reluctant graduate, *Management Today,* November

LOCAL GOVERNMENT TRAINING BOARD, 1976, Training and development of training officers, *Training recommendation 17,* Local Government Training Board

MAGER R F, 1962, *Preparing instructional objectives,* Fearon, California

MAGER R F, 1968, *Developing attitude toward learning,* Fearon, California

MANPOWER RESEARCH UNIT, 1968, *Growth of office employment,* in Manpower Studies, No 7, HMSO

MANPOWER SERVICES COMMISSION, 1975, *Vocational preparation for young people,* Manpower Services Commission

MANPOWER SERVICES COMMISSION, 1976(a), *Towards a comprehensive manpower policy,* Manpower Services Commission

MANPOWER SERVICES COMMISSION, 1976(b), *Training for vital skills – a consultative document,* Manpower Services Commission

MANPOWER SERVICES COMMISSION, 1977(a), *Young people at work,* Manpower Services Commission

MANPOWER SERVICES COMMISSION, 1977(b), *Review and plan,* Manpower Services Commission

MANPOWER SERVICES COMMISSION, 1978(a), *Training Services Agency – a five year plan,* Manpower Services Commission

MANPOWER SERVICES COMMISSION 1978(b), *Training Services Division, Training of trainers,* First report of the training of trainers committee. Manpower Services Commission

MANPOWER SERVICES COMMISSION, 1978(c), Sponsored survey into management training in London and the South East, *Personnel Management,* June, Vol 10, No 6

MANPOWER SERVICES COMMISSION, 1979, *Giving you the chance to give them a future,* Manpower Services Commission

MANT A, 1970, *The experienced manager – a major resource,* British Institute of Management

MARKS W R, 1974, *Induction – acclimatizing people to work,* Institute of Personnel Management

MARKWELL D S and ROBERTS T J, 1969, *Organization of management development programmes,* Gower Press

MARSHALL G L, 1971, Predicting academic achievement, Unpublished thesis, quoted in Livingston, J S, Myth of the well educated manager, *Harvard Business Review,* January-February

MASLOW A H, 1954, *Motivation and personality,* Harper

McGEHEE W and THAYER P W, 1961, *Training in business and industry,* Wiley

McGREGOR D, 1960, *The human side of the enterprise,* McGraw Hill

MEGGINSON D and BOYDELL T, 1979, *A manager's guide to coaching,* British Association for Commercial and Industrial Education

MELROSE-WOODMAN J, 1978, *Profile of the British manager,* BIM management survey No 38, British Institute of Management

MORRIS J and BURGOYNE J, 1976, *Developing resourceful managers,* Institute of Personnel Management

MOSS A, 1971, The technician, a social-structural approach, *Industrial Training International,* May, Vol 6, No 5

MUKHERJEE S, 1970, *Changing manpower needs: a study of industrial training boards,* Broadsheet 523, Political and Economic Planning

MUKHERJEE S, 1974, *There's work to be done,* Manpower Services Commission, HMSO

NADLER L, 1971, Assessment of needs, *Industrial Training International,* April, Vol 6, No 4

NATIONAL ECONOMIC DEVELOPMENT OFFICE, 1968, *Grow your own sales staff,* A guide to the selection and training of sales staff in the smaller shop, HMSO

NATIONAL ECONOMIC DEVELOPMENT OFFICE, 1974, *Career development in retail distribution,* Distributive Trades Economic Development Council

NELSON J, 1966, The criteria inventory, *Industrial Training International*, Vol 1, No 8 *et seq*

NEWSHAM D B, 1969, The challenge of change to the adult trainee, *Training Information Paper* No 3, HMSO

NISBET J D, 1957, Intelligence and age, Retesting with twenty four years interval, *British Journal of Educational Psychology*

OTTO C P and GLASER R O, 1970, *The management of training,* Addison Wesley

PAGE G T, 1967, *The Industrial Training Act and after,* A Deutsch

PAPER AND PAPER PRODUCTS INDUSTRY TRAINING BOARD, 1969, Assessment of training needs, *Training guide* No 1, Paper and Paper Products, ITB

PAPER AND PAPER PRODUCTS INDUSTRY TRAINING BOARD, 1970(a), Preparation of training programmes, *Training guide* No 2, Paper and Paper Products ITB

PAPER AND PAPER PRODUCTS INDUSTRY TRAINING BOARD, 1970(b), Implementation of training programmes, *Training guide* No 3, Paper and Paper Products ITB

PAPER AND PAPER PRODUCTS INDUSTRY TRAINING BOARD, 1971(a), Training in accident prevention, *Training recommendation,* No 4, Paper and Paper Products ITB

PAPER AND PAPER PRODUCTS INDUSTRY TRAINING BOARD, 1971(b), First year training for engineering craftsmen and technicians in the paper and paper products industry, *Training recommendation* No 2, Paper and Paper Products ITB

PARKIN N, 1978, Apprenticeship: outmoded or undervalued? *Personnel Management,* May, Vol 10, No 5

PEDLER M, BURGOYNE J AND BOYDELL T H, 1978, *Managers' guide to self development,* McGraw-Hill

PERRY P J C, 1972, *Vocational training in the European Economic Community,* British Association for Commercial and Industrial Education

PERRY P J C, 1976, *The evolution of British manpower policy from the Statute of Artificers, 1563, to the Industrial Training Act, 1964,* BACIE

PERRY P J C, 1978, Is TOPS tops? *British Association for Commercial and Industrial Education Journal,* July, Vol 32, No 7

PETROLEUM INDUSTRY TRAINING BOARD, 1970, *The training of petroleum salesmen,* Petroleum ITB

POWELL L S, 1978, *A guide to the use of visual aids,* British Association for Commercial and Industrial Education

PRICE B, 1978, Whatever happened to business graduates? *Personnel Management,* April, Vol 10, No 4

PUGH D S, HICKSON D J and HININGS C R, 1971, *Writers on organizations – an introduction,* Penguin

RACKHAM N, HONEY P and COLBERT M, 1971, *Developing interactive skills,* Wellens
278

RANDELL G A, PACKARD P M A, SHAW R L and SLATER A J, 1974, *Staff appraisal,* Institute of Personnel Management

REDDIN W J, 1968, Training and organizational change, *British Association for Commercial and Industrial Education Journal,* March, Vol 2, No 1

REDDIN W J, 1970, *Managerial effectiveness,* McGraw-Hill

ROAD TRANSPORT INDUSTRY TRAINING BOARD, 1968, *Training recommendations for forecourt sales staff and vehicle sales staff,* Road Transport ITB

ROAD TRANSPORT INDUSTRY TRAINING BOARD, 1978, *Vehicle trades apprentice,* Road Transport ITB

ROBBINS REPORT, *Report of the Committee on Higher Education,* 1963, HMSO

RODGER A, MORGAN T and GUEST D, 1971, *The industrial training officer – his background and his work,* Institute of Personnel Management

ROGERS T G P, and WILLIAMS P, 1970, *The recruitment and training of graduates,* Institute of Personnel Management

ROSE REPORT, *Management education in the 1970s – growth and issues,* 1970, HMSO

SEYMOUR W D, 1954, *Industrial training for manual operatives,* Pitman

SEYMOUR W D, 1966, *Industrial skills,* Pitman

SEYMOUR W D, 1968, *Skills analysis training,* Pitman

SHEPHERD R A, 1978, Picking up the EITB's gauntlet, Comment in *Personnel Management,* May, Vol 10, No 5

SINGLETON W T (editor), 1978, The study of real skills: Volume 1, The analysis of practical skills, MTP Press

SHIPBUILDING INDUSTRY TRAINING BOARD, 1979, Training policy statement No 8, *Recommendations for the training and development of Commercial and Clerical staff,* Shipbuilding ITB

SINGER E J and MACDONALD I D, 1970, *Is apprenticeship outdated?* Institute of Personnel Management

SINGER E J, 1977, *Training in industry and commerce,* Institute of Personnel Management

SINGER E J, 1979, *Effective management coaching,* 2nd edition, Institute of Personnel Management

SOFER C, 1970, *Men in mid-career, A study of British managers and technical specialists,* Cambridge University Press

SPENCER G A, 1971, *Letter to the London Times,* 3 March

STAMMERS R and PATRICK J, 1975, *The psychology of training,* Methuen

STARBUCK W H, 1971, *Organizational growth and development,* Penguin

STEWART R, 1968, Management education and our knowledge of managers' jobs, *International Social Science Journal,* Vol 20, No 1

STEWART R, 1970, *Managers and their jobs,* Pan Books

STEWART R, 1975, Classifying different types of managerial jobs, *Personnel Review,* Vol 4, No 2

STRINGFELLOW C D, 1968, Education and training, *Industrial Training International,* August, Vol 3, No 2

SUPER D E and JORDAAN J P, 1973, Career development theory, *British Journal of Guidance and Counselling,* January, Vol 1, No 1

SWANN REPORT, *The flow into employment of scientists, engineers and technologists,* 1968, HMSO

TALBOT J R and ELLIS C D, 1969, *Analysis and costing of company training,* Gower Press

TANNEHILL R E, 1970, *Motivation and management development,* Butterworths

TAVERNIER G, 1971, *Industrial training systems and records,* Gower Press

TECHNICAL AND SUPERVISORY STAFF, 1978, *The qualified engineers – the way forward,* TASS

TECHNICIAN EDUCATION COUNCIL, 1974, *Policy statement,* TEC

THAKUR M, BRISTOW J and CARBY K, 1978, *Personnel in change – Organization development through the personnel function,* Institute of Personnel Management

THOMAS B, BOXHAM J and JONES J A G, 1969, A cost benefit analysis of industrial training, *British Journal of Industrial Relations,* July, Vol VII, No 2

THOMAS L F, 1962, Perceptual organization in industrial inspectors, *Ergonomics,* Vol 5

THOMPSON, N, 1968, Introducing the concept of 'do-it-yourself' training, *Industrial Training International,* July, Vol 3, No 7

THURLEY K E and HAMBLIN A, 1963, *The supervisor and his job,* HMSO

TONKINSON E, 1962, *Commercial apprenticeship,* editor Oakley C A, University of London Press

TRACEY W R, 1968, *Evaluating training and development systems,* American Management Association

TRAINING SERVICES AGENCY, 1977(a), *An approach to the training of staff with training officer roles,* Training Services Agency

TRAINING SERVICES AGENCY, 1977(b), *A discussion document on management development,* Training Services Agency

VAN GELDER R, 1967, *Induction,* The Industrial Society

VAUGHAN T D, 1970, *Education and vocational guidance,* Routledge and Kegan Paul

VENABLES P, 1969, 1970, Technical and higher education — the changing pattern, *British Association for Commercial and Industrial Education Journal,* Part I December 1969, Part II March 1970

WALKER M, 1970, The training of clerical workers, *Industrial and Commercial Training,* October, Vol 2, No 10

WARR P B and BIRD M W, 1968, Identifying supervisory training needs, *Training Information Paper* No 2, HMSO

WARR P, BIRD M and RACKHAM N, 1970, *Evaluation of management training,* Gower Press

WELLENS J, 1963, *The training revolution,* Evans Brothers

WELLENS J, 1968, The exploitation of human resources, Article in *The Times* (London), 26 August

WELLENS J, 1970, An approach to management training, *Industrial and Commercial Training,* February, Vol 2, No 2

WELLENS J, 1976, Experiential learning, *Industrial and Commercial Training,* July, Vol 8, No 7

WELLENS J, 1979, *Training in physical skills,* Wellens Publishing

WHEATCROFT M, 1970, *The revolution in British management education,* Pitman

WHITAKER G, (ed.), 1965, *T-Group training – group dynamics in management education* Association of Management Teachers Occasional Paper No 2, Blackwell

WHITELAW M, 1972, *The evaluation of management training – a review,* Institute of Personnel Management

WHITE PAPER, 1961, *Better opportunities in technical education,* HMSO

WILD R, 1979, UK Engineering training, *Industrial and Commercial Training,* Vol 11, No 1

WILLIAMS G, 1963, *Apprenticeship in Europe – the lesson for Britain,* Chapman and Hall

WILLIAMS E H, 1969, *Training for retailing,* Macdonald

WILLIAMS S, 1978, reported in the *Financial Times,* 30 March

WILSON M T, 1970, *Managing a sales force,* Gower Press

WISE A C, 1970, An adaption of the group training concept for commercial and clerical workers, *Industrial and Commercial Training,* Vol 2, No 7, July

WOMEN'S ENGINEERING SOCIETY, 1978, *Evidence to the Finniston Committee of Inquiry into the Engineering Profession,* Women's Engineering Society

WOODWARD J, 1965, *Industrial organization – theory and practice,* Oxford University Press

WRIGHT D S and TAYLOR A, 1970, *Introducing psychology – an experimental approach,* Penguin Education

YOUNGMAN M B, *et al,* 1978, *Analysing jobs,* Gower Press

Index

Performance
  annual appraisal, 84
  appraisal linked to job training, 145
  appraisal of managers, 220-1
  behaviour, 3
  improved by training, 16, 18, 84
  records, 84
Personnel departments
  harmonizing training policies, 55-6
  integration of training, 23-5
  participation in training needs assessment, 46
Personnel management, growth of function, 1
Policies
  development, 55-8
  dissemination to employees, 58
  necessity for, 54-5
  province of top management, 22
  review procedure, 55
  written statements, 56, 57-8
Positive transfer, 94
Practice periods in training, 92
  in variety of settings, 94
Priorities
  assigning, 58
  criteria, 52
  in allocationg training resources, 44,
Problem-centred analysis, 70-1
Professional associations, training courses, 62
Programmed learning, 92
  for retail sales staff, 157
Promotion plans and training, 25

Qualifications, 114
  lack of, effect on work prospects, 107,
  related to historical social conditions, 139
  see also Academic qualifications; Vocational qualifications
Quality control departments, participation in training needs assessment, 49

Race relations, 39-40
'Reaction evaluation', 102
Records
  in job analysis, 68
  of personnel, 25
  of trainees' progress, 11
  performance, 84
  use in training needs assessment, 44
Recruitment—selection
  against job specification, 83
  inclusion of feedback from training, 24-5
  of craft apprentices, 173
  of graduates, 120
  of ready-trained staff, 44
  of school leavers for offices, 142
  of technicians, 185
  of technologists, 199-200

of young people, 113-14
  role of training department, 24
Reinforcement in training programmes, 88-90
Remuneration, reflecting success in training, 25
Research and development departments, 49
Retail sales staff, 149-60
  job knowledge, 154-60
  training
    junior assistants, 158-60
    problems, 150
    requirements, 152-6
Retraining, 35, 257
  for existing staff, 17
Role analysis, 71
Role playing, 156, 263

Safety, see Accident reduction; Health and Safety at Work Act (1974)
Sales representatives, training, 160-5
Sales staff, training, 149-65
Sandwich courses
  company sponsorship, 118-19
  for technologists, 200, 201-2
Schools
  careers education function, 109
  curricula deficiencies in basic skills, 111, 134
  involvement in craft training, 178
  links with employers, 107-8
  provision of vocational training, 108
Science Research Council, 'teaching factory', 199
Secretarial posts, 145-6
  see also Office workers
Selection see recruitment
Self-development of managers, 223
Selling skills, 153-4
Semi-skilled work, 67, 126-32, 166
Service, length of, 47-8
Sewing machinists, training programme, 130-1
Shop stewards, union training courses, 64
Short courses, 3
Skill, as job component, 67-8
Skill Centres, 63, 243
  adult trainees, 169
Skill training
  for office machine operators, 146-7
  in retailing, 153-4
  modular approach (craft apprentices), 173-5
Skilled labour see Craftsmen
Social benefits of training, 17
Social skills see Interpersonal skills
Special Programmes Division, 243
Sponsorship
  for students, 118-19
  for technologists, 200
Stimuli—cues
  in manual skills analysis, 79

287